JAGUAR E TYPE 1961-72 AUTOBOOK

Workshop Manual for
Jaguar E Type 3.8 litre 1961-65
Jaguar E Type 4.2 litre 1964-68
Jaguar E Type 4.2 litre 2 + 2 1966-68
Jaguar E Type 4.2 litre series 2 1968-71
Jaguar E Type 4.2 litre 2 + 2 series 2 1968-71
Jaguar E Type 4.2 litre 2+2 series 3 1971-72

by

Kenneth Ball G I Mech E
and the
Autopress team of Technical Writers

AUTOPRESS LTD   GOLDEN LANE   BRIGHTON   BN1 2QJ   ENGLAND

The AUTOBOOK series of Workshop Manuals is the largest in the world and covers the majority of British and Continental motor cars, as well as all major Japanese and Australian models. For a full list see the back of this manual.

CONTENTS

ISBN 0 85147 337 7

First Edition   1970
Reprinted   1970
Reprinted   1971
Second Edition, fully revised   1972
Third Edition, fully revised   1972
Reprinted   1973

Printed and bound in Brighton England for Autopress Ltd by G Beard & Son Ltd

ACKNOWLEDGEMENT

My thanks are due to Jaguar Cars Ltd. for their unstinted co-operation and also for supplying data and illustrations.

I am also grateful to a considerable number of owners who have discussed their cars at length and many of whose suggestions have been included in this manual.

Kenneth Ball G I Mech E
Associate Member Guild of Motoring Writers

Ditchling Sussex England.

INTRODUCTION

This do-it-yourself Workshop Manual has been specially written for the owner who wishes to maintain his car in first class condition and to carry out his own servicing and repairs. Considerable savings on garage charges can be made, and one can drive in safety and confidence knowing the work has been done properly.

Comprehensive step-by-step instructions and illustrations are given on all dismantling, overhauling and assembling operations. Certain assemblies require the use of expensive special tools, the purchase of which would be unjustified. In these cases information is included but the reader is recommended to hand the unit to the agent for attention.

Throughout the Manual hints and tips are included which will be found invaluable, and there is an easy to follow fault diagnosis at the end of each chapter.

Whilst every care has been taken to ensure correctness of information it is obviously not possible to guarantee complete freedom from errors or to accept liability arising from such errors or omissions.

Instructions may refer to the righthand or lefthand sides of the vehicle or the components. These are the same as the righthand or lefthand of an observer standing behind the car and looking forward.

CHAPTER 1

THE ENGINE

1:1 Description

All the models of E type Jaguar covered by this manual have an engine that is based on the traditions and design of the race-bred XK engine. The differences between the 4.2 engine and the 3.8 engine are only minor and the increased capacity of the 4.2 is gained by using a larger bore in the cylinders.

A longitudinal section of the 4.2 litre engine is shown in **FIG 1:1**. From this it can be seen that the engine is a six cylinder in-line having hemispherical combustion chambers and overhead valves. **FIG 1:2** shows the details of the cylinder block assembly and **FIG 1:3** gives the cylinder head details. Details of bore and stroke are given in Technical Data at the end of this manual, together with a extensive coverage of further technical information. It should be noted that there is a choice of compression ratios but the cylinder head is not changed and the compression ratio is governed by the type of piston fitted.

From the exploded views details of the basic engine construction can be seen. The valves are mounted in two inclined banks on either side of the cylinder head. The exhaust valves are in one in-line bank on the lefthand side of the cylinder head and the inlet valves are all in-line on the other side. The valves are directly operated by the camshafts, one camshaft for each bank of valves, and the camshafts are chain driven from the crankshaft. Details of the valve operating gear will be given in the relevant section.

The crankshaft is supported in seven main bearings. Both the main bearings and the big-end bearings are fitted with renewable steel-backed shell bearings. The front of the crankshaft carries a gear which provides the drive for the distributor and oil pump. Also mounted on the front of the crankshaft is a damper which helps to damp out the torsional vibrations in the relatively long crankshaft.

1:2 Engine and gearbox removal

Most operations can be carried out on the engine without removing it from the car. The sump can be removed while the engine is still in the car, so big-end bearings can be changed without taking out the engine. The timing chain cover is similarly removable, so again the valve timing gear can be serviced without removing the engine. However, the gearbox cannot be removed separately so the engine and gearbox unit must be removed for any work requiring attention to the clutch, flywheel or crankshaft.

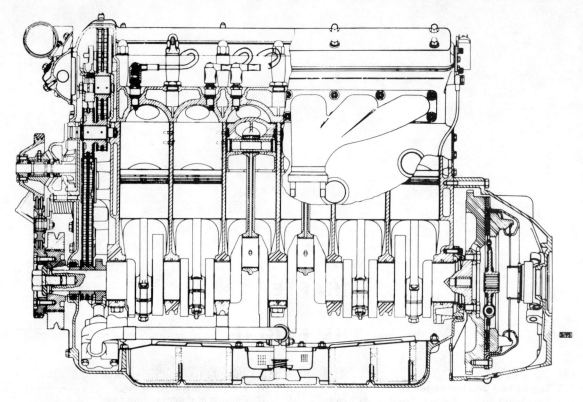

FIG 1:1   Longitudinal section of the 4.2 litre engine

The engine and gearbox unit is removed from above, but if a pit is not available the front of the car must be raised to give access room underneath. **It must be stressed that any supports used must be firmly based and not likely to collapse during the operation, or serious injury could result**, apart from any damage to the car.

If the operator is not a skilled automobile engineer it is suggested that he will find much useful information in 'Hints on Maintenance and Overhaul' at the end of this manual and that he should read it before starting work.

1   Remove the bonnet (see **Chapter 13**). Disconnect the battery leads. Drain the cooling system and remove the radiator and header tank (see **Chapter 4**). Drain the oil out of the engine sump and gearbox.

2   Disconnect the air cleaner and carburetter controls. Remove the carburetters (see **Chapter 2**). Dis-

connect the heater hoses and brake vacuum hose.

3   Disconnect the electrical cables to the following: starter motor and solenoid, generator or alternator, oil pressure and temperature transmitters. If the colours have faded on the cables, label each one to ensure that it will be correctly reconnected when refitting the engine. Do not disconnect the cables for the tachometer generator 38 but instead remove the unit from the cylinder head. Disconnect the engine earthing strap.

4   Drain and remove the oil filter canister (see **Section 1:8**). Slacken the generator, or alternator, mounting bolts and free the fan belt. Undo the four bolts 37 and remove the crankshaft pulley 36 and washer 41. Mark the damper 29 to facilitate lining it up with the key 35 on reassembly. Undo the bolt 39 and use two levers to remove the damper. A sharp tap with a hammer on the securing cone 30 will help to free the damper. To

Key to Fig 1:2   1 Cylinder block   2 Core plug   3 Timing cover   4 Setscrew   5 Copper washer   6 Plug
7 Dowel   8 Dowel   9 Stud   10 Dowel stud   11 Cover   12 Ring dowel   13 Setscrew   14 Bolt
15 Banjo bolt   16 Copper washer   17 Sealing ring   18 Gauze filter   19 Drain tap   20 Copper washer
21 Fibre washer   22 Mounting bracket   23 Crankshaft   24 Plug   25 Bush   26 Thrust washer   27 Main bearing
28 Main bearing   29 Crankshaft damper   30 Cone   31 Distance piece   32 Oil thrower   33 Sprocket
34 Gear   35 Key   36 Pulley   37 Bolt   38 Locking washer   39 Bolt   40 Washer   41 Tabwasher
42 Connecting rod   43 Bearings   44 Flywheel   45 Dowel   46 Dowel   47 Setscrew   48 Locking plate
49 Piston   50 Compression ring   51 Compression ring   52 Scraper ring   53 Gudgeon pin   54 Circlip
55 Oil sump   56 Gasket   57 Seal   58 Cork seal   59 Baffle plate   60 Stud   61 Filter basket   62 Adaptor
63 Gasket   64 Stud   65 Hose   66 Clip   67 Dipstick   68 Pointer   69 Bracket   70 Bracket   71 Engine mounting
72 Plate   73 Link   74 Bush   75 Stepped washer   76 Stepped washer   77 Rubber mounting   78 Bracket   79 Bracket
80 Support bracket   81 Rubber mounting

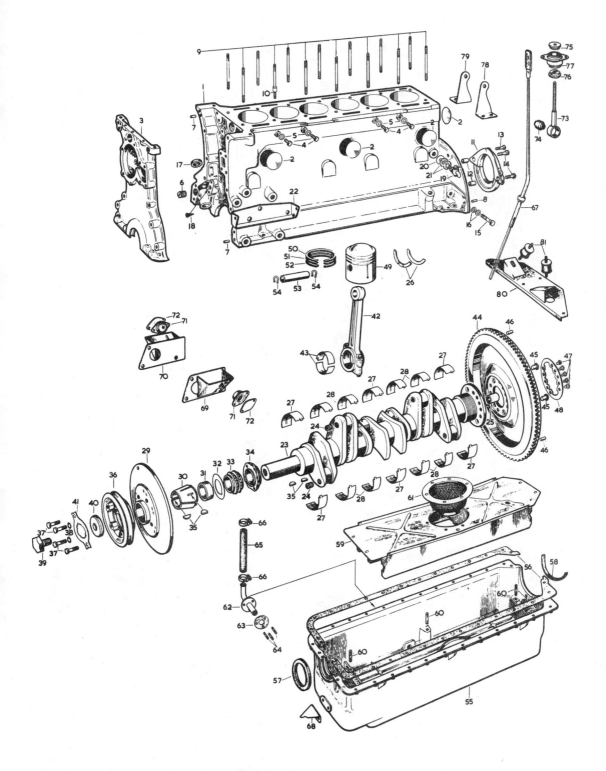

FIG 1:2 Cylinder block details

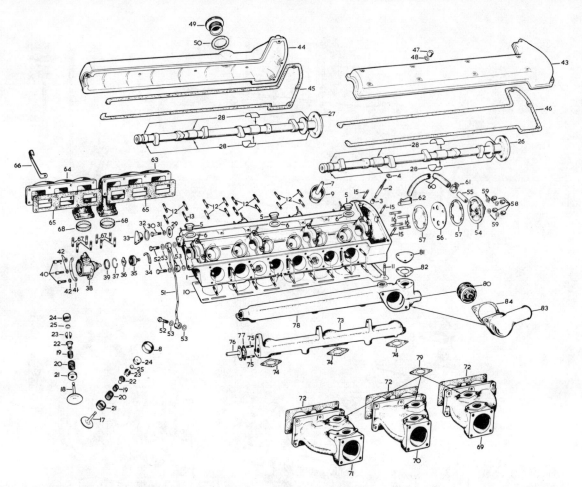

FIG 1:3 Cylinder head details

Key to Fig 1:3   1 Cylinder head   2 Stud   3 Ring dowel   4 D-washer   5 Plug   6 Copper washer
7 Valve guide   8 Valve insert   9 Tappet guide   10 Gasket   11 to 16 Studs   17 Inlet valve   18 Exhaust valve
19 Valve spring   20 Valve spring   21 Seat   22 Collar   23 Collet   24 Tappet   25 Adjusting pad
26 Inlet camshaft   27 Exhaust camshaft   28 Bearing   29 Oil thrower   30 Setscrew   31 Copper washer
32 Sealing ring   33 Sealing plug   34 Seal   35 Adaptor   36 Driving dog   37 Circlip   38 Generator
39 Sealing ring   40 Screw   41 Plate washer   42 Lockwasher   43 Inlet camshaft cover   44 Exhaust camshaft cover
45 Gasket   46 Gasket   47 Dome nut   48 Copper washer   49 Filler cap   50 Fibre washer   51 Oil pipe
52 Banjo bolt   53 Copper washer   54 Breather housing   55 Pipe   56 Baffle   57 Gasket   58 Dome nut
59 Spring washer   60 Flexible pipe   61 Clip   62 Clip   63 Exhaust manifold   64 Exhaust manifold   65 Gasket
66 Clip   67 Stud   68 Sealing ring   69 Inlet manifold   70 Inlet manifold   71 Inlet manifold   72 Gasket
73 Air balance pipe   74 Gasket   75 Stud   76 Adaptor   77 Gasket   78 Water pipe   79 Gasket
80   Thermostat   81 Plate   82 Gasket   83 Elbow   84   Gasket

save it becoming damaged also remove the ignition timing pointer 68.

5 Remove the four nuts and bolts securing each exhaust downpipe to the exhaust manifolds. Unclip the downpipes at the silencer assembly and withdraw them. Discard the sealing rings between the pipes and manifolds as new sealing rings should be fitted on reassembly.

6 Remove the seats, gearlever knob and radio/ashtray console. Remove the trim and take off the gearbox cover. On the 2+2 the central armrest will have to be removed. Raise it and take out the bottom panel when the five self-tapping, securing screws will be exposed. On all other cars the trim is also held in place by the two seat belt attachments.

7 Remove the gearbox top cover with the gearlever. Blank the orifice with carboard to prevent the ingress of dirt into the gearbox. The reversing light cables should be disconnected from the switch on the cover before removing it. Disconnect the speedometer cable. Disconnect the propeller shaft from the gearbox flange. Remove the clutch slave cylinder from the

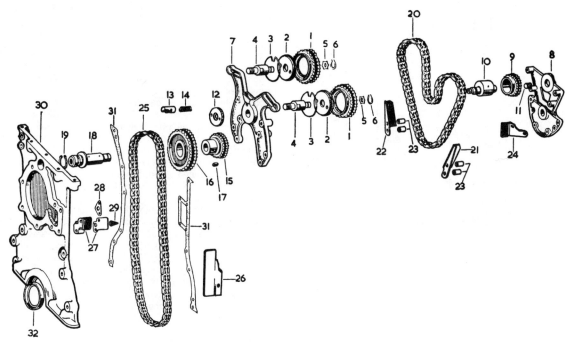

FIG 1:4   Valve timing gear details

Key to Fig 1:4   1 Camshaft sprocket   2 Adjusting plate   3 Circlip   4 Guide pin   5 Star washer   6 Circlip
7 Timing gear front mounting bracket   8 Timing gear rear mounting bracket   9 Idler sprocket   10 Eccentric plug   11 Plug
12 Adjustment plate   13 Plunger pin   14 Spring   15 Intermediate sprocket of top timing chain
16 Intermediate sprocket of lower timing chain   17 Key   18 Shaft   19 Circlip   20 Top timing chain
21 Damper for top timing chain (lefthand)   22 Damper for top timing chain (righthand)   23 Distance piece
24 Intermediate damper   25 Bottom timing chain   26 Vibration damper   27 Hydraulic chain tensioner   28 Shim
29 Filter gauze   30 Front timing cover   31 Gasket   32 Oil seal

bellhousing. There is no need to disconnect the hydraulic pipe but wire the slave cylinder safely out of the way.

8 **Automatic transmission.** If this is fitted ignore the details given in operation 7 and proceed as instructed in this operation. Withdraw the transmission dipstick and unscrew the tube from the transmission oil pan. Set the selector to L and working underneath the car disconnect the selector cable adjustable ball joint from the transmission lever by removing the securing nut. Free the cable from the abutment bracket. Disconnect the speedometer cable. Disconnect the propeller shaft. Disconnect, and then remove from the car, the transmission oil cooler pipes leading to the righthand side of the radiator block. Disconnect the kickdown cable at the rear of the cylinder head.

9 **The front suspension torsion bars are held by the same bolts which support the tie plate and if the following procedure is not carried out these bolts will have their threads stripped necessitating their renewal and resetting of the torsion bars in the front suspension.** On each side of the car remove the lower nut securing the torsion bar tie plate. Tap the bolt back until it is flush with the tie plate and a silver steel bar is in its place. Remove the nuts from the top securing bolts.

Have a second operator, using a lever between the head of the bolt just released and the torsion bar, relieve the tension on the upper bolt. The upper bolt can then be tapped back, with the air of a silver steel drift so it too is flush with the face of the tie plate. Similarly tap back the other side bolt and then tap the tie plate off the four bolts. **Leave the silver steel drift in place.**

10 Attach a sling to the engine. On earlier cars a lifting plate Churchill No. J.8 must first be attached to the engine but later engines have a lifting eye already embodied in the cylinder head. Slide a trolley jack under the front of the car and support the gearbox. Remove the rear engine mounting plate (item 80 in **FIG 1:2**). Use lifting tackle and the sling to take the weight of the engine. Refer to **FIG 1:2** and remove the self-locking nut from above the stepped washer 75 on the stabilizing link 73. Remove the stepped washer 75. Undo the bolts on the front engine mountings 71.

11 Check that all connections between the engine/gearbox unit and the car are disconnected. Raise the engine slightly in the level position, and move it forwards. Make sure the water pump pulley clears the top crossmember and that the bellhousing clears the torsion bar anchor brackets. Carefully tilt the gearbox end downwards and withdraw the engine from the car.

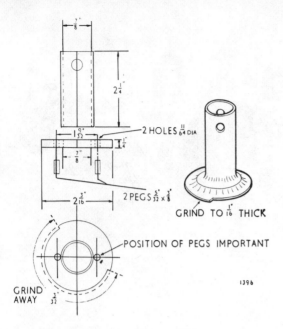

FIG 1:5 Dimensions of tool for adjusting top timing chain

2 HOLES $\frac{11}{64}$" DIA

2 PEGS $\frac{5}{32}$" x $\frac{3}{8}$"

GRIND TO $\frac{1}{16}$" THICK

POSITION OF PEGS IMPORTANT

GRIND AWAY $\frac{1}{32}$"

1396

Take care not to foul the bonnet drain channel or damage the brake pipes.

Refitting the engine is the reversal of the removal procedure. On automatic transmission cars the kickdown cable and selector cable must be readjusted as described in **Chapter 7**.

On all cars the engine stabilizer must be correctly set otherwise the engine will either vibrate or foul in the gearbox cover. Refer to **FIG 1:2**. If the link 73 was not inserted back through the rubber mounting 77 when the engine was refitted, the link will have to be freed from the engine bracket and then refitted correctly. Screw the bottom stepped washer 76 up the threads of the link 73 until its flange contacts the lower face of the rubber mounting 77. Slots are provided in the face of the lower stepped washer so that it can be turned by inserting a thin screwdriver down the bore of the rubber mounting. Replace the upper stepped washer and tighten it into place with the self-locking nut.

1:3 Removing and replacing the cylinder head

The cylinder head can be removed and replaced without removing the engine from the car. **FIG 1:3** shows the details of the cylinder head, and the details of the valve timing gear are shown in **FIG 1:4**. Two timing chains are used to drive the camshafts and the upper timing chain is tensioned by rotating the eccentric shaft 10 which moves the idler sprocket 9 further away or nearer to the chain to tension it. The eccentric shaft 10 is connected to the plate 12 which is turned by a special tool, details of which are shown in **FIG 1:5**, to slacken or tension the top timing chain. The method is shown in **FIG 1:6**, after slackening the locknut. **Before removing the cylinder head or**

carrying out any work on it the following points should be noted:

1 The cylinder head is manufactured from aluminium alloy and is therefore much softer than steel. Failing to clean out blind threaded holes or the use of undue force on studs, nuts or bolts can strip threads from holes in the cylinder head. Steel thread inserts are available to fit most holes but extra expense and inconvenience will be caused by having to fit these so do not use undue force.

2 When the valves are open they protrude below the face of the cylinder head so never lay the head on a flat surface. Support it on wooden blocks at either end. For the same reason the crankshaft or camshafts should never to be rotated when the camshaft sprockets have been disconnected otherwise the valves will hit the piston crowns.

3 As the banks of valves are inclined towards each other the individual camshafts should not be rotated otherwise the valves will hit each other. If it is necessary to rotate one camshaft either remove the other camshaft or slacken its bearing cap nuts to the fullest extent.

4 Once slackened the sparking plugs should turn freely by hand. Use a tap, or old sparking plug with crosscuts down the threads, to clean out dirty threads. Lubricate the sparking plug threads with graphite grease to prevent them seizing. If the threads are stripped or the sparking plug is inserted crossthreaded a steel thread insert will have to be fitted. **FIG 1:7** gives the dimensions for machining to fit a steel insert.

Remove the cylinder head as follows:

1 Remove the bonnet. Disconnect the battery and drain the cooling system. Disconnect the air cleaner, fuel supply pipe and controls from the carburetters (see **Chapter 2**). Disconnect the electrical cables from the tachometer generator 38, the ignition coil, the distributor and the water temperature bulb. Remove the ignition coil. Disconnect the HT leads from the sparking

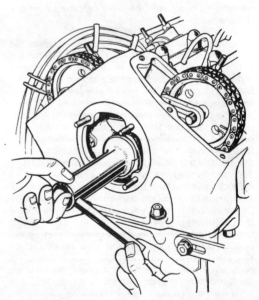

FIG 1:6 Method of adjusting top timing chain tension

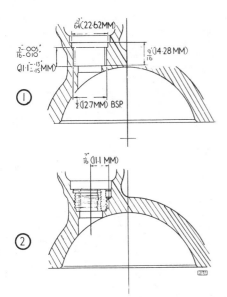

FIG 1:7 Dimensions for fitting a sparking plug insert. A ⅛ inch (3.17 mm) diameter hole is drilled and reamed ³⁄₁₆ inch (4.76 mm) deep at the dimension shown for the locking pin.

plugs and remove the HT lead carrier from the cylinder head studs. Disconnect all the water hoses to the cylinder head and inlet manifold. Remove the exhaust manifolds from the cylinder head, or else disconnect the exhaust pipes from the manifold flanges.

2 Remove the four nuts 58 and washers 59. Withdraw the breather cover 54, two gaskets 57 and the baffle plate 56. Note that the baffle plate 56 is fitted so that the large holes are in vertical alignment. Use the special tool and slacken the top timing chain tension. Remove the eleven domed nuts 47 and washers 48 securing each timing cover 43 or 44 and remove the covers with the gaskets 45 and 46. The camshafts 26 and 27 are bolted to the timing sprockets by two wire-locked bolts on each camshaft. Break the wire-locking and remove the accessible bolt from each camshaft. Turn the engine until the other two bolts are accessible and remove these. **Do not turn the engine or the camshafts after this.** Slide the camshaft sprockets along the support brackets and wire-lock them out of the way.

3 **Slacken the cylinder head nuts half a turn at a time and in the order shown in FIG 1:8.** If this precaution is not carried out the cylinder head will become distorted causing the head gasket to fail prematurely and regularly. Remove the cylinder head by lifting it squarely up the studs after disconnecting the two camshaft oil feed pipes. Free a difficult head by tapping on the sides, using a block of wood to hammer on. Aluminium alloy heads can often be very stubborn. In really difficult cases break the seal by turning the engine over and letting the cylinder compression slightly lift the head. Lay strips of rag around the cylinder head studs, soak them with penetrating oil and leave overnight.

Refitting the cylinder head:

This is basically the reversal of the removal process, while noting the following points:

1 To prevent leaks use new gaskets throughout. These are available in kits. The cylinder head gasket is fitted with the marking 'Top' uppermost and smeared lightly on both sides with grease as an additional seal.

2 Leave the camshafts as near as possible to the position in which they were removed and provided that the engine has not been turned the valve timing will not be lost. **If there is any doubt whatsoever the valve timing should be reset.** Turn the engine until No. 6 piston is at TDC. **It should be noted that No. 6 is the front piston as Jaguars count from the rear of the engine.** Check that the cylinder is on the firing stroke by seeing that the rotor arm is pointing at the contact in the distributor cap for No. 6 cylinder. If required, the exact position of TDC can be determined by mounting a DTI on the cylinder block and turning the engine until No. 6 piston is at its highest position. Turn each camshaft, noting the warning given earlier, until the keyway on the front of each camshaft is pointing vertically outwards from the camshaft cover mounting face. Refit the cylinder head and place the camshaft sprockets in position on the camshaft flanges. Tension the top timing chain until there is just a little give in it and it is not bar tight. Place the timing gauge on the camshaft keyway, as shown in **FIG 1:9.** Tap the sprockets off the camshaft flanges and check that the engine has not turned from its TDC position. Referring to **FIG 1:4,** remove the circlips 3 from the camshaft sprockets and tap out the adjusting plates 2. Replace the sprockets 1 and chain onto the camshaft flanges. Exactly and precisely align the holes in the adjuster plates 2 with the threaded holes in the camshafts, and press the serrated adjuster plates back into the serrations in the sprockets. The securing holes in the adjusting plates are slightly offset from the tooth centre line so, if the plate is difficult to engage, turn it through 180 degrees to ensure easy fitting and exact alignment of the holes. Replace the circlips 3 and secure the sprockets to the camshaft using the two bolts on each and wire-locking all four bolts after assembly. Under no circumstances must the crankshaft

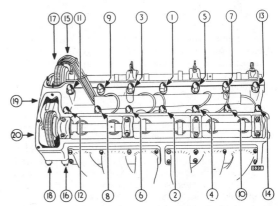

FIG 1:8 Tightening sequence for the cylinder head nuts

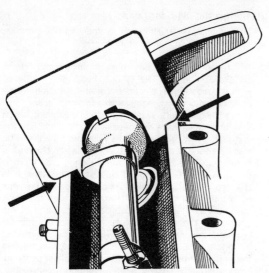

FIG 1:9 Valve timing gauge fitted to camshaft. Ensure that the gauge seats at the points indicated by the arrows

or camshafts be rotated from their set positions while setting the valve timing.

3 Tighten the cylinder head nuts progressively and evenly in the order shown in **FIG 1:8** to a torque of 54 lb ft (7.5 kg m). Make sure all connections are reconnected and start the engine. Check for leaks and allow the engine to reach its normal temperature. With the engine hot again torque load fourteen domed cylinder head nuts. After running the car for about 500 miles the torque load on the cylinder head nuts should again be rechecked with the engine hot.

1:4 Servicing the cylinder head

Remove the cylinder head as described in the previous section. Tape the ends of all free hoses and block waterways and oil passages in the cylinder block with goodsized pieces of rag to prevent the ingress of dirt or carbon chippings. It is extremely important to be methodical and careful when dismantling or reassembling parts. The camshaft bearing caps are marked for position but the tappet parts are not. **Whenever parts are removed they should be laid out on clean paper, or stored in several small tins so that they can be returned to the exact position from which they were removed.** This instruction applies particularly throughout the whole of this section, though it is equally applicable to all operations.

The camshafts:

The end float of the camshaft is taken on the flanges on either side of the front bearing, and each camshaft runs in four sets of renewable steel-backed bearing shells held in place by numbered bearing caps. The camshaft is removed by evenly and progressively slackening all the nuts securing the four bearing caps. The steel-backed bearings are unlikely to wear except after long service, when new ones should be refitted. No undersize shell bearings are

supplied and in the unlikely event of wear on the camshaft journals the bearing caps must not be filed in an attempt to take up wear. Apart from cleaning off any protective, the shell bearings are fitted exactly as supplied and must neither be bored or scraped.

It should be noted that when the camshaft covers 43 and 44 are refitted they should only be lightly secured by the nuts 47 until the tachometer generator 38 and sealing plug 33 have been fully refitted. The camshaft cover nuts may then be fully tightened.

The valves:

A more detailed view of the valve assembly is shown in **FIG 1:10** and this should be used in conjunction with **FIG 1:3**. The valve stems operate in normal valve guides fitted to the cylinder head. The valves are returned to the closed position by double valve springs 19 and 20 which are secured to the top of the valves by the collars 22 and collets 23. The valves are opened by the tappet 24 being forced downwards by the cam on the camshaft. The tappet slides in a renewable sleeve fitted into the cylinder head and the valves seat into renewable steel seats 21 fitted into the combustion chambers. Though these are renewable, accurate machining and very close tolerances are required, so if either the tappet guides or the valve seats require renewing the task should be entrusted to a reliable service station. Tappet clearance is set by the thickness of the shims 25.

Removing and replacing the valves:

Remove both camshafts as described earlier. Make up a shaped block of wood which fits snugly inside the combustion chamber and holds both valves firmly shut when the cylinder head is laid on a flat surface. The cylinder head can be laid on a flat clean surface once both camshafts have been removed as all the valves will be in the closed position. Remove all the tappets 24, using a magnet to draw them out, and the shims 25. Lay each

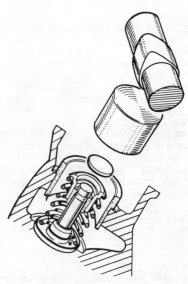

FIG 1:10 Valve tappet details

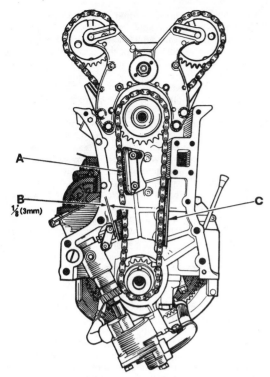

FIG 1:11 The timing gear arrangement on the 4.2 litre engine. If the timing chain is worn the dimension B should be increased to ensure that the chain does not foul the cylinder block. Note the position of the oil pump

combustion chamber in turn over the shaped block of wood. Press firmly down on the collar 22 and when the collets 23 are free, remove them with a thin screwdriver. The springs 19 and 20 and the collar 22 can then be removed, and the valves 17 or 18 slid out from the combustion chamber. Check all the valve springs against the dimensions given in Technical Data and if they are shorter than the free length given, or weak,renew the complete set. Check the valve guides as detailed later and service the valves. Replace the valves in the reverse order of dismantling, using valve spring compressor No. J.6118 mounted on the front or rear camshaft bearing studs to compress the valve springs and refit the collets.

Servicing the valves and seats:

1 Remove all the valves as just described. Make sure that they are stored in their correct order. Examine the valve stems. They should be straight, (check with a metal straightedge), and not show signs of wear, scoring or 'picking up'. Provided the stems are satisfactory remove the carbon and deposits from the valve head. Leave the carbon around the top of the machined portion of the valve stem as this acts as an oil seal. An easy way of cleaning the valves is to mount the stem in a lathe or electric drill and use worn emerycloth to remove the deposits. Great care must be taken not to damage the valve seat or stem.
2 Examine the seat in the cylinder head and on the valve. If either are deeply pitted the worn seat should be

reground using garage equipment. The use of grinding paste would only remove excess metal from the other seat as well. The cylinder head seats must be recut if new valve guides have been fitted to ensure concentricity. If, after regrinding, the head seats are too wide new seat inserts should be fitted.
3 To grind-in valves put a light spring under the valve head and use medium-grade carborundum paste, unless the seats are in very good condition, in which case fine-grade paste may be used immediately. Use a suction cup tool to hold the valve head and grind with a semi-rotary motion, letting the valve rise off the seat occasionally by the pressure of the spring. Use grinding paste sparingly, and when the pitting has been removed, clean away the old paste and transfer to using fine-grade paste. When the seats have a matt grey, even finish clean away every trace of grinding paste from the valves and ports. After grinding-in the valves the tappet clearances will have to be reset.

Setting the tappet clearances:

This operation can be carried out with the cylinder head fitted to the engine, but it will be much easier before refitting the cylinder head.
1 Remove one camshaft. This is only necessary when the camshafts are disconnected from the timing sprockets. Turn the other camshaft and use feeler gauges to measure the clearance between the back of each cam and its tappet. Note the readings on a piece of paper. Remove the second camshaft and replace the first camshaft and again note the clearances for this camshaft.
2 Remove the fitted camshaft. Withdraw all the tappets 24 and the shims 25, laying them out in the correct order. The correct tappet clearances are as follows:

Normal touring
| Inlet | .004 inch (.10 mm) |
| Exhaust | .006 inch (.15 mm) |

Racing
| Inlet | .006 inch (.15 mm) |
| Exhaust | .010 inch (.25 mm) |

New shims 25 will have to be fitted to obtain the correct tappet clearance.

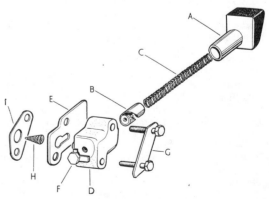

FIG 1:12 Bottom timing chain tensioner details

Key to Fig 1:12   A Slipper head   B Restraint cylinder
C Spring   D Body   E Backplate   F Plug
G Lockplate and securing bolts   H Filter   I Shim

3 The shims 25 are etched on the face with an identifying letter, but if this is worn away a micrometer gauge will have to be used to measure the actual thickness of the shim. The letter A indicates a shim of .085 inch (2.16 mm) thickness. Each succeeding letter upwards indicates an increase of thickness of .001 inch up to the letter Z which therefore is a shim .110 inch (2.79 mm) thick.

4 When a clearance is found to be incorrect check the thickness of the shim fitted. A new shim will have to be fitted so that the difference in thickness between the shims corresponds to the error in the tappet clearance. After replacing the shims and tappets refit each camshaft in turn and check that the valve clearances are now correct.

Decarbonizing :

Remove the cylinder head and dismantle it as described previously. It is suggested that the cylinder head studs be removed from the cylinder, using either a stud extractor or a spanner on two nuts locked together. The face of the block should be checked for truth. Use either a long metal straightedge or engineers' blue on a surface table or plate glass (never window glass as this is not flat). At the same time check the face of the cylinder head. High spots can be removed by the careful use of a scraper. Minor distortion can be removed by lapping on fine grinding paste spread over a sheet of plate glass, but major distortion will have to be removed by grinding on a surface grinder.

Since both the cylinder head and pistons are machined out of aluminium alloy, and the pistons are tin coated, sharp or hard metal tools must not be used to remove the carbon. Use a sharpened stick of solder or hardwood to remove very carefully the major deposits, and finish cleaning and polishing using worn emerycloth and paraffin as a lubricant. **Never use a wire brush.**

Before cleaning the pistons, smear a little grease around the tops of the bores as the dirt will stick to this and be easily removable. Turn the engine until a pair of pistons are nearly at TDC and spring an old piston ring into the bore to protect the carbon around the periphery of the piston and the top of the bore. This carbon should not be removed as it acts as a heat shield and oil seal. Repeat the process on the other two pairs of pistons and finally clean away all dirt and remove the pieces of rag from the water passages and oilways.

Valve guides :

These should be checked using a new valve. The clearance new is .001 to .004 inch (.025 to .10 mm) and if this dimensions if exceeded by more than a few 'thou' the valve guide should be renewed. Valve guides are available in four different grades, the size increasing with the number of identifying grooves. Only standard (no groove) and first oversize (one groove) guides are fitted on production. First oversize valve guides can be refitted directly in place of the standard valve guides but all the other oversizes require extremely accurate reaming of the bore for the valve guide. If the owner has any doubt about his ability to ream a hole to $+.0005$ and $-.0002$ inch tolerances he is advised to leave the task to a garage. The dimensions and tolerances for the valve guides are given in Technical Data.

All valve guides must be fitted so that they protrude $\frac{5}{16}$ inch (8 mm) above the spot facing of valve spring seat. Later valve guides are fitted with a circlip so that the guide is driven in from the top, the circlip fitted and the guide driven down until the circlip is firmly against the spring seat.

Heat the cylinder head by boiling it in water for 30 minutes. Use a piloted drift and if a circlip is fitted drive the guide slightly out of the head to free and then remove the circlip. Drive the old guide down and out into the combustion chamber. Ream the bore to the dimension given in Technical Data. Again heat the cylinder head for 30 minutes in boiling water. Coat the new guide with graphited grease and drive it into place from the combustion chamber and using the piloted drift. Set the protrusion as described earlier. If a circlip is fitted the guide is driven in from the top.

Oil seals are fitted to the valve guides after engine No. 7E.11668 and another groove is machined above the circlip groove to take the oil seal.

1 : 5 Servicing the valve timing gear

Tensioning the top timing chain and setting the valve timing have already been dealt with in **Section 1 : 3**. The timing chains and tensioners can be removed with the engine still fitted to the car.

1 Disconnect the battery. Remove the bonnet (see **Chapter 13**). Drain the cooling system, remove the radiator, the header tank and its bracket (see **Chapter 4**). Remove the water pump from the timing cover (see **Chapter 4**). Remove the crankshaft damper (see operation 4 in **Section 1 : 2**) and then remove the split cone by carefully opening it with a screwdriver in the slot and sliding it off the crankshaft. Remove the sump (see **Section 1 : 6**). Remove the cylinder head (see **Section 1 : 3**).

2 Remove the timing cover (item 3 in **FIG 1 : 2**) by taking out the securing bolts and pulling the cover forward off the two dowels 7. The timing gear will then be as shown in **FIG 1 : 11**. The figure illustrated the 4.2 litre engine and the main difference in the 3.8 litre engine is that the damper A acts on the opposite side of the chain.

3 Remove the bottom automatic chain tensioner A (item in **FIG 1 : 4**). This automatic hydraulic tensioner is shown in detail in **FIG 1 : 12**. Remove the plug F from the body and insert through the hole an .125 inch AF Allen key. Fit the Allen key into the hexagonal hole in the end of the restraint cylinder B and turn the cylinder in a 'clockwise' direction until the slipper head B is in the retracted position. Remove the plate and bolts G and detach the tensioner parts from the engine. Take care not to lose the small conical filter H.

4 Use **FIG 1 : 4** for reference. Remove the four setscrews securing the front mounting bracket 7 to the cylinder block. Remove the two screw-headed setscrews that secure the intermediate damper 24 and the rear mounting bracket 8 to the cylinder block. The timing gear assembly can now be removed, levering off the crankshaft sprocket from the crankshaft so that the bottom timing chain 25 is not distorted.

5 Completely unscrew the locking nut from the front of the eccentric shaft 10. Remove the serrated adjusting plate 12, the plunger 13 which locks the adjusting

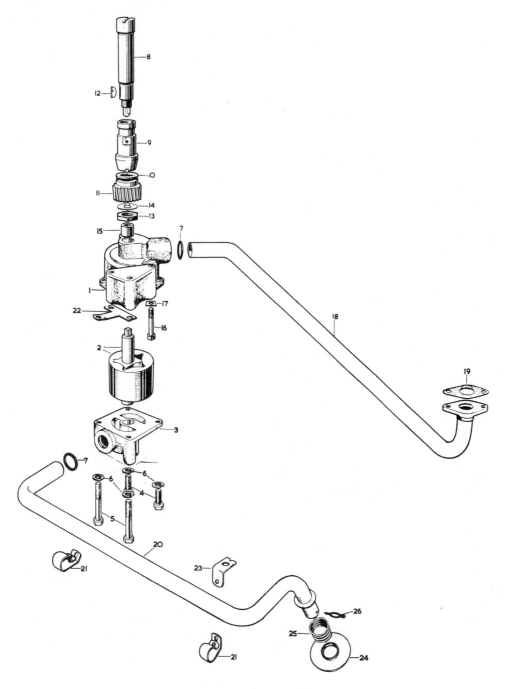

FIG 1:13 Oil pump and distributor drive details

Key to Fig 1:13   1 Body   2 Rotor assembly   3 Cover   4 Setscrew   5 Setscrew   6 Washer   7 O-ring
8 Drive shaft   9 Bush   10 Washer   11 Helical gear   12 Key   13 Nut   14 Tabwasher   15 Coupling
16 Dowel bolt   17 Tabwasher   18 Oil delivery pipe   19 Gasket   20 Oil suction pipe   21 Clip   22 Strut
23 Strut   24 Plate   25 Spring   26 Splitpin

plate and the spring 14. Remove the four nuts which hold the front mounting bracket 7 to the rear bracket 8 and lift off the front bracket 7. Lift off the bottom timing chain 25 from the sprocket 16. Remove the eccentric shaft 10 and idler sprocket 9 and lift out the top timing chain 20. Remove the circlip 19 and press out the shaft 18 from the bracket to free the intermediate sprockets 15 and 16. On later engines these are manufactured in one piece but on earlier engines they can be separated by pressing them apart. Note that on earlier engines the two sprockets are keyed together with the key 17. The camshaft sprocket assemblies can be dismantled by removing the circlips 3 and 6.

Clean all the parts with petrol or paraffin, using an old toothbrush to clean out crevices. Shake the timing chains in a tin full of solvent. Dry all the parts and examine them for wear. If the timing chains have stretched or worn they should be renewed. Carefully examine all the sprockets and renew any that show 'hooking' wear of the teeth. Renew the dampers if the pads are worn. Reassemble the parts and then refit them in the reverse order of dismantling, but noting the following points.

1 Use new gaskets throughout. The cost of new gaskets and seals is little compared with the inconvenience of finding an old gasket leaking and having to repeat the whole operation. If the distance piece (item 31 in **FIG 1 : 2**) on which the seal 32 operates is scored or worn renew it otherwise it will be a source of oil leakage. Use non-setting jointing compound on the gaskets. Make sure the seal 32 is firmly in its recess in the timing cover 30 before refitting the cover.

2 Lubricate all bearing surfaces and the timing chains with clean engine oil.

3 Do not adjust or refit the automatic timing chain tensioner 27 until the bottom timing chain 25 is in position. The tensioner is refitted in the reverse order of dismantling using shims I to ensure that the slipper head A runs centrally on the timing chain. Lock the bolts with the tab G. On the 3.8 litre engine an Allen key is used to turn the restraint cylinder B clockwise only until the slipper pad is in contact with the chain. **Never try to force the slipper pad A back and never turn the restraint cylinder B anticlockwise.** The 4.2 litre engine is similarly adjusted but the gap B is set at $\frac{1}{8}$ inch as shown and the other dampers are then set to just contact the chain, as shown in **FIG 1 : 11**. Refit the plug F and lock it in place.

4 Once the cylinder head has been refitted the top timing chain tension will have to be set and the valve timing reset.

1 : 6 The sump

Refer to **FIG 1 : 2**. Before removing the sump it must be drained of oil by removing the drain plug and catching the oil in a suitable container. The oil will run more easily if it is hot, so take the car for a run to heat the oil before draining. After draining remove the crankshaft damper 29 (operation 4 in **Section 1 : 2**) and disconnect the return hose 65 from the oil filter. It may be necessary to slacken the locknut and bottom stepped washer 76 on the engine stabilizer assembly to allow the rear of the engine to be raised to remove the sump. Unscrew the twenty-six setscrews and four nuts securing the sump in place. Lower the sump and remove it.

Before refitting the sump dismantle it by taking off the nuts securing the baffle plate 69 and filter basket 61. Use newspapers to remove the worst of the sludge and oil, then clean the parts with petrol or paraffin. Remove the gaskets 56 and the rear seal 58 and discard them. Clean the mating faces of the sump and cylinder block free from bits of gasket or jointing compound. Reassemble the sump.

Secure the new gaskets 56 to the sump with a little jointing compound. Fit a new seal 58 into the recess on the cover 11. This operation will be made easier, time permitting, if the seal is rolled into a coil held by string and left for a few hours.

Refit the sump to the engine, taking care not to displace the gaskets or seals 57 and 58. The short setscrew is fitted to the righthand front corner of the sump.

Refit the damper, connect the return hose from the oil filter and fill the sump to the correct level with clean engine oil. If the stabilizer has been slackened, reset it as described at the end of **Section 1 : 2**.

1 : 7 The oil pump

The details of the oil pump are shown in **FIG 1 : 13**. The pump has the fullflow of oil passing through it and is unlikely, unless the oil filter is choked and the engine oil dirty, to wear much in service or cause trouble. The most likely wear will be excessive end float or scoring of the cover 3. If, after a long period of service, this occurs, damage can be removed and the correct end float restored by lapping the parts with fine grinding paste spread on a sheet of plate glass.

To remove the oil pump first remove the sump as described in the previous section. Remove the clips 21 and remove the inlet pipe 20. Disconnect the oil delivery pipe 18 at the flange and also remove this pipe. Free the tab-washers 17 and unscrew the bolts 16 securing the pump to the front main bearing cap. Withdraw the pump and collect the coupling sleeve 15.

Dismantle the pump by removing the bolts 4 and 5. Wash the parts in clean petrol and reassemble them dry, leaving off the cover 3. Use feeler gauges to measure the clearance between the rotors, as shown in **FIG 1 : 14**. This clearance should not exceed .006 inch (.15 mm). Similarly measure the clearance between the outer rotor and the body 1, checking to see that it does not exceed .010 inch (.25 mm). Lay a straightedge across the base of the body 1 and check that the end clearance between the rotors and the straightedge does not exceed .0025 inch (.06 mm).

Reassemble the pump fully in the reverse order of dismantling, ensuring that the outer rotor is inserted chamfered end leading into the body of the pump. Well lubricate the rotors with clean engine oil before replacing the end cover. Fit the coupling sleeve 15 to the end of the drive shaft 8 and refit the pump so that the squared end of the rotor shaft also fits into the coupling sleeve. Replace the remainder of the parts in the reverse order of dismantling.

1 : 8 The oil filter and relief valve

The components of these are shown in **FIG 1 : 15**. The element 9 can either be a paper type or felt element. The paper type element should be renewed at every oil change. This is normally every 2500 miles but in adverse

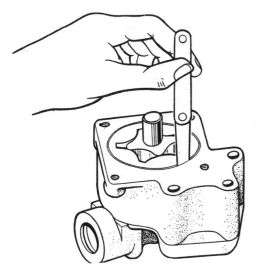

FIG 1:14 Measuring the clearance between the inner and outer rotors

seal 10 back into the filter head, making sure the seal is not twisted and is fully and squarely fitted into the recess. Renew or replace the cleaned element 9 into the case 1 and refit the case back onto the filter head. Replace the drain plug 19. Fill the engine to the correct level with fresh oil and start the engine. Check for leaks immediately. When satisfied switch off the engine and leave for one minute at least. Provided the car is on level ground an accurate reading of the oil level can be taken on the dipstick. Top up the level to replace the oil required for filling the oil filter casing.

The filter head 11 contains the relief valve assembly, from where surplus oil is returned directly to the sump by the external rubber hose, and a balance valve 12. The balance valve is fitted to allow oil to be passed to the engine if the oil filter element 9 is choked with dirt. When this occurs there will be an oil pressure drop of approximately 10 lb/ sq in.

A drop in oil pressure can sometimes also be caused by the relief valve assembly. Unscrew the adaptor 17 and withdraw the parts. Carefully clean both the valve 14 and its seat in the head, in case dirt has been trapped under the valve and is holding it open. If, after long service, it is suspected that the relief spring 15 has weakened refit the parts using a new spring.

1:9 The clutch and flywheel

Full instructions on servicing the clutch will be given in **Chapter 5**, so this section will deal only with clutch removal and replacement. The gearbox has to be removed to gain access to these parts. As the gearbox cannot be removed separately, the complete unit will have to be taken out from the car and the gearbox then separated from the engine (see **Section 1:2** and **Chapters 6** and **7**). With the gearbox removed examine the outer flange of the clutch and flywheel. The letter B will be found

conditions, such as very cold weather or much stop start driving, the period should be decreased to 1000 miles. The felt type element should be renewed every other oil change but before replacing it, it should be washed in clean fuel and allowed to dry completely.

Place a container under the oil filter and remove the drain plug 19. Unscrew the central bolt 6 and remove the container 1 with the internal parts and the element 9. With a small pointed tool prise out the sealing ring 10 from the filter head 11. Wash out the container 1 with clean petrol. If required renew the seal 7 and felt washer 4. Fit a new

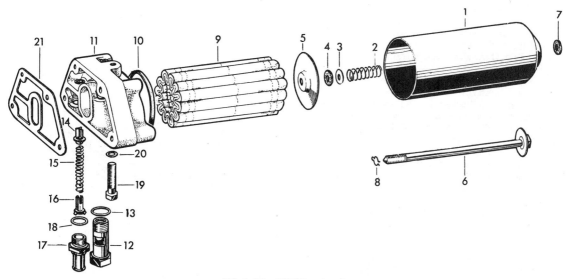

FIG 1:15 Oil filter details

Key to Fig 1:15   1 Canister   2 Spring   3 Washer   4 Felt washer   5 Pressure plate   6 Bolt   7 Washer
8 Spring clip   9 Element   10 Sealing ring   11 Filter head   12 Balance valve   13 Washer   14 Relief valve
15 Spring   16 Spider and pin   17 Adaptor   18 Washer   19 Drain plug   20 Washer   21 Gasket

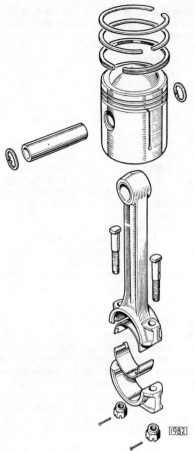

FIG 1:16 Piston and connecting rod details

side' facing the flywheel, and must be centralized, using a mandrel, while progressively tightening the clutch securing setscrews. Tighten the flywheel securing bolts 47 to a torque of 67 lb ft (9.2 kg m). Do not forget to align the B mark on the clutch flange with the B mark on the flywheel and remember to replace the balance weights in their respective positions.

1:10 Pistons and connecting rods

These can be removed with the engine still fitted to the car. To change the big-end bearings, only the sump need be removed (see **Section 1:6**) but as the pistons will not pass downwards past the crankshaft the cylinder head will have to be removed (see **Section 1:3**). Though not necessary, it is also recommended that the oil pump be removed (see **Section 1:7**) to give more access room and to prevent damage to the oil pump pipes. The details of the parts are shown in **FIG 1:16**. Refer also to **FIG 1:2**.

Big-end bearings:

The bearing caps should already be marked for both position and order with stamped numerals, but if they are not marked do so with light punch marks.

1 Turn the engine so that a pair of throws are in a convenient position for working on. Remove the splitpins from the bearing cap nuts and undo the nuts. Pull off the bearing caps complete with their shell bearings.

2 Slide the connecting rods and pistons up the bore of the cylinders to clear the connecting rods from the crankpins. Slide out the shell bearings from the caps and connecting rods and lay the parts out in order. Tap the bolts out of the connecting rods.

3 Turn the engine and similarly disconnect the remaining four big-ends, laying the parts out in order as they are removed.

4 Examine all the shell bearings and if any are pitted, scored or worn the complete set should be renewed. If a bearing has actually 'run' and the steel backing is

stamped on both, indicating the balance point. Under some of the clutch securing bolts small balance weights may be found. These and the clutch cover will be stamped with matching numbers.

Progressively and evenly slacken the six setscrews securing the clutch cover to the flywheel and remove the clutch assembly and driven plate. Free the tabs on the locking plate 48 and remove the ten flywheel securing bolts 47, shown in **FIG 1:2**. Tap the flywheel off the crankshaft using a rawhide hammer, preferably having a second operator to support the flywheel 44 as it comes free.

The starter ring gear is integral with the flywheel so if the teeth are worn or damaged the flywheel will have to be renewed. After renewing the flywheel the clutch and flywheel assembly must be rebalanced. Mount the assembly on a mandrel and rest the mandrel on parallel horizontal knife-edges. The assembly always stopping in the same place indicates that the heavy point is at the bottom. Remove the clutch and, if required, drill $\frac{3}{8}$ inch (9.5 mm) balance holes not more than $\frac{1}{2}$ inch (12.7 mm) deep at a distance of $\frac{3}{8}$ inch (9.5 mm) from the edge of the flywheel at the heavy point.

Refit the flywheel with the Nos. 1 and 6 pistons at TDC and the flywheel B mark as near BDC as possible. The clutch driven plate is fitted with the marking 'Flywheel

FIG 1:17 8:1 compression ratio piston showing the markings on the piston crown

showing through the bearing material, the engine should be further dismantled and a new connecting rod fitted. New shell bearings are fitted as received, apart from cleaning off any protective, and should not be scraped or bored.

5 Examine and measure the crankpins with a micrometer gauge. If they are worn oval or tapered in excess of .003 inch (.08 mm) the crankshaft must be removed and the crankpins reground. New undersize bearing shells will then also have to be fitted.

6 Reconnect the big-ends in the reverse order of dismantling. Make sure the tags on the shell bearings are seated in the recesses provided and lubricate them with clean engine oil. It is strongly advised that new nuts and bolts are fitted. Make sure that the markings on the caps and connecting rods are on the same side and tighten the cap nuts to a torque of 37 lb ft (5.1 kg m). **Never file the bearing caps or connecting rods in an attempt to take up wear in the bearings or crankpins.**

Cylinder bores:

When the pistons and connecting rods have been removed, examine the bores of the cylinders for wear. Ideally a Mercer dial gauge should be used to measure the bore, but by using judgement and a set of feeler gauges as a guide the wear can be estimated fairly accurately. The maximum wear will occur near the top of the bore across its thrust axis, leaving an unworn ring around the top of the bore. If the wear exceeds .006 inch (.15 mm) the cylinders should be rebored and oversized pistons fitted. The maximum limit for reboring is .030 inch (.76 mm) and if this is exceeded the dry liners should be pressed out and new liners fitted. These liners can then be bored to take standard pistons again.

If the wear is not sufficient to warrant reboring but new piston rings are to be fitted, the unworn ridge around the top of the bore should be removed using garage equipment. The remainder of the bore should also be lightly honed or scuffed to remove the hard glaze and assist in bedding-in new piston rings.

Pistons:

The pistons are made of low-expansion aluminium alloy coated with tin and are of the semi-split skirt type. A typical 8:1 compression ratio piston is shown in **FIG 1 :17**. The 9:1 compression ratio piston is similar but the dome on the crown is larger. The piston is marked with the word 'Front' and must always be fitted to the engine so that this faces forwards. In addition to this the crown is also marked with a grade letter or oversize. The various grades of standard piston and their matching bores are given in Technical Data.

The gudgeon pins are fully floating, matched to the pistons, and secured in place by the two circlips. The pistons are removed and replaced on the connecting rods by taking out the circlips and heating the piston in oil at a temperature of 110°C (230°F). The gudgeon pin can then easily be slid in or out. Use new circlips when refitting the piston.

Piston rings:

Three rings are fitted to each piston; two compression rings and one oil control ring. The top compression rings are tapered and chromium plated. On the 4.2 litre engine these rings are supplied 'Cargraphed'. This is a red material which assists in the bedding-in of the ring. **This red material should not be removed with solvents or degreasing fluid.** The second compression is not chrome-plated but may be tapered. All tapered rings have the marking 'T' or 'Top' on them which must be fitted uppermost on the piston. On the 3.8 litre engine the oil control ring is of one piece construction and can be fitted either way up. The oil control ring of the 4.2 litre engine is made in three parts.

A piston ring expanding tool will greatly facilitate removing the rings from the pistons, but it is not essential. Remove the rings from the top of the piston by sliding a thin piece of metal, such as a discarded .020 inch feeler gauge, under one end and passing it around the ring, at the same time pressing the raised part onto the piston land above. Use three equi-spaced shims to protect the piston when sliding the rings on or off.

Clean carbon and dirt from the ring grooves by using a piece of broken ring, taking great care not to remove metal or the oil consumption will be increased. Carefully clean out the oil drain holes behind the oil control ring. Refit the rings and check that the side clearance in the grooves is .001 to .003 inch (.025 to .076 mm). If this clearance is exceeded either new rings, or in bad cases new pistons and rings, will have to be fitted.

Before fitting new piston rings check that the gaps between the ends are correct when the rings are fitted in the bore. Fit the ring only as far down the bore as possible and press it square with a piston. Measure the gap between the ends with feeler gauges. The clearances should be as follows, and if they are not correct the ends of the rings should be carefully filed to make the correct gap.
All top compression rings .015 to .020 inch (.38 to .51 mm)
Second compression ring 3.8 .015 to .020 inch (.38 to .51 mm)
Second compression ring 4.2 .010 to .015 inch (.254 to .38 mm)
Oil control ring 3.8 .011 to .016 inch (.28 to .41 mm)
Maxiflex oil control ring 4.2 .015 to .045 inch (.38 to 1.143 mm)
Later engines are fitted with Hepworth and Grandage pistons which have a solid skirt. The oil control ring for these pistons must have the ends of the expander ring butting and not overlapping otherwise the scrapers cannot be fitted correctly. The earlier type of oil control rings is supplied held together by adhesive for easier fitting and should not be separated. The adhesive will dissolve in the hot engine oil.

Connecting rods:

The big-end bearings are renewable as already instructed. The gudgeon pin runs in a renewable phosphor/bronze bush. If new bushes are fitted they require to be jig-reamed to a very close tolerance, so renewal of the phosphor/bronze bushes is an operation best left to a garage. Whenever the connecting rods are removed they should also be checked for twist and bend. Again, since accurate jigs are required, this should be left to a garage.

To avoid fatigue failures the connecting rods should be renewed after long service or the failure of a big-end bearing. The cost is minor compared to the cost of repairs when a connecting rod breaks and thrashes through the side of the crankcase.

Refitting the pistons and connecting rods:

Assemble the pistons to their respective connecting rods so that the 'Front' mark on the piston will face forwards and the connecting rods will also face the same direction from which they were removed. The connecting rods should be centralized between the bosses of the piston so that there is no side load when the big-ends are reconnected. Turn the piston rings so that the gaps are evenly spaced around the piston. Lightly oil the rings and compress them into the piston with a piston ring clamp. In emergency a large Jubilee type clip can be used instead of the proper ring clamp. Lower the connecting rod down the bore of the cylinder and carefully enter the skirt of the piston into the bore. Press the piston down gently into the bore, allowing the clamp to slide off the rings as they enter. Do not force the piston and carefully check that no rings are jammed otherwise the rings will be snapped. Reconnect the big-ends as described earlier.

1:11 The crankshaft and main bearings

1 Remove the engine and gearbox from the car (see **Section 1:2**). Part the engine from the gearbox and remove the clutch and flywheel (see **Section 1:9**). Remove the cylinder head (see **Section 1:3**), the sump (see **Section 1:6**), the oil pump (see **Section 1:7**) and the valve timing gear (see **Section 1:5**). Disconnect the big-ends (see **Section 1:10**) and though it is not necessary, remove the pistons and connecting rods for examination. Remove the cylinder head studs and invert the engine on a clean flat surface. Use a thick layer of old newspapers to rest the block on to prevent damage.

2 Refer to **FIG 1:2**. Check that all the main bearing caps are number stamped and that the number corresponds with the one stamped on the bottom face of the crankcase. Free all the tabwashers securing the main bearing bolts and remove the bolts on all the main bearings, save the centre bearing which has the thrust washers fitted. Lift off the main bearing caps and slide out the shell bearings from them. Store the parts in the correct order for reassembly. Remove the bolts which secure the bottom half of the seal housing 11 to the top half bolted to the rear of the crankcase. The two halves are located by hollow dowels.

3 Either mount a DTI in the crankcase or use feeler gauges to measure the crankshaft end float. The end float should be .004 to .006 inch (.10 to .15 mm) and if this is exceeded new thrust washers will have to be fitted on either side of the centre main bearing cap. +.004 inch oversize thrust washers are available if the end float is really excessive. It is permissible to use one standard thrust washer and one oversize thrust washer to cure moderate amounts of end float.

4 Refer to **FIG 1:13**. Free the tabwasher 14 and remove it and the nut 13. Tap the squared end of the distributor drive shaft 8 through the gear 11, noting that they are keyed together by key 12. Remove the gear 11 and thrust washer 10 and withdraw the drive shaft from the top.

5 Undo the bolts and remove the centre main bearing cap, collecting the thrust washers from either side of it.

Lift out the crankshaft. Remove the upper row of bearing shells from their recesses in the crankcase and lay all the parts out in the correct order for reassembly. Examine the shell bearings and renew them all if any are scored, worn or pitted.

6 Examine and measure, with a micrometer gauge, the crankshaft journals. The crankshaft must be reground if the journals are scored or worn oval or tapered in excess of .003 inch (.08 mm). Undersize new main bearing shells must then be fitted. **Never file the main bearing caps in an attempt to take up wear on the journals or bearings.**

7 Clean all the parts in petrol or paraffin. Blow through the oilways in the crankshaft using paraffin under pressure followed by dry compressed air after removing the Allen screws. This is particularly important if a bearing has 'run' or if the crankshaft has been reground.

8 Refit the shell bearings into their appropriate places, making sure that the tags on the shells fit into the recesses provided. Lubricate the shells with clean engine oil. Lay the crankshaft back in place and secure it with the centre main bearing cap only. Refit the thrust washers on either side of the cap so that the whitemetal faces the crankshaft. Tighten the bolts to a load of 83 lb ft (11.5 kg m). Check that the crankshaft end float is correct, as described earlier. When satisfied replace the remainder of the main bearing caps, torque loading all the securing bolts to a load of 83 lb ft (11.5 kg m). Check that the crankshaft spins without binding. The rear cover and distributor drive gearing will have to be replaced before the engine can be reassembled in the reverse order of dismantling. Secure the main bearing bolts with the locktabs, noting that the lockwashers for the rear bolts are larger than the others.

Distributor drive gear:

Refer to **FIG 1:12** for part numbers. If the bush 9 is worn the old one should be drifted out and a new bush pressed into place. After fitting, the bush must be reamed to a diameter of .75 + .0005 — .00025 inch (19.05 + .012 — .006 mm).

Turn the crankshaft until Nos. 1 and 6 crankshaft throws are at TDC. Insert the drive shaft 8 and key 12 through the bush 9 so that it fits with the offset as shown in **FIG 1:18**. Withdraw the drive shaft slightly, without turning it, and place the thrust washer 10 and drive gear 11 on the end of the shaft. Press the drive shaft back down and secure the parts with a new tabwasher 14 and the nut 13.

Before locking the nut 13 check the end float. This should be .004 to .006 inch (.10 to .15 mm). If the end float is too little then the drive gear 11 will have to be replaced. As an emergency measure, if a new drive gear 11 is unobtainable, it is permissible to cure no end float by rubbing down the thrust washer 10 on fine emerycloth spread on plate glass or a surface table.

Rear oil seal:

A scroll is machined on the rear of the crankshaft and this acts in the rear cover 11 to drive the oil back into the engine. For effective operation it is essential that the clearance of .0025 to .0055 inch (.06 to .14 mm) is maintained between the scroll and the cover. Bolt the two halves of the cover together and slightly slacken the

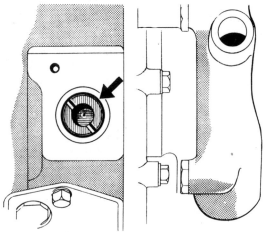

FIG 1:18 The position of the distributor drive shaft offset when No. 6 (front) piston is at TDC

bolts that hold the assembly to the cylinder block. Use feeler gauges to check the gap and tap the cover into place with a rawhide hammer. Tighten the securing bolts when the clearance is correct and even all round.

1:12 Reassembling a stripped engine

The order for dismantling the engine has already been given in the previous section. All dismantling and reassembly operations have been given in detail in the various sections, so it is simply a matter of tackling the task in the correct sequence.

Always fit new gaskets and seals. Make sure that all parts are scrupulously clean before reassembly and lubricate bearing surfaces with clean engine oil. **Cleanliness is essential.** Dirt will cause premature wear and early failure of the parts as well as preventing the engine from reaching the peak of its performance.

Start by refitting the crankshaft, distributor drive gear and rear oil seal cover. Next replace the connecting rods and pistons. Refit the valve timing gear, oil pump and sump. The engine can then be turned over and stood on the sump while the flywheel and clutch are refitted. Refit the cylinder head. Mate the gearbox to the engine and then replace the accessories such as generator, distributor starter motor and manifolds. The accessories should be left till last as they will only make the engine difficult to handle and also stand less chance of being damaged if there is a mishap.

Torque wrench loads for all important fixings are given in the relevant sections and Technical Data.

When the engine has been refitted to the car fill the gearbox and engine sump with oil, the cooling system with water and the clutch hydraulics with hydraulic fluid. Check for leaks both before and after starting the engine.

1:13 Modifications

After engine No. 7E.9210 4.2 litre and No. 7E.50963 2+2 the cylinder head gasket was changed from copper/asbestos to steel/asbestos. The new type of gasket is covered on both sides with a varnish that eliminates the need for jointing compound. The new gasket can be fitted

in place of the old type but if the top timing chain cannot be satisfactorily adjusted, because of the increased thickness of the new gasket, a replacement idler eccentric shaft (item 10 in **FIG 1:4**) part number C.27189 must be fitted.

The torque load on the cylinder head nuts is changed to 58 lb ft (8.0 kg m) when the later type of cylinder head gasket is fitted.

1:14 Fault diagnosis

(a) Engine will not start

1 Defective coil
2 Faulty distributor capacitor
3 Dirty, pitted or incorrectly set ignition contact points
4 Ignition wires loose or insulation faulty
5 Water on sparking plug leads
6 Battery discharged, corrosion on terminals
7 Faulty or jammed starter
8 Sparking plug leads wrongly connected
9 Vapour lock in fuel pipes (hot weather only)
10 Defective fuel pump
11 Overchoking or underchoking
12 Blocked petrol filter or float chamber needles
13 Leaking valves
14 Sticking valves
15 Valve timing incorrect (this fault can cause damage to engine)
16 Ignition timing incorrect

(b) Engine stalls

1 Check 1, 2, 3, 4, 5, 10, 11, 12, 13 and 14 in (a)
2 Sparking plugs defective or gaps incorrect
3 Retarded ignition
4 Mixture too weak
5 Water in fuel system
6 Petrol tank vent blocked
7 Incorrect valve clearance

(c) Engine idles badly

1 Check 2 and 7 in (b)
2 Air leak at manifold joints
3 Carburetter jet setting wrong (not applicable on emission controlled engines)
4 Worn piston rings
5 Worn valve stems or guides
6 Weak exhaust valve springs

(d) Engine misfires

1 Check 1, 2, 3, 4, 5, 10, 12, 13, 14, 15 and 16 in (a) also check 2, 3, 4 and 7 in (b)
2 Weak or broken valve springs

(e) Engine overheats (see Chapter 4)

(f) Compression low

1 Check 14 and 15 in (a); 4 and 5 in (c) and 2 in (d)
2 Worn piston ring grooves
3 Scored or worn cylinder bores

(g) Engine lacks power

1 Check 3, 10, 11, 13, 14, 15, and 16 in (a); 1, 2, 3 and 6 in (b); 4 and 5 in (c) and 2 in (d). Also check (e) and (f)
2 Leaking cylinder head gaskets
3 Fouled or worn out sparking plugs
4 Automatic advance not operating
5 Piston sticking in carburetter

(h) Burnt valves or seats

1 Check 14 and 15 in (a); 6 in (b) and 2 in (d). Also check (e)
2 Excessive carbon around valve seat and head

(j) Sticking valves

1 Check 2 in (d)
2 Bent valve stem
3 Scored valve stem and guide
4 Incorrect valve clearance
5 Gummy deposits on valve stem

(k) Excessive cylinder wear

1 Check 11 in (a) and also check (e)
2 Lack of oil
3 Dirty oil
4 Piston rings gummed up or broken
5 Badly fitting piston rings
6 Connecting rods bent

(l) Excessive oil consumption

1 Check 4 and 5 in (c) and also check (k)
2 Oil return holes in pistons choked with carbon
3 Oil level too high
4 External oil leaks

(m) Crankshaft and connecting rod bearing failure

1 Check 2 and 3 in (k)
2 Restricted oilways
3 Worn journals or crankpins
4 Loose bearing caps
5 Bent connecting rod
6 Extremely low oil pressure

(n) Low oil pressure

1 Check 2 and 3 in (k) and 2, 3 and 4 in (m)
2 Choked oil filter
3 Weak relief valve spring
4 Faulty gauge or connections

(o) 'Pinking'

1 Using too low a grade of fuel
2 Ignition too far advanced
3 Excessive carbon in the cylinder head

(p) Engine 'knocks'

1 Worn big-ends
2 Worn main bearings
3 Excessive crankshaft end float
4 Worn small-end bushes or piston bosses
5 Piston knock (slap)
6 Incorrectly adjusted tappet clearances

(q) Internal water leakage (see Chapter 4)

(r) Poor water circulation (see Chapter 4)

(s) Corrosion (see Chapter 4)

(t) High fuel consumption (see Chapter 2)

CHAPTER 2

THE FUEL SYSTEM

2:1 Description

Multiple constant-vacuum variable choke carburetters are fitted to all models of E type Jaguar. The standard version has triple SU carburetters, and the emission-controlled version for the American market is fitted with twin Stromberg 175 CD2SE carburetters.

The inlet manifold for the emission-controlled version has been progressively modified to allow homogeneous mixing of the fuel and air with the minimum loss of full power output.

All models are fitted with electric fuel pumps but the pump fitted to the 3.8 litre version is totally different from that fitted to the 4.2 litre model. The fuel pump fitted to the 3.8 litre version is a sealed unit immersed in the fuel tank and the only adjustment available is setting the fuel pressure, whereas the fuel pump on the 4.2 litre model is mounted separately from the fuel tank and may be dismantled for repairs.

All the carburetters and the fuel pump are individually fitted with wiremesh filters and an additional fuel line filter is fitted to ensure that the fuel is free from sediment and particles when it reaches the carburetters.

As there are so many interdependent variables the correct setting of triple carburetters is a difficult task. If the

owner has any doubts about his ability to carry this out accurately he is strongly advised to take the car to a reliable and experienced garage.

The emission-controlled carburetters cannot be set by ear alone. Exhaust gas analyser equipment is absolutely essential and incorrect or unauthorized tampering with the carburetters will almost certainly result in the car failing to meet the stringent demands of the US Federal law.

2:2 Routine maintenance

1 At periodic intervals unscrew the hexagonal plug from on top of each carburetter and remove the damper. Check the damper oil level and replenish it as required. The Stromberg carburetter oil well is filled with 'Zenith Lube pack' or SAE.20 engine oil to within $\frac{1}{4}$ inch of the end of the rod. On the SU carburetter the hollow piston spindle is filled with SAE.20 engine oil.

2 Every 10,000 miles the drain plug on the 3.8 litre fuel tank should be removed and the fuel drained into a clean container. Clean the wiremesh filter around the drain plug and replace the plug, checking that the filter fits evenly around the inlet pipe to the pump. Discard any dirty fuel and check that the cork washer and O-ring are both in good condition.

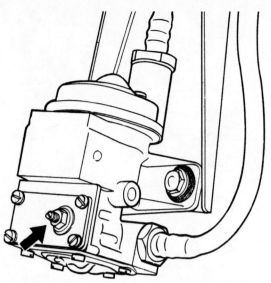

FIG 2:1 3.8 litre fuel pump relief valve adjusting screw

3 At intervals depending on the sediment in the bowl, the glass sediment bowl should be freed from the fuel line filter and the bowl and wiremesh filter washed in clean fuel. Later models of the 4.2 litre are fitted with a renewable fibre filter element. This type of element cannot be cleaned and a new element must be fitted every 12,000 miles.

4 If the fuel line filter is regularly and rapidly filled with sediment all the fuel should be drained out of the tank and the fuel lines blown through with dry compressed air. **Disconnect the fuel lines from the fuel pump before blowing through, otherwise the valves in the fuel pump may be damaged.** In exceptionally bad cases the fuel tank will have to be removed and cleaned out internally.

5 At regular intervals, depending on climatic conditions, brush loose dirt off the air cleaner element, with either a soft brush or compressed air, and clean out the casing. Beyond this the air cleaner element cannot be cleaned and when dirty it must be renewed.

6 The linkages and controls on the emission-controlled carburetters (Stromberg) should be checked regularly for freedom of movement and correct operation. Idling and mixture settings should also be checked regularly but the proper test equipment must be used. After every 24,000 miles the new parts supplied in the Red Emission Pack kit should be fitted to the carburetters. It is advisable to fit reconditioned or new carburetters to the car every 48,000 miles.

PART I FUEL PUMPS

2:3 The centrifugal impeller type pump

This is the type of pump fitted to all 3.8 litre models. The unit is sealed and contains an electric motor driving a centrifugal impeller. A relief valve, arrowed in **FIG 2:1**, is adjusted to set the correct fuel pressure. If sediment blocks the valve it can be cleaned out by removing the cover securing the relief valve.

The pump is fitted to a bracket inside the fuel tank, and is removed from the tank by taking off the cover and bracket 17 shown in **FIG 2:2**. The inlet pipe to the pump passes through the sump assembly 2 to draw fuel from the tank through the filter on the filter and drain plug assembly 4.

The fuel pump is turned on with the ignition but is protected by a separate 5 amp fuse. If the pump fails to operate, first check the fuse and then that the supply is reaching the terminals on the motor. A junction box is fitted in the spare wheel compartment to connect the pump cables to the car wiring and this will provide a convenient point for testing. Connect a first-grade 0–20 voltmeter across the connections and a good quality 0–5 ammeter in series in the circuit. Switch on the ignition and check that the operating current of the pump does not exceed 1.8 amps at 12 volts. If this current is exceeded the pump will have to be removed and a new unit fitted.

Removing and replacing the pump:

1 Disconnect the battery. Raise the boot lid and remove the carpet from the boot floor. The two floor panels are removed after taking out the retaining setscrews.

2 Remove the cover from the junction box and disconnect the pump cables. Remove the banjo bolt 27 from on top of the fuel pump and carefully move the fuel pipe 26 out of the way.

3 From underneath the car drain the fuel tank by removing the filter and drain plug assembly 4.

4 Undo the eight screws securing the carrier plate 17 to the fuel tank and lift out the pump and carrier plate assembly. Undo the union securing the fuel delivery pipe to the carrier bracket and then the nut securing the braided electrical cables to the carrier bracket. The pump itself is held by two bolts to the carrier bracket.

The pump is replaced in the reverse order of removal but note the following points:

1 A metal star-washer is fitted onto one of the rubber grommets on the pump mounting feet. **This washer must be fitted,** as it provides the earth path for the fuel pump and prevents the dangerous build-up of static electricity on the pump.

2 Check all seals and gaskets as they are replaced. Any that are damaged or liable to leak should be renewed, otherwise there will be excessive fuel losses or fuel fumes in the car

3 If the fuel inlet pipe 19 has been removed from the pump make sure it is refitted so that it fits centrally and smoothly in the sump assembly 2 and drain plug and filter assembly 4.

Testing the fuel pump:

The current consumption checks with the pump fitted to the car have already been described earlier. If all the carburetters tend to flood and no fault can be found with the carburetter float chamber needles, suspect the fuel pump of delivering fuel at too high a pressure. Remove the pump from the car and connect it to a 12 volt battery, using an on/off switch in the circuit, and connecting the black pump lead to the battery positive terminal. Connect a pressure gauge to the delivery pipe on the fuel pump. This test can be carried out with the pump still fitted to the car, (in which case a union must be made up to insert the pressure gauge into the fuel lines) but the pump will

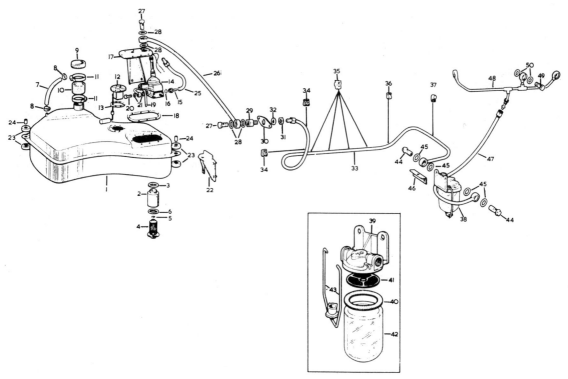

FIG 2:2   3.8 litre fuel system details

Key to Fig 2:2   1 Fuel tank   2 Sump assembly   3 Washer   4 Filter and drain plug assembly   5 O-ring
6 Washer   7 Hose   8 Clip   9 Filler cap   10 Hose   11 Clip   12 Tank element   13 Gasket   14 Fuel pump   15 Union
16 Fibre washer   17 Mounting bracket   18 Gasket   19 Pipe   20 Banjo bolt   21 Washer   22 Mounting bracket
23 Rubber pad   24 Distance piece   25 Pipe   26 Pipe   27 Banjo bolt   28 Fibre washer   29 Connector
30 Mounting plate   31 Nut   32 Brass washer   33 Pipe   34 to 37 Clips   38 Filter assembly   39 Filter casting
40 Sealing washer   41 Filter gauze   42 Bowl   43 Retaining strap   44 Banjo bolt   45 Fibre washer
46 Mounting bracket   47 Pipe   48 Feed pipe   49 Banjo bolt   50 Fibre washer

still have to be removed if it requires adjusting. Immerse
the pump in a container of clean paraffin and set it
running by using the switch, to prevent the danger of any
sparks. **Make sure that all naked lights or flames
are out.** The pump should give a pressure reading of 2
to $2\frac{1}{2}$ lb/sq in (.14 to .17 kg/sq cm). On later models a
pump delivering at a higher pressure of 3 to $3\frac{1}{2}$ lb/sq in
(.2 to .25 kg/sq cm) is fitted. This pump can replace the
earlier type of pump provided the carburetter float chamber
needles are of the later 'Delrin' type.

If the fuel pump is not delivering within the correct
pressure limits, slacken the locknut on the relief valve
shown in **FIG 2:1**. To reduce the pressure turn the relief
valve in an anticlockwise direction. When the pressure is
correct tighten the locknut and refit the pump back into
the fuel tank.

2:4 The reciprocating diaphragm fuel pump

This is the type of fuel pump fitted to all 4.2 litre models,
and is situated as shown in **FIG 2:3**. The components
of the pump are shown in **FIG 2:4**.

When the pump is first switched on, and the carburetter
float chambers are low, the current flows through the
contact blade 22 and the contacts on the rocker assembly
15 to energize the coil in the housing 6. The armature and

diaphragm 2 are drawn towards the coil and a suction is
set up in the body 1 allowing fuel to be drawn in through
the inlet valve 37. The rocker mechanism 15 has a
throw-over action so that the points are opened when
the diaphragm reaches the end of its stroke. Arcing across
the points is prevented by the action of the capacitor 25
and as soon as the current is cut off the coil de-energizes,
allowing the diaphragm to return under the action of the
return spring 5. The fuel in front of the diaphragm is then
forced out to the carburetters through the outlet valve 38.
Fluctuations in the fuel delivery pressure are damped out
by a diaphragm 57 and spring 59 assembly connected to
the atmosphere on the non-fuel side of the diaphragm. As
the diaphragm reaches the end of its pumping stroke the
throw over action of the rocker again closes the contacts
to energize the coil and the complete cycle is rapidly
repeated until the carburetter float chambers are full.
Fuel pressure then holds the diaphragm back against
the pressure of the return spring until more fuel is
required. When the ignition is switched on, the pump
should tick rapidly and then slow down as the carburetters
fill until eventually it is ticking about once a minute. With
the engine started and running it should tick regularly and
slowly. Each stroke of the pump will also show as a movement on the ammeter needle. The pump continuing to
operate rapidly indicates either low fuel level or a fault.

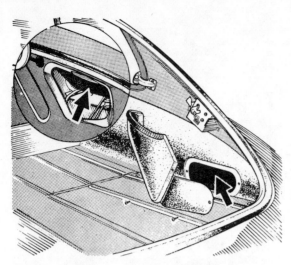

FIG 2:3 Location of fuel pump on 4.2 litre models. Inset shows position in open 2-seater model

Removing and replacing the pump :

Remove the trim and cover over the pump. Disconnect both fuel pipes from the pump body and the supply cable to the terminal. Remove the two self-locking nuts and washers securing the pump. Withdraw the pump leaving the grommets on the bracket, after disconnecting the earth wire from the earth tag on the pump body.

Replacing the pump is the reversal of the removal procedure. If the rubber grommets are worn they should be renewed as otherwise the pump will be noisy in operation.

Dismantling the pump :

1 Remove the cover 29 by undoing the nut 32. Note the relative positions of the parts before removal. Remove the screw 24 and take out contact blade 22. Unclip the capacitor 25.
2 Separate the body 1 assembly from the coil housing 6 by undoing the ring of screws 7. **Use a well fitting thick-bladed screwdriver for these screws otherwise the slots in the heads will be damaged.** Hold the housing 6 over a box, to catch the eleven rollers 3 as they fall out, and unscrew the diaphragm and spindle assembly 2. **Do not separate the diaphragm from the spindle as they are renewed as one unit.** Remove the spring 5.
3 Collect the washer 21 and remove the nut 20. Cut the flattened lead washer 19 to remove it. Remove the two screws 28 securing the pedestal 16 to the housing 6, noting that the earth wire tag 13 and capacitor clip 26 are held by these screws. Tilt the pedestal to remove the cable tags from the terminal screw 17 and remove the pedestal 16 and rocker assembly 15. Separate these two by withdrawing the hardened steel pin 14.
4 Remove the two screws 35 securing the clamp plate 34 and remove the valve components, including the inlet filter 40. The inlet air bottle cover 45 and its associated parts can be removed by undoing the screw 48 but the cover 51 should not be removed unless the

flow smoothing assembly is leaking. If the flow smoothing assembly is dismantled the pump must be pressure checked after reassembly.

Examining the parts :

1 Remove any gum deposits by soaking the affected metal parts in methylated spirits and then scrubbing them to remove the deposit. If there are thick gum deposits both diaphragms should be examined as these residues, left after the evaporation of fuel, will attack neoprene.
2 Brush the parts in clean fuel to remove any sediment and dirt. Renew the filter 40 if the mesh is damaged.
3 Examine the pedestal 16 for cracks or damage, especially on the narrow ridge at the edge of the rectangular hole where the contact blade fits. Renew the part if it is damaged.
4 Examine the contact points. If these are burnt or pitted the complete rocker assembly 15 and contact blade 22 must be renewed.
5 Examine the inlet and outlet valves. The best method of testing them is to hold them in the mouth and blow and suck through them. Check that the little brass tongues on the cage that retain the actual valves are not damaged and distorted and that they allow the valves approximately $\frac{1}{16}$ inch (1.6 mm) free lift.
6 Check the non-return valve 42 to ensure that it is clear and that the ball is free to move.
7 Renew all seals and gaskets, including the lead washer 19. Renew any rollers 3 that show signs of wear on the periphery. Pitting or irreparable corrosion in the valve recesses means that a new body 1 must be fitted.

Reassembling the pump :

1 Reassemble the valves and parts to the body 1 in the reverse order of dismantling, noting that the recess for the inlet valve is deeper than the recess for the outlet valve. If the flow smoothing device has been dismantled this too should be reassembled in the reverse order of dismantling. Refit the spring 59 and end cap 58 to the cover 51 and compress the spring. Use a bent piece of stiff wire in the slot of the end cap and through the hole in the cover 51, to keep the spring compressed while refitting the cover. Turn the wire through 90 degrees to free the small bent end from the slot and pull it out of the cover when the parts are secured.
2 Reassemble the rocker mechanism to the pedestal, **using only a correct hardened steel pin 14** and secure the assembly back to the housing 6. **Do not overtighten the securing screws 28 or the pedestal 16 will crack.** Reassemble with all the parts except the contact blade 22. Hold the earth tag 13 to prevent it rotating with the screw and breaking the wire.
3 Check that the impact washer 4 is in place and refit the diaphragm and spindle assembly 2 by screwing the threaded portion of the spindle into the trunnion in the centre of the rocker assembly with the spring 5 in place. Screw the diaphragm in until the rocker will not throw over, making sure that the armature does not jam on the internal steps in the coil housing. Hold the pump in one hand with the rocker assembly facing downwards

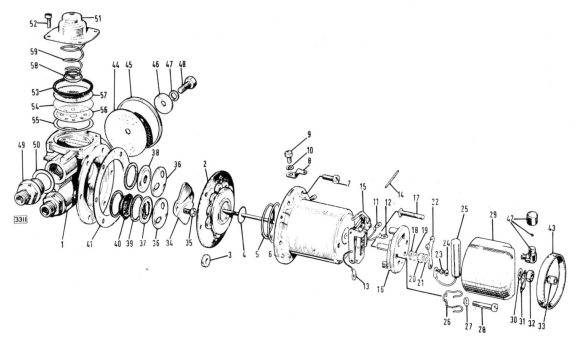

FIG 2:4   4.2 litre fuel pump details

Key to Fig 2:4   1 Pump body   2 Diaphragm and spindle assembly   3 Armature centralizing roller   4 Impact washer
5 Armature spring   6 Coil housing   7 2 BA screw, securing housing   8 Earth connector   9 4 BA screw   10 Spring washer
11 Terminal tag   12 Terminal tag   13 Earth tag   14 Rocker pivot pin   15 Rocker mechanism   16 Pedestal
17 Terminal stud   18 Spring washer   19 Lead washer   20 Terminal nut   21 Washer   22 Contact blade
23 Washer   24 Screw   25 Condenser   26 Clip   27 Spring washer   28 Screw   29 End cover   30 Shakeproof washer
31 Lucas connector   32 Nut   33 Insulating sleeve   34 Clamp plate   35 Screw   36 Valve cap   37 Inlet valve
38 Outlet valve   39 Sealing washer   40 Filter   41 Gasket   42 Vent valve   43 Sealing band   44 Joint
45 Inlet air bottle cover   46 Dished washer   47 Spring washer   48 Screw   49 Outlet connection   50 Fibre washer
51 Cover   52 Screw   53 O-ring   54 Diaphragm barrier   55 Sealing washer   56 Diaphragm plate   57 Diaphragm
58 Spring end cap   59 Diaphragm spring

while using the other hand to turn back the diaphragm edge and slip the eleven rollers 3 into place.

4 Taking care not to allow the rollers 3 to fall out, refit the contact blade 22, set the correct clearances and then remove the blade again. The correct clearances are shown in **FIG 2:5**. Fit the contact blade so that the contacts are a little above the contacts on the rocker in the closed position and mate squarely at the point of the contacts opening. Slotted securing holes are provided for this adjustment. The blade 22 should be tensioned so that when the points are opened the blade just rests on the ridge at the edge of the rectangular hole in the pedestal 16. Bend the blade carefully to suit. The .035 inch clearance will be correct with the correct tension on the blade. Carefully bend the stop finger on the rocker to set the .070 inch clearance to the correct limits. Carefully remove the blade as instructed.

5 Hold the coil housing horizontal in one hand, holding the diaphragm and hence the rollers in place with the thumb of the other hand. Carefully unscrew the diaphragm and check, by pushing the diaphragm firmly in with the thumb, until the rocker assembly just throws over. Establish this position accurately. Unscrew the diaphragm further until the next set of holes in the body accurately align with the holes in the diaphragm and unscrew it a further 4 holes (two-thirds

of a complete turn). Press the diaphragm firmly in and insert a forked wedge under the rocker assembly. This wedge is to hold the diaphragm in and prevent the rollers becoming displaced when reassembling the pump.

6 Refit the housing assembly to the body assembly, ensuring that the cast lugs on the housing are at the bottom and tighten the six screws 7 finger tight only. **Remove the retaining wedge from under the rocker** and make sure none of the rollers 3 are displaced. Tighten the securing screws in a diametric sequence. Correctly replace the contact blade 22. Connect the pump to a 12 volt battery and briefly run it in air to check that the pump operates correctly. Replace the cover and refit the pump to the car. Check for leaks and ensure that the pump only operates at long intervals when the carburetter float chambers are filled and the engine is not running.

PART II CARBURETTERS

2:5 Operating principles of a constant-vacuum carburetter

A typical carburetter consists of a body, with a choke tube running through it for the passage of the engine air, and a float chamber. The purpose of the float chamber is to

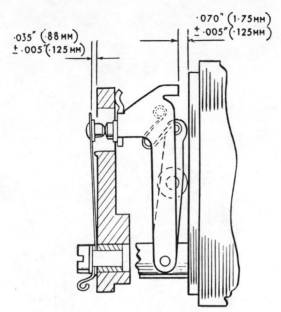

·035" (·88MM)
± ·005" (·125MM)

·070" (1·75MM)
± ·005" (·125MM)

FIG 2:5   4.2 litre fuel pump rocker and contact clearances

maintain the correct fuel level at the jets. A butterfly valve, connected to the accelerator pedal, is fitted to the bore nearest the engine and controls the quantity of air to the engine and hence its power. The bore is also closed by an air valve which is lifted by suction. The suction to lift the air valve is taken internally from the carburetter and since the weight of the air valve assembly is constant it will rise until the vacuum in the carburetter is also constant. As the throttle is opened and more air is required by the engine, the air valve will rise to allow the extra volume of air to pass, and the height of the air valve will be proportionate to the volume of air passing.

A tapered needle, calibrated for the particular engine characteristics, is fixed to the underside of the air valve and operates in a concentric fixed-area jet. As the air valve rises the effective area of the jet increases, the needle being tapered, and as the fuel level is constant and the suction also, the amount of fuel drawn out through the jet will be proportional to the area of the jet. The greater the volume of air passing to the engine the higher the air valve rises, increasing the effective area of the jet and the amount of fuel drawn through it.

A hydraulic damper fitted to the air valve serves the dual purpose of damping out rapid fluctuations of the air valve and of an accelerator pump. On acceleration the damper holds the air valve back and since the volume of air is made to pass through a slightly reduced opening the suction will increase. This increased suction draws more fuel out through the jet to provide a richer mixture for acceleration.

All the carburetters fitted to the E type Jaguar operate on this principle though there are differences in design, and compensating devices between the Stromberg and SU carburetters. The SU carburetter uses a piston operating in a suction chamber to raise the air valve while the Stromberg uses a diaphragm. The mixture strength both for cold starts and for normal running is adjusted on the SU carburetter by raising or lowering the fixed area jet, thus letting it operate on a different range of the tapered needle. The Stromberg carburetter has the fixed jet fixed in place and a separate sealed bleed screw to adjust the differences between carburetters, this screw being set at manufacture only. A trim screw is provided to adjust the mixture strength between very narrow limits. Enrichment for cold starts is achieved by raising the air valve physically.

2:6 SU carburetter removal

3.8 litre model :

1 Remove the air cleaner elbow by taking off the two butterfly nuts at the carburetter trumpets. Remove the trumpet plate from the carburetters by undoing the six sets of nuts and bolts.
2 Remove the triple branch fuel pipe by undoing the union to the main fuel pipe and taking out the three banjo bolts securing it to the carburetter float chambers. Loosely replace the banjo bolts in the float chambers to prevent the loss of the fibre washers or float chamber filters.
3 Remove the float chamber drain pipe clip from the oil filter. Remove the three butterfly return springs and disconnect the three throttle links from the clips on the throttle spindle levers.
4 Disconnect the mixture control cables. Remove the vacuum advance pipe from the front carburetter.
5 Remove the nuts and spring washers holding each carburetter to the manifold. Lift off the return spring brackets and remove the three carburetters together. The mixture control linkage may be removed from each carburetter by taking out the splitpins and withdrawing the clevis pins.

Replace the carburetters in the reverse order of removal, and use new gaskets on either side of the thick insulator on the manifold. If the gaskets between the carburetter flanges and the trumpet plate are damaged these should also be renewed. If the carburetter flanges are damaged scrape or lap them flat to ensure an airtight seal.

4.2 litre model :

1 Remove the air cleaner elbow, trumpet plate, triple branch fuel pipe, mixture control cables and vacuum advance pipe as described 1 to 4 in 3.8 litre carburetter removal.
2 On cars fitted with automatic transmission, disconnect the kick-down cable at the rear of the cylinder head.
3 Isolate the battery and partially drain the cooling system. Disconnect the water hoses to the inlet manifold. Disconnect the electrical cables from the thermostat switch in the header tank and the oil pressure switch. Disconnect the throttle linkage at the rear carburetter.
4 Remove the inlet manifold complete with the carburetters. Remove the nuts and washers holding the carburetters to the manifold, remove the return spring brackets, and slide off all three carburetters together. The mixture control linkage may be disconnected by removing the clevis pins.

Replace the carburetters in the reverse order of removal. Renew gaskets as instructed for the 3.8 litre model and check the carburetter flanges. Refill the cooling system and reconnect the battery.

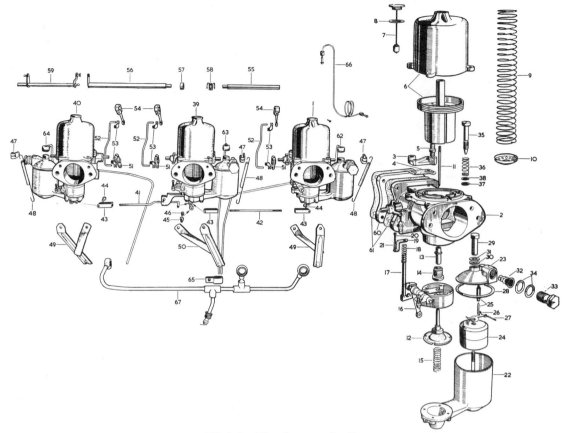

FIG 2:6 SU carburetter details

Key to Fig 2:6   1 Front carburetter assembly   2 Carburetter body   3 Adaptor   4 Gasket   5 Union
6 Suction chamber and piston assembly   7 Damper   8 Washer   9 Spring   10 Skid washer   11 Jet needle
12 Jet   13 Jet bearing   14 Locking nut   15 Spring   16 Jet housing   17 Pushrod assembly   18 Spring
19 Plate   20 Screw   21 Spring   22 Float chamber   23 Lid   24 Float   25 Needle and seat   26 Lever
27 Pin   28 Gasket   29 Cap nut   30 Serrated fibre washer   31 Alum washer   32 Filter   33 Banjo bolt
34 Fibre washer   35 Slow-running valve   36 Spring   37 Gland washer   38 Dished washer
39 Centre carburetter assembly   40 Rear carburetter assembly   41 Connecting rod   42 Connecting rod   43 Fork end
44 Clevis pin   45 Adaptor   46 Screw   47 Lever   48 Return spring   49 Bracket   50 Bracket   51 Lever
52 Rod   53 Clip   54 Lever   55 Slave shaft   56 Slave shaft   57 Distance piece   58 Coupling   59 Slave shaft
60 Insulator   61 Gasket   62/63/64 Overflow pipe   65 Clip   66 Suction pipe   67 Petrol feed pipe

2:7 Servicing the SU carburetter

The details of the SU carburetters and their linkages are shown in **FIG 2:6**.

Float chambers:

1 Remove the float chamber by undoing the four screws securing it to the base of the carburetter. If the float chamber is being removed because the carburetter is flooding, this can be done with the carburetter still fitted to the engine but the appropriate banjo bolt must also be removed. Flooding will be shown by fuel dripping from the overflow pipe 62.

2 Remove the bolt 29 to separate the parts of the float chamber. Lift out the float 24 and check that it is not punctured or partially filled with fuel. Renew it if it is damaged.

3 Withdraw the pin 27 and lift out the lever 26. Unscrew the seat 25 taking care not to lose the needle. Examine the needle and if it is worn the whole assembly 25 should be renewed. Earlier models were fitted with all-metal needles. At engine No. RA.2464 on the 3.8 litre engine new Delrin float chamber needles were fitted. The needle has a white plastic body and a spring-loaded plunger to prevent 'flutter' and consequent flooding at slow-running. A modified float chamber lid 23 and lever 26 were also fitted. The new needle assembly can be fitted in place of the old one, but not the other way around. The new type of lid will have AUD 2883 or 2884 embossed on the inside.

On later type 4.2 litre models the needle was changed to the Viton tipped sort, identifiable by a black rubber tip. These are interchangeable with the earlier type of needle.

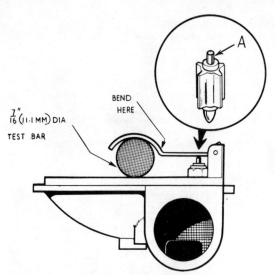

$\frac{7}{16}''$ (11·1 MM) DIA

TEST BAR

BEND HERE

A

FIG 2:7 Checking float lever setting. Insert shows Delrin type float chamber needle with spring-loaded plunger A

Never replace the needle alone, but replace both needle and seat assembly.

4 Clean the parts with clean fuel. A small speck of dirt under the float chamber needle can cause flooding of the carburetter. Examine the filter 32 and renew it if the mesh is broken.

5 Refit the needle assembly 25, lever 26 and pin 27. Invert the assembly and place the shank of a $\frac{7}{16}$ inch twist drill in position as shown in **FIG 2:7**. The lever forks should both rest on the twist drill and the flat portion of the lever just touch the needle without compressing the spring-loaded plunger in the needle. If required carefully bend the lever to the correct setting. Bend the lever at the start of the forked section and take care to keep the straight portion flat.

6 The float chamber can now be fully reassembled, and if required, refitted to the carburetter in the reverse order of dismantling.

Suction chamber and air valve assembly:

1 If the carburetter is still fitted to the engine, first remove the trumpet plate assembly. Remove the damper assembly 7 from the top of the suction chamber. Through the air intake, raise the piston of the the air valve and allow it to drop. It should fall freely and hit the bridge in the air intake with an audible click. If the piston sticks either dirt is holding it, the needle is bent or the jet requires centralizing.

2 Carefully mark the flanges, to ensure correct position on reassembly, and remove the screws securing the suction chamber. Lift off the suction chamber, remove the spring 9 and skid washer 10 and withdraw the piston and needle assembly. **Take great care of all these parts as they are machined to very close tolerances. Take care not to damage or bend the needle 11.**

3 Wash the piston and suction chamber parts 6 with clean fuel or methylated spirits. **Do not use any form of abrasive on the parts** otherwise the accurate clearance between them will be altered. Very lightly oil the piston rod and insert the piston back into the suction chamber. Check that the piston slides freely in the chamber. Any damage which prevents this will require renewal of both parts. Remove the piston from the suction chamber.

4 Examine the needle 11. If it is bent or scored it must be renewed using a new needle of the correct size. The needle is secured to the piston by a small screw. Refit the needle so that the lower edge of the groove on the needle is flush with the base of the piston.

5 Reassemble the parts in the reverse order of dismantling. If a new needle has been fitted, or the piston still does not fall freely the jet 12 requires centralizing.

Throttle spindle seals:

These are fitted to the throttle spindles to prevent air leakage from upsetting the slow-running of the engine. They do not normally require servicing but, if they are worn, the throttle butterfly valve and then the spindle will have to be removed in order to replace the seals.

Centralizing the jet:

1 Remove the carburetter from the car. Undo the four securing screws and remove float chamber assembly 22 and the jet housing 16. Remove the damper assembly 7. Withdraw the jet 12 from the base of the carburetter.

2 Use a ring spanner to slacken the locking nut 14 by half a turn. Leave the ring spanner in place and refit the jet 12. Turn the jet 12 so that the holes in the diaphragm accurately align with the securing holes in the body of the carburetter. **Mark both the body and the jet with a soft pencil to ensure that the jet will always be replaced in exactly the same position.**

3 Press the air valve firmly down, using a pencil or similar tool through the damper hole. Press the jet 12 firmly up into the carburetter as far as it will go and carefully tighten the locking nut 14. Raise the air valve and check that it falls freely while tightening the nut.

4 Press the jet up as far as it will go. Raise the air valve and let it fall. Note the noise it makes when it hits the bridge. Repeat the test with the jet at its lowest position. If the click is louder and clearer when the jet is down, then the jet is not accurately centralized and the process will have to be repeated. In difficult cases slacken the screw securing the needle 11 to the piston and pull the needle down to a lower position. Tighten the securing screw and centralize the jet. **The needle must be replaced in the correct position after centralizing the jet.**

5 Remove the jet, free the ring spanner and refit the jet ensuring that the correct securing holes are used by aligning the pencil marks. Refit the jet housing and float chamber before replacing the carburetter on the engine.

2:8 Tuning the SU carburetters

The carburetters cannot be satisfactorily tuned if the engine is in poor condition, the ignition timing incorrect or the carburetters themselves worn. The adjustment screws for setting the carburetters are shown in **FIG 2:8**.

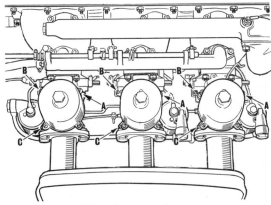

FIG 2:8 SU carburetter adjustment screws

Key to Fig 2:8
A Slow-running screws
B Fast-idle screws
C Mixture adjustment screws

1 Start the engine and run it until it reaches its normal operating temperature. Disconnect the mixture control linkage rods and remove the air cleaner. If the carburetters have been serviced and the correct settings lost, then set them approximately. Screw in all three slow-running screws A until they are just on their seatings, and then unscrew each one two complete turns. Raise the piston through the air intake and unscrew the mixture adjusting screws C until the top of the jet is flush with the bridge in the carburetter. Screw each mixture screw C down two and a half turns. These will provide accurate enough settings for the engine to be started and run. Switch off after it reaches its normal working temperature.

2 Slacken the pinchbolts clamping the two-piece throttle levers to the throttle spindles on the carburetters. Rotate the throttle spindle in a clockwise direction, viewed from the front, to close the butterfly valves in each carburetter. Keep the two-piece throttle lever in the midway position and tighten the pinchbolts. Operate the accelerator pedal and check that all three throttle spindles move simultaneously.

3 Ensure that each jet lever is firmly against its stop for the choke off position. Turn each fast-idle screw B until a .002 inch (.051 mm) feeler gauge is just nipped between the end of the screw and the interconnection lever. After final setting and reconnecting, this setting should ensure that the engine speed rises to 1000 rev/min before the mixture adjusting screws C begin to move.

4 Start the engine. Set all models, except the 4.2 litre manual gearbox version, to slow run at 500 rev/min. The slow-running speed for the 4.2 litre model fitted with a manual gearbox should be 700 rev/min. Adjust each screw A until the engine is running at the correct speed and the hiss in each of the three intakes is equal. **Once set, the slow-running must only be adjusted by turning each of the three screws A by an equal amount.**

5 Check the mixture strength of each carburetter in turn by lifting the air valve $\frac{1}{32}$ inch, using either the lifting pin or a thin-bladed screwdriver through the air intake. On a correctly set carburetter the engine speed will rise

momentarily. If the engine continues to run faster, then the mixture on that carburetter is too rich. A weak mixture is indicated by the engine speed decreasing. Turn the appropriate screw C down to enrich the mixture and up to weaken. The slow-running speed may rise or fall once the mixture is adjusted and it should be reset by turning the three screws A by an equal amount.

6 **The three carburetters are interdependent and once all three have been set they should all be rechecked.** When the overall mixture is correct the engine should be running with a smooth even beat.

7 Reconnect the mixture control linkage, adjusting the fork ends if required so that all three jet levers are against their stops simultaneously. Reconnect the mixture control cable so that there is $\frac{1}{16}$ inch (1.6 mm) free movement of the facia control upwards before the jet levers start to move. The facia control should be halfway through its range of movement before the screws C start to move and the engine should be running at 1000 rev/min (hot). Refit the air cleaner.

2:9 Servicing the Stromberg carburetters

All the parts required to service the carburetters at 24,000 mile intervals are supplied in the appropriate Red Emission Pack. They should not be tampered with; the correct procedures must be followed, and the correct test equipment used to set and adjust the carburetters. The Stromberg carburetter details are shown in **FIG 2:9**. Service the carburetters individually to avoid mixing up the parts. The parts required for servicing the carburetters at 12,000 mile intervals are supplied in the appropriate Yellow Emission Pack.

1 Undo the securing screws and remove the float chamber cover 30. Withdraw the pin 31 and lift out the floats 29. Unscrew the jet assembly 28, and the needle valve assembly 33. Discard all old seals and washers, and wash the parts in clean fuel. Reassemble in the reverse order of dismantling, using the new seals and washers supplied. At the 24,000 mile service discard the old needle valve assembly 33 and fit the new one supplied in the Red Emission kit. Before refitting the float chamber cover 30 invert the carburetter and check the dimension A shown in **FIG 2:10**. On the earlier type the dimension should be 16.5 ± .5 mm, and on the later type where the manifold is connected by a duct to the exhaust hot spot, the dimension should be $\frac{11}{16}$ inch. This covers the 12,000 mile service.

2 Remove the damper assembly 1. Break the lead seal, remove the four screws securing the cover 3 and lift off the cover. Carefully remove the spring 5 and lift out the air valve assembly. Drain the oil from the piston rod. Remove the diaphragm 41 by taking off the retaining ring 4. Slacken the screw 6 and discard the needle 36. Refit the new diaphragm supplied to the piston 40, ensuring that the locating tag on the diaphragm seats in the slot in the piston. Check the spring action in the head of the new needle and insert the needle partially into the piston so that the flat portion faces the securing screw 6, as shown in **FIG 2:11**. Place a straightedge against the small shoulder of the needle, **not the casing**, and use the straightedge to press the needle into the piston until the small shoulder on the needle, not the casing, aligns with the face of the

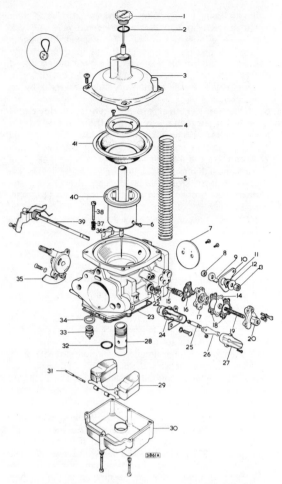

FIG 2:9 Stromberg carburetter details

Key to Fig 2:9   1 Hydraulic damper   2 O-ring
3 Cover 4 Diaphragm securing ring 5 Piston return spring
6 Needle securing screw   7 Butterfly   8 Bush
9 Pick-up lever   10 Floating lever   11 Washer
12 Shakeproof washer   13 Nut   14 Diaphragm
15 Idle trim screw   16 Gasket   17 Bypass valve
18 Gasket   19 Spring   20 Cover   21 Seal   22 Seal
23 Gasket   24 Temperature compensator housing
25 Tapered plug   26 Bi-metallic blade   27 Plastic cover
28 Jet assembly   29 Float assembly   30 Float chamber
31 Pivot pin   32 O-ring   33 Needle valve
34 Special washer   35 Choke assembly   36 Needle
37 Spring   38 Throttle stop screw   39 Throttle spindle
assembly 40 Piston 41 Diaphragm Inset—Lead seal

piston. Lightly tighten the securing screw 6 so as not to crush the housing on the needle. **If the operation is carried out correctly the needle will be biased towards the throttle with its shoulder flush with the face of the piston.** Carefully refit the air valve assembly back to the carburetter. Guide the needle into the jet, check that the transfer ports on the piston face the throttle and hold the piston in position with a finger through the air intake while refitting the spring 5 and cover 3.

3 Remove the two screws securing the temperature compensator housing 24 to the body and remove the temperature compensating assembly. Renew the two seals 21 and 22 and refit the compensator assembly. Take off the cover 27 by removing the two smaller screws. Carefully, so as not to distort the bi-metal spring 26, pull back the tapered plug 25 and ensure that it returns freely to its seat. If the valve sticks take off the nut and remove the spring and plug. Clean the parts with a fuel-moistened cloth. Refit the parts so that the plug is concentric in its seat and tighten the nut so that the tapered plug just seats. **Do not tighten the nut any further.** Refit the cover 27.

4 Remove the throttle bypass valve assembly 17, do not dismantle it. Prise out the throttle spindle seal under it and renew the seal. Replace the bypass valve assembly using a new gasket 16. Prise out the other throttle spindle seal from the other side of the carburetter and renew this also.

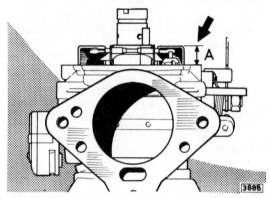

FIG 2:10 Checking float height on Stromberg carburetter

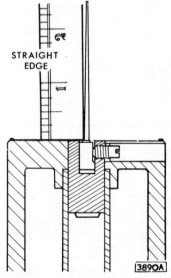

FIG 2:11 Correct method of fitting the fuel metering needle to the piston on the Stromberg carburetter

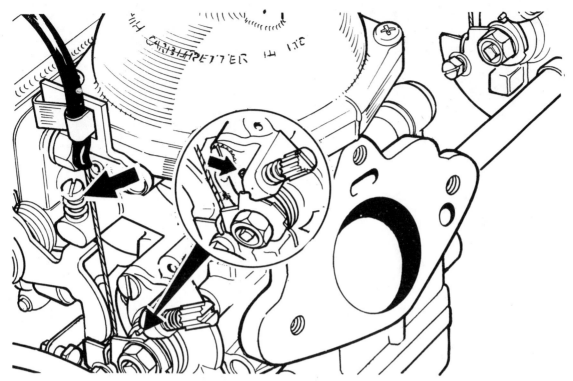

FIG 2:12 Short arrow indicates the slow-running adjustment screw. Inset shows the choke limiting spindle at the summer setting and the long arrow indicates the position for winter setting

2:10 Tuning the Stromberg carburetters

Before attempting to tune the carburetters the engine condition must be checked and if necessary rectified. **The only way to do this satisfactorily is to use an electronic tester such as 'Sun' or 'Crypton'. The ignition timing must be set dynamically, using a stroboscope. Exhaust gas analyser equipment is also essential for setting the carburetters. Failure to use the correct equipment will almost certainly result in the car failing to meet the stringent requirements of local law in some areas.**

The accelerator pedal should not be touched when starting the car from cold and an adjustment is provided to vary the choke between winter and summer conditions. This is shown at the arrow and inset of **FIG 2:12**. The inset shows the summer position.

1 Remove the air cleaner and run the engine until it reaches its normal operating temperature. Check that the damper is correctly filled and fitted. Adjust the slow-running speed on both carburetter adjustment screws (arrowed in **FIG 2:12**) so that the manual gearbox version is idling at 750 rev/min and the automatic gearbox version is idling at 650 rev/min. **A balance meter must be used to balance the airflow through each carburetter.**

2 Ensure that the choke control cam on the rear carburetter is in the fully off position, as shown in **FIG 2:13**. Slacken the locknut and turn the screw until

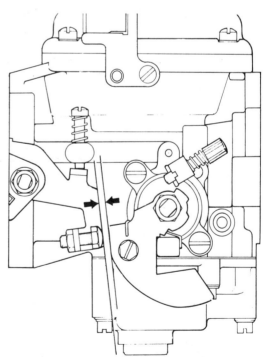

FIG 2:13 Fast-idle adjustment. Gap should be .067 inch

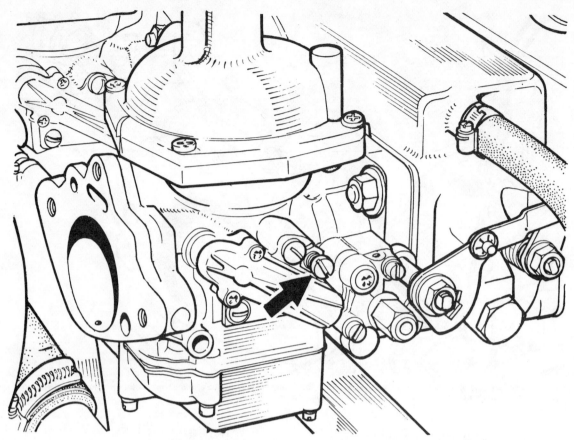

FIG 2:14 Idling mixture adjustable trim screw

the gap between the head of the screw and cam is .067 inch. Retighten the locknut.

3 The carburetters are made to such a high standard that a sealed trim screw is sufficient to adjust all carburetters to a constant datum on manufacture. To cater for different conditions of the engine, such as new and tight or run-in, another trim screw is fitted. **The screw is arrowed in FIG 2:14 and must only be adjusted using exhaust gas analyser equipment to check the correct mixture strength.**

PART III EMISSION CONTROL

2:11 The emission-controlled manifold

A typical inlet manifold is shown in **FIG 2:15**. The earlier type of manifold is very similar except that there is no duct leading the air and fuel mixture to and from the hot spot on the exhaust manifold. The point where the duct should join the inlet manifold is blanked over by a special plate.

The manifold is divided into two parts, separated by a secondary throttle valve interconnected with the normal throttle valve in the carburetter. At full throttle openings the secondary throttle is also wide open, allowing the mixture to pass straight through to the combustion chambers. Exhaust emission is low at wide throttle openings and by allowing a cold charge to be drawn into the cylinders the high power range of the engine is not restricted.

At lower speeds, such as city driving, the secondary throttle is fully shut. The air/fuel mixture is thus made to pass through the length of the heated manifold before passing to the engine. On the earliest engines the manifold and secondary thottle box were heated by hot water from the engine. Later models used the duct shown to carry the mixture over a hot spot on the exhaust manifold, and this system was again later modified to include a water heated secondary throttle box. This heating and movement of the incoming mixture ensures that the fuel and air are thoroughly mixed so, because of more efficient combustion, the engine will run using a weaker mixture.

The latest model covered by this manual is further modified to heat a proportion of the incoming air to the carburetters. Some of the air is taken from a stainless-steel shroud over the exhaust manifold and through a duct over the engine to a mixing valve. A thermal sensor fitted to the air intake adjusts the valve to control the proportions of hot and cold air to produce the right temperature at the carburetters. The system is so designed that only cold air is drawn to the carburetters at full throttle. The arrangement is shown in **FIG 2:16**.

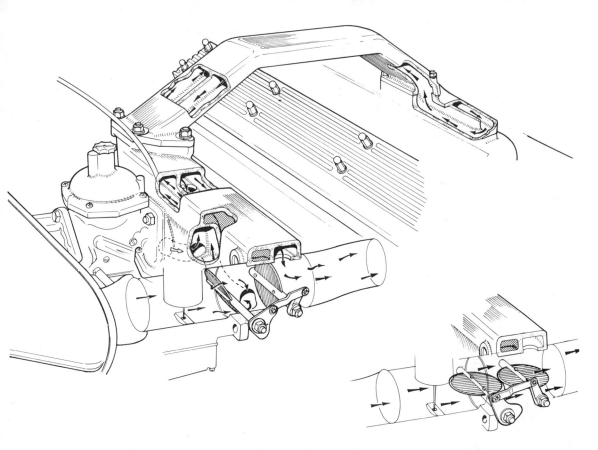

FIG 2:15   Typical Duplex manifold system fitted to exhaust emission- controlled cars

2:12 Crankcase fumes

The breather on the front of the engine is modified with a flame trap and is connected to the inlet on the carburetters. The slight suction caused when the engine is running is sufficient to draw the fumes from the crankcase so that they are drawn in with the air/fuel mixture and burnt in the combustion chambers.

2:13 Fuel fumes

For 1971, in order to satisfy certain State legislation, a system was introduced whereby fuel fumes from the tank and carburetters are not vented to atmosphere but eventually burnt in the engine. The carburetter float chambers are vented to the engine side of the air cleaner and the fumes are therefore trapped when the engine is stationary and burnt with the mixture when the engine is running.

The fuel tank is sealed, the filler cap being of the non-vented type. Three pipes, from the top of the extreme corners of the tank, lead the fumes to a separate small expansion tank. This tank is connected by a pipe to a special activated-carbon packed canister, shown in **FIG 2:17**. When the engine is not running the fumes are trapped by the activated-carbon. The canister is connected to the breather on the engine and as soon as the engine starts air is drawn through the canister so that the

activated-carbon is purged of fuel fumes. The fuel fumes are then drawn into the engine where they are burnt. The quantity of fuel involved is very small so the mixture strength of the carburetters is not altered. The tank can of course draw air through the container to replace the fuel as it is used.

2:14 Fault diagnosis

(a) Leakage or insufficient fuel delivered

1 Fuel pipes choked
2 Air vent to fuel tank restricted
3 Air leaks at pipe connections
4 Pump filter blocked
5 Fuel line filter choked
6 Faulty centrifugal pump (3.8 litre)
7 Faulty pump valves (4.2 litre)
8 Faulty pump diaphragm (4.2 litre)
9 Fuel vaporizing in pipelines due to heat

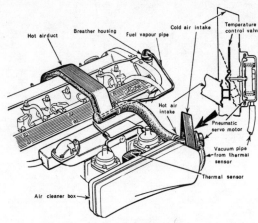

FIG 2:16 Latest design of Duplex manifold

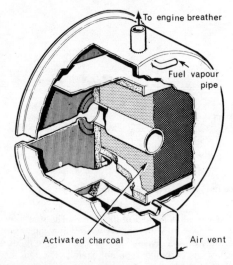

FIG 2:17 Activated-carbon packed canister fitted to latest models to prevent fuel fumes from the tank reaching the atmosphere

(b) Excessive fuel consumption

1 Carburetters require adjusting
2 Fuel leakage
3 Dirty air cleaner
4 Sticking carburetter controls
5 Excessive engine temperature
6 Brakes binding
7 Tyres under-inflated
8 Idling speed too high
9 Car overloaded

(c) Idling speed too high

1 Rich fuel mixture (SU only)
2 Carburetter controls sticking
3 Incorrect slow-running adjustment
4 Worn throttle valve assembly

(d) Noisy fuel pump

1 Worn mounting grommets
2 Air leaks on suction side (4.2 litre)
3 Obstruction in fuel pipeline
4 Clogged pump filter

(e) No fuel delivery

1 Float needle stuck shut
2 Tank vent blocked
3 Blown pump fuse and/or faulty electrical connections
4 Pump contacts dirty (4.2 litre)
5 Pipeline obstructed
6 Choked filter or filters
7 Pump diaphragm stiff or damaged (4.2 litre)
8 Pump inlet valve stuck open (4.2 litre)
9 Pump faulty (3.8 litre)
10 Bad air leak on suction side of pump (4.2 litre)

CHAPTER 3

THE IGNITION SYSTEM

3:1 Description

The 3.8 litre engine is fitted with a Lucas DMBZ.6A distributor and the 4.2 litre engine is fitted with a Lucas 22D6 distributor. The distributor fitted to exhaust emission controlled engines is of a similar type to the one fitted to the 4.2 litre engine but the timing characteristics are different.

All the models are similar in that they incorporate automatic timing control by the use of a centrifugal advance mechanism and a vacuum-operated unit. A vernier adjustment is provided to enable fine alterations to the ignition point to be made by hand. These alterations can compensate for changes in engine condition or for the use of various grades of fuel.

The weights of the centrifugal device fly out against the tension of small springs as the engine speed rises. This movement advances the contact breaker cams relative to the distributor driving shaft to give advanced ignition. The vacuum unit is connected to the inlet manifold by a small-bore pipe. The suction in the manifold is proportional to the throttle openings and engine load so that the vacuum unit rotates the base plate of the contact breakers to set the ignition point for the engine demands.

The details of the Lucas DMBZ.6A distributor are shown in **FIG 3:1**. A typical Lucas 22D6 distributor is shown in **FIG 3:2**, though it should be noted that no tachometer drive is fitted to the distributor on Jaguars and parts 15, 16 and 17 are omitted with no provision made for them.

3:2 Routine maintenance

Ensure that the outside of the distributor, the HT leads and top of the ignition coil are always kept clean and dry. Wipe away moisture with a clean, dry cloth, paying particular attention to the crevices between the HT leads on the distributor cap.

Remove the distributor cap and carefully pull off the rotor arm. The lubrication points for the Lucas 22D6 distributor are shown in **FIG 3:3**, and the Lucas DMBZ.6A distributor is lubricated in a similar manner. Pour a few drops of engine oil into the top of the cam as shown at 1. The screw should not be removed as a clearance is provided around it to allow the oil to pass through. Put a single drop of oil onto the contact pivot 2. Work the moving contact to and fro to ensure that it is free, and allow the oil to spread evenly. If the contact sticks the points will have to be removed and the pivot lightly polished with a piece of fine emerycloth. Pour a few drops of oil down the gap 3 to lubricate the centrifugal advance mechanism. Lightly grease around the face of

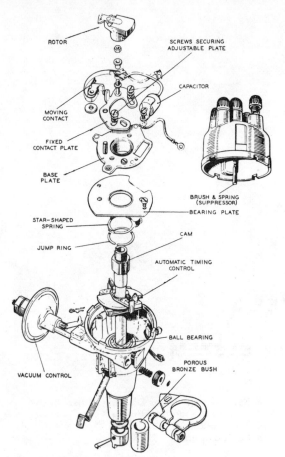

ROTOR

SCREWS SECURING
ADJUSTABLE PLATE

CAPACITOR

MOVING
CONTACT

FIXED
CONTACT PLATE

BASE
PLATE

BRUSH & SPRING
(SUPPRESSOR)

BEARING PLATE

STAR-SHAPED
SPRING

CAM

JUMP RING

AUTOMATIC TIMING
CONTROL

BALL BEARING

POROUS
BRONZE BUSH

VACUUM CONTROL

FIG 3:1   Details of Lucas DMBZ.6A distributor fitted
to 3.8 litre engine

the cam 4, using petroleum jelly or Mobilgrease No. 2
Wipe off any surplus oil, and make sure that there is no oil
on the contact points. Wipe out the inside of the distributor
cap and rotor arm before replacing them.

Adjusting the contact breaker points:

Remove the distributor cap and turn the engine until
a lobe on the cam is below the foot of the moving contact
point, so that the points are at their widest gap. Slacken
the screw(s) securing the fixed contact to the base plate.
Move the fixed contact until the gap between the contacts is .014 to .016 inch (.36 to .41 mm), as measured
with feeler gauges. On earlier types of distributor the
fixed contact will have to be moved into position. Later
types of Lucas DMBZ.6A distributor are fitted with an
eccentric screw for adjusting the fixed contact, and the
Lucas 22D6 distributor has a slot in the base plate and
another matching slot in the fixed contact. Insert a
screwdriver between the two slots and turn it to adjust
the gap between the points. Tighten the fixed contact
securing screw(s) and check that the contact gap has not
altered. Replace the rotor arm and distributor cap.

Cleaning the contact breaker points:

The surfaces should have a clean, grey, frosted
appearance. If they are dirty or partially worn cleaning
only will be sufficient, but if they are excessively pitted or
worn they should be renewed. Use a fine contact file
to remove dirt and face the contacts so that they meet
evenly and squarely. The points should not be dressed
smooth but left with a slightly roughened surface. Never
use emerycloth or sandpaper as abrasive particles are
likely to become imbedded in the points and cause
arcing.

The moving contact is removed by taking off the nut on
the spring securing pillar. Lift off the insulated bush
followed by the two terminals of the supply cable and
capacitor cable. The moving contact can then be lifted
out. Note the positions of the two insulated washers on
top of the fixed contact and then lift these out. The fixed
contact can be removed after taking out the securing
screw(s). If required the capacitor can also be removed
by taking out the single cross-headed securing screw.

Reassemble the parts in the reverse order of dismantling,
**and make sure the insulated washers and insulated
bush are replaced in their correct positions.** If new
points are being fitted remove any protective from them
using either methylated spirits or clean fuel.

3:3 Ignition faults

If the engine runs unevenly, although the carburetters
are correctly adjusted, set the engine to idle at a fast speed.
Use the choke control on the facia to increase the idling
speed but do not move it far enough to enrich the mixture.
Take care not to touch any metal parts on the HT leads,
preferably using a pair of insulated tongs, and disconnect
each HT lead in turn from its sparking plug. Disconnecting
the lead from a sparking plug that is firing properly will
make the uneven running more pronounced, while disconnecting a sparking plug which is not firing will make
no difference. If, when replacing the HT lead, the engine
runs smoothly when there is a small gap for the spark to
jump across between the lead and the top of the sparking
plug, then that plug is badly fouled.

Having located the faulty cylinder stop the engine and
remove any shroud or insulator fitted to that HT lead.
Start the engine and, taking care to avoid shocks, hold the
metal end of the lead about $\frac{3}{16}$ inch (5 mm) away from a
clean metal part of the engine. A strong regular spark
shows that the fault may lie with the sparking plug,
although note that a sticking engine valve will produce
similar symptoms. Stop the engine, remove the sparking
plug and either clean it, as described in **Section 3:8**, or
else substitute it with a new sparking plug.

If the spark is weak or irregular check that the HT lead
is not cracked or perished. If the lead is found to be faulty
renew it and repeat the test. If there is no improvement,
remove the distributor cap and wipe the inside with a
soft clean cloth, especially between the contacts for the
HT leads. Check that the carbon brush is undamaged and
that it protrudes from the moulding. Also check that the
brush moves freely against the pressure of the internal
spring. Examine the inside surface of the distributor cap
for cracks or 'tracking'. 'Tracking' will be seen as a thin
black line between the electrodes or to some metal part in
contact with the cap. The only permanent cure in either
case it to renew the distributor cap.

Testing the low-tension circuit :

Before carrying out any electrical tests, confirm that the contact points are clean and correctly set.

1 Disconnect the low-tension cable between the distributor and the coil at the CB terminal on the coil. Connect a low-wattage 12 volt test bulb between the cable and the terminal. Switch on the ignition and turn the engine over slowly by hand. To turn the engine, remove the sparking plugs and try turning it by pulling on the generator driving belt. If the engine is too stiff for this method, engage a gear, jack up one rear wheel and turn the engine by rotating the jacked-up rear wheel. The bulb should light when the contacts close and extinguish as they open. If the lamp stays on continuously either there is a shortcircuit in the distributor or the capacitor is faulty.

2 If the lamp fails to light at all then no supply is reaching the distributor. Remove the test bulb and reconnect the cable to the CB terminal on the ignition coil. Disconnect the other low-tension cable to the ignition coil at the SW terminal and connect the test bulb between this cable and a good earth on the car. When the ignition is switched on the bulb should light and stay on continuously. If the lamp now lights as it should then the ignition coil is faulty and must be renewed. The bulb still failing to light shows that there is a fault in the wiring circuit.

3 The fault in the wiring circuit must be found by checking through using either the test bulb or a 0–20 voltmeter. The tests given so far should not have taken a long time but since further ones will be more protracted the fuel pump on the 3.8 litre should be isolated, either by disconnecting the wires or by removing the appropriate fuse. Before tracing through the circuit, with the help of the appropriate wiring diagram in Technical Data, check to see if the brake warning light is on. If this functions normally, then the circuit is satisfactory as far as the live side of the fuse box. Note that neither the ignition circuit nor the brake warning light are fused but are tapped from the permanently live side of the fuse. If the brake warning light does not light check the battery terminals and battery condition before carrying out any further tests.

Capacitor (Condenser) :

The capacitor is made up of metal foil insulated with paper. If the insulation breaks down the sparks tend to erode away the metal foil in the surrounding area, preventing a shortcircuit, though a shortcircuit in the distributor may sometimes be caused by a faulty capacitor.

An open circuit capacitor is more difficult to diagnose without specialized equipment but it may be suspected if the points are badly burned or 'blued' and starting is difficult. Check by substituting the suspect capacitor with one either new or known to be satisfactory.

3:4 Removing the distributor

Free the distributor cap and swing it out of the way still attached to the ignition leads. Disconnect the low-tension cable from the terminal and the vacuum pipe from the vacuum unit. **Note the exact position of the rotor arm.** Remove the setscrew securing the distributor clamp plate to the engine and withdraw the distributor.

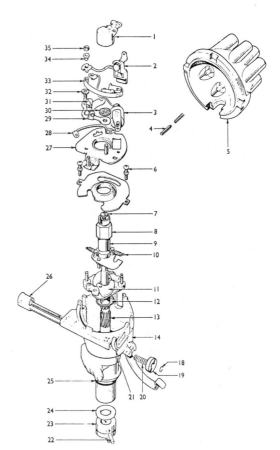

FIG 3:2 Details of a typical Lucas 22D6 distributor as fitted to 4.2 litre engines

Key to Fig 3:2 1 Rotor 2 Terminal block 3 Capacitor
4 High-tension carbon brush 5 Cover 6 Side screw
7 Cam spindle screw 8 Cam 9 Cam spindle
10 Control spring 11 Weight 12 Distance collar
13 Shaft and action plate 14 Body 18 Circlip
19 Micrometer adjustment nut 20 Spring
21 Ratchet spring 22 Driving dog pin 23 Driving dog
24 Thrust washer 25 Rubber O-ring 26 Vacuum timing control 27 Moving plate 28 Moving plate earth lead
29 Fixed contact 30 Large insulation washer
31 Lock screw 32 Small insulation washer
33 Moving contact 34 Insulation piece 35 Nut

Do not slacken the clamp plate pinch bolt or the ignition timing will be lost and do not rotate the engine after the distributor has been removed.

Replacing the distributor is the reversal of the removal procedure. Renew the cork washer in the engine housing if it is damaged. Provided that the engine has not been turned the rotor arm should be in the same position as before removal.

3:5 Servicing the Lucas 22D6 distributor
Dismantling :

1 Disconnect the spring of the vacuum unit 26 from the peg on the moving plate 27. Slide out the terminal 2

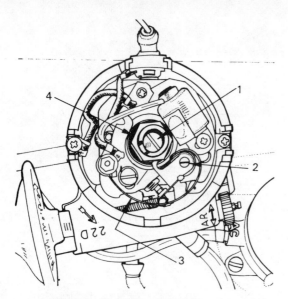

FIG 3:3 Distributor lubrication points

and remove the complete contact breaker assembly after undoing the two screws 6. The contact breaker assembly can be dismantled by removing the contacts and capacitor as described in **Section 3:2**. The moving plate 27 is held to the fixed plate by spring washers.

2 Remove the circlip 18 and unscrew the nut 19 to free the vacuum unit 26. Take care not to lose the springs 20 or 21.

3 Use feeler gauges to measure the end float of the distributor shaft in the body. If the end float exceeds .002 to .006 inch then the nylon spacer 12 and thrust washer 24 will have to be renewed on assembly. **Note accurately the relationship of the rotor arm driving slot in the cam 8 and the offset on the driving dog 23.** Drive out the pin 22 and remove the driving dog 23 and thrust washer 24.

4 Clean any burrs off the end of the shaft 13 and slide the driving shaft assembly up out of the distributor body. Carefully, in order not to distort or bend them, remove the springs 10. Note accurately the relation of the cam 8 to the driving shaft 13 and remove the cam spindle 9 from the driving shaft 13 by taking out the screw 7.

Reassembling:

Reassemble the parts in the reverse order of dismantling. Wash all the metal parts in clean fuel and renew any that are worn. Lightly lubricate all bearing surfaces with clean engine oil. Ensure that the driving slot in the cam is correctly positioned relative to the offset on the driving dog.

Distributors for emission-controlled engines should be checked on specialized garage equipment to ensure that they are within the correct performance limits before refitting to the car.

3:6 Servicing the Lucas DMBZ.6A distributor

This distributor (fitted to 3.8 litre engines) is dismantled and reassembled in a very similar manner to the Lucas 22D6 type (see **Section 3:5**). However the following points should be noted:

1 The vacuum unit is fitted to the moving plate by a link and spring clip.

2 The drive shaft turns in a ballbearing in a porous bronze bush. Neither of these should be removed unless they are worn. Use a drift on the inner journal of the ballbearing to drive the old one out and similarly use a drift to remove the old bush.

3 Replace the ballbearing using a stepped mandrel which fits over both the inner and outer journals of the bearing.

4 Before fitting, a new porous bronze bush must be soaked in clean engine oil for 24 hours. The period can be shortened in an emergency, by heating the oil to 100°C (temperature of boiling water) and allowing the bush to soak hot for 2 hours and to cool in the liquid before removal. A stepped mandrel is required to fit the bush. The end that fits in the bush should be hardened and polished and should be .0005 inch greater in diameter than the distributor drive shaft. Use a press to fit the bush, not a hammer, and fit a stripping washer between the mandrel and bush to prevent the mandrel drawing the bush back out as the mandrel is withdrawn. This method will ensure that the fit and finish of the bush are correct, but **the bush must in no circumstances be reamed or bored.**

3:7 Setting the ignition timing

The timing marks on the crankshaft damper are shown in **FIG 3:4**. When the edge of the pointer is aligned with the zero mark on the damper Nos. 1 and 6 pistons are at TDC.

1 Remove the sparking plugs and turn the engine as described in **Section 3:3**. Turn the engine until No. 6 (front) piston is coming up on the compression stroke. This is easily determined by blocking the sparking plug hole in No. 6 cylinder with a thumb and turning the engine until a strong pressure rise is felt in the cylinder. Carry on turning the engine until the edge of the pointer is exactly on the correct static timing position for the model. Remove the distributor cap and check that the rotor arm is pointing at the electrode in the cap connected to No. 6 sparking plug.

2 The correct static ignition settings are as follows:

8:1 compression ratio (all standard models) 9 deg. BTDC

9:1 compression ratio (all standard models) 10 deg. BTDC

All emission-controlled engines (approx only) 5 deg. BTDC

3 Slacken the distributor clamp pinch bolt. Connect a low-wattage test bulb between the low-tension cable from the distributor and the CB terminal on the ignition coil. Switch on the ignition and rotate the distributor about its position until the contacts have just opened, indicated by the test lamp having just gone out. Tighten the clamp plate pinch bolt to hold the distributor in position. The settings will be accurate enough to start emission-controlled engines so ignore the remaining operations, except for replacing the sparking plugs.

4 Turn the engine one complete revolution in a clockwise direction and just before the full revolution watch the test lamp. Stop turning the engine the instant the lamp extinguishes. Check that the pointer is again aligned with the correct mark and adjust if required. The engine can then be turned clockwise another full turn to bring No. 6 (front) piston back to the firing position for a final check. Replace the sparking plugs.

Stroboscopic method of setting the ignition timing:

This method may be used on all models, but it is essential for emission-controlled engines as the static method of setting is not accurate enough for these. On standard models it is sufficient to run the engine at idling speed and add 2 deg. to the static setting to allow for advance in the distributor and any backlash. **Emission-controlled engines are adjusted to 10 deg. BTDC at 1000 rev/min.** Mark the appropriate point on the crankshaft damper with a thin white line and similarly mark the edge of the timing pointer.

Connect the stroboscopic light as instructed by the instrument maker and set it so that it will shine on the timing marks. Start the engine and after allowing it to warm up set the correct idling speed. Adjust the ignition using the vernier on the distributor until the white line on the damper appears exactly aligned with the white line on the pointer.

The stroboscopic light can also be used to check that the advance and retard mechanisms are functioning. The limits for the distributors on emission-controlled engines are:

Engines without exhaust hot spot heated inlet manifold

Engine rev/min	Crankshaft degrees
1200	13 to 17
1600	22 to 26
2900	29 to 33
4400	37 to 41

Engines with exhaust hot spot heated inlet manifold

1200	8 to 12
1600	17 to 21
2900	24 to 28
4400	32 to 36

3:8 The sparking plugs

Inspect, clean and adjust sparking plugs at regular intervals. The inspection of the deposits on the electrodes is particularly useful because the type and colour of the deposit gives a clue to conditions inside the combustion chambers, and is therefore most useful when tuning the engine.

Remove the sparking plugs by loosening them a couple of turns and blowing away loose dirt from the plug recesses, either with compressed air or with a tyre pump, before removing them completely. Store the sparking plugs in the order of removal. Examine the gaskets and renew them if they are less than half their original thickness.

Examine the firing end of the sparking plug to note the type of deposit. Normally the deposit should be powdery

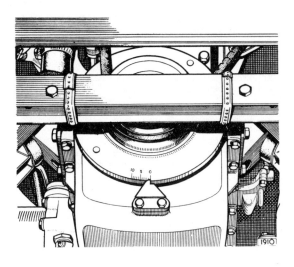

FIG 3:4 Ignition timing scale on crankshaft damper

and range in colour from brown to greyish tan. There will also be light wear on the electrodes and the general effect is one which comes from mixed periods of high-speed and low-speed driving. Cleaning and resetting the gaps is all that is required. If the deposits are white or yellowish they will indicate long periods of constant-speed or low-speed city driving. Again the treatment is straightforward.

Black, wet deposits are caused by oil entering the combustion chambers past worn pistons, rings or down worn valve guides or valve stems. Hotter running sparking plugs may help to alleviate the problem, but the only cure is an engine overhaul.

Overheating sparking plugs have a white, blistered look about the centre electrode and the side electrode may be badly eroded. This may be caused by poor cooling, incorrect ignition, running with too weak a mixture, incorrect grade of sparking plugs or sustained high speeds with heavy loads.

Dry, black, fluffy deposits are usually caused by running with too rich a mixture. Incomplete combustion may also be a cause and this can often be traced to excessive idling or defective ignition.

Have the sparking plugs cleaned on an abrasive-blasting machine and then tested under pressure after attention to the electrodes. File these until they are clean, bright and parallel. Set the electrode gap to .025 inch (.64 mm) on all models and for all conditions. **Do not bend the centre electrode.** Sparking plugs should be renewed every 12,000 miles.

Before refitting the sparking plugs clean the threads only with a wire brush and smear them with a little graphite grease to prevent them from binding in the cylinder head. Never use ordinary grease or oil on threads as this will bake hard. If it is found that the sparking plugs cannot be screwed into place by hand, run a tap down the threads of the cylinder head. Failing a tap, use an old sparking plug with crosscuts down the threads. Grease the tool well to prevent chips or dirt from falling down the cylinder bore. **Take great care when fitting sparking plugs as the cylinder head is made of aluminium**

alloy and the threads can easily be stripped. Clean the insulator on the sparking plug with a fuel-moistened rag to remove all traces of dirt or grease. Screw the sparking plug fully into place by hand and then tighten it to a torque of 27 lb ft (3.73 kg m). If a torque wrench is not available tighten the plug with a deep well-fitting box spanner through half a turn.

HT cables:

Earlier models were fitted with tinned-copper cored cables, but later models are fitted with resistive type of cables. **The correct type must be used for replacing cracked or perished cables.** Resistive cables have a resistance of approximately 420 ohms per inch so an ohmeter can be used to check if they are serviceable. The later types of cable often have a short length of tinned-copper wire inserted in the end as a pick-up but they can easily be identified by rolling them between the fingers. The resistive type will feel as if the core is made of granules, which in fact it is.

The cables run in a conduit fixed to the top of the cylinder head. They should be fitted into the distributor cap in the firing order (1–5–3–6–2–4) in an anticlockwise direction. **Note that Jaguars count the rear cylinder as No. 1 and count forward to the front cylinder No. 6**

3:9 Fault diagnosis

(a) Engine will not fire

1 Battery discharged
2 Distributor points dirty, pitted or out of adjustment
3 Distributor cap dirty, cracked or 'tracking'
4 Carbon brush inside distributor cap not in contact with rotor arm
5 Faulty cable or loose connection in low-tension circuit
6 Distributor rotor arm cracked or not replaced after dismantling
7 Faulty ignition coil
8 Broken contact breaker spring
9 Contact points stuck open
10 Faulty capacitor
11 Water on HT leads, distributor cap or ignition coil

(b) Engine misfires

1 Check 2, 3, 5 and 7 in (a)
2 Weak contact spring
3 HT leads cracked or perished
4 Sparking plug loose
5 Sparking plug insulation cracked
6 Sparking plug gap incorrect
7 Ignition timing too far advanced

CHAPTER 4

THE COOLING SYSTEM

4:1 Description

All the models covered by this manual have a pressurized cooling system. The natural thermo-syphon flow of the water is augmented by a centrifugal-type pump driven by a belt from the crankshaft. The heated water from the cylinder head passes out around the inlet manifolds and when sufficiently hot, the thermostat valve fitted in the water gallery opens and allows the hot water to pass through the radiator, where it is cooled before returning to the engine through the water pump. When the water is cold the thermostat valve remains shut and the water is bypassed back around the engine, ensuring a shorter warm-up period.

Earlier models are fitted with a radiator and separate header tank mounted in front of the radiator. The filler cap, mounted on the header tank, contains two concentric spring-loaded valves. One valve limits the pressure in the cooling system and opens above this set pressure to allow excess air or water to pass through the valve and out through an overflow pipe. When the coolant cools and the pressure drops the other valve opens, allowing air to be drawn in through the overflow pipe and preventing a vacuum forming in the cooling system.

Later models of the 4.2 litre no longer use a header tank. A plain non-pressure cap is fitted to the radiator top tank and the top tank is connected by a hose to an expansion tank, shown in **FIG 4:1**. The expansion tank is fitted with a similar type of cap as fitted to earlier model header tanks. It should be noted that this system is filled through the radiator top tank cap but the level is always checked at the expansion tank, when the system is cold.

The pressure of the cooling system, controlled by the cap fitted, was progressively raised from the pressure used in earlier models. The correct pressures for the various models are given in Technical Data. The caps cannot be confused as they are stamped on top with the pressure at which they release. **Do not fit a higher pressure cap than is called for, as the system is not designed to stand the stress of a higher pressure.**

When the car is stationary, or travelling slowly, the passage of air through the radiator may not be sufficient to provide adequate cooling. An electrically driven fan on the 3.8 litre model (two separate electrically driven fans on the 4.2 litre models) is fitted to promote the circulation of cooling air under these conditions. The fan(s) are controlled by a thermostatic switch in the header tank.

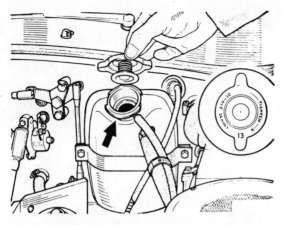

FIG 4:1 Expansion tank fitted to sealed cooling system on later 4.2 litre models. Inset shows the cap fitted when the car is fitted with air-conditioning equipment

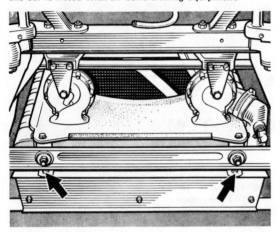

FIG 4:2 4.2 litre radiator attachments. Arrows indicate nuts securing radiator to subframe shield. Main securing nuts are just above those arrowed as shown in figure

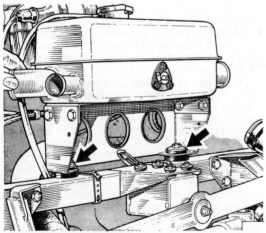

FIG 4:3 4.2 litre radiator header tank attachments. Note thermostatic switch in front of header tank

On earlier 3.8 litre cars a relay was fitted between this switch and the fan motor but this was later discarded. On 4.2 litre models fitted with air-conditioning equipment a relay is fitted to override the operation of the switch when the air-conditioning equipment is in use.

On 4.2 litre models fitted with automatic transmission an oil cooler for the transmission is mounted with the radiator. This may be removed after disconnecting and plugging the oil hoses.

The air-conditioning hoses fitted to some models of the 4.2 litre must not under any circumstances be disconnected. The condenser may be released from its mountings and swung out of the way, still attached to its hoses. Any work that requires disconnecting of the air-conditioning hoses must be left to a garage equipped and qualified to deal with air-conditioning systems.

4:2 Protective maintenance

There is no lubrication point on the cooling system.

The cooling system should be flushed through at regular intervals, either using clean water or a proprietary compound.

Draining:

Set the heater control to hot and remove the filler cap from the radiator, on later 4.2 litre models, or the header tank on all earlier models. Open the drain tap on the bottom of the radiator and the tap on the rear of the left-hand side of the cylinder block. If antifreeze has been added the coolant should be drained into a clean container for re-use.

Flushing:

If a proprietary compound is used follow the instructions given on the tin. To flush with clean water first drain the cooling system as previously instructed. Insert a hosepipe into the filler and when the system is full, balance the flow through the hosepipe so that it equals the flow out through the drains. Start the engine and set it to idle at 1000 rev/min. Carry on flushing with the engine running until the water comes out clean from the drain taps. Stop the engine and when all the water has drained out close the drain taps.

Filling:

Leave the heater control on hot and make sure the drain taps are closed. Fill the system with soft clean water to just below the bottom of the filler neck. Run the engine and allow it to cool before checking the level and topping up if required. On later models of the 4.2 litre half-fill the expansion tank and top up to this level at the expansion tank and not at the radiator. **Two caps are fitted to this sealed system and they must be replaced in their correct positions, the non-pressure cap on the radiator. Never remove a cap from the cooling system when the engine is hot.**

4:3 The radiator

The water flow through the earlier types of radiator is crossflow but on the radiator fitted to sealed cooling systems the water passes downwards through the radiator.

Removing the radiator :

Drain the cooling system and disconnect all the hoses to the radiator. On the latest models of the 4.2 litre the bonnet will have to be removed (see **Chapter 13**). On earlier models disconnect the radiator top support stays, on the later models disconnect the cowl from the radiator by undoing the six setscrews. A view from underneath on the radiator on the 4.2 litre model is shown in **FIG 4 : 2**. All the other models are basically similar. Undo the two bolts securing the radiator closing bracket, shown arrowed, to the radiator. Undo the bottom nuts securing the radiator to the subframe and carefully lift the radiator out from the top, taking care not to damage the fins. Collect the packing washers.

Replace the radiator in the reverse order of removal.

4 : 4 The header tank

The 4.2 litre model header tank is shown in **FIG 4 : 3**. The arrows indicate the support bracket mounting points. The header tank on the 3.8 litre models differs only in the mounting to the support bracket, and the position of the thermostatic switch (on top instead of on the side as shown). Also it is only connected by a single hose to the radiator top, whereas the 4.2 litre model is connected by two hoses to the radiator top and both are also connected by one hose to the cylinder head.

4 : 5 The driving belt

On the earliest models of the 3.8 litre the driving belt is adjusted to have $\frac{1}{2}$ inch (12.7 mm) movement on either side of the normal line by slackening the generator adjust-

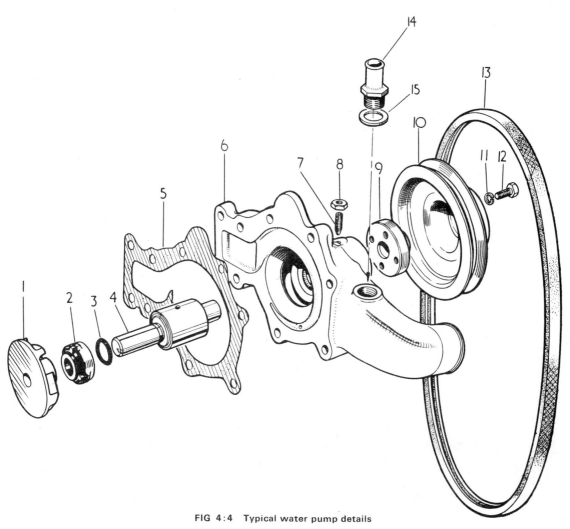

FIG 4 : 4 Typical water pump details

Key to Fig 4 : 4   1 Impeller   2 Seal   3 Thrower   4 Spindle and bearing assembly   5 Gasket   6 Pump body
7 Allen-headed lockscrew   8 Locknut   9 Pulley carrier   10 Pulley   11 Spring washer   12 Setscrew
13 Drive belt   14 Adaptor for heater return pipe   15 Copper washer

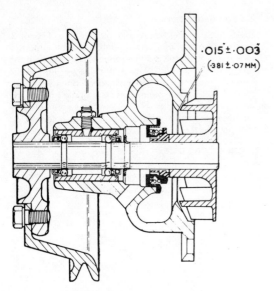

FIG 4:5 Sectioned view of water pump

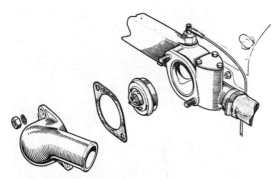

FIG 4:6 3.8 litre thermostat and housing details

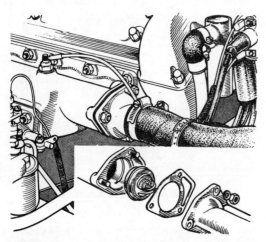

FIG 4:7 4.2 litre thermostat and housing details

ment and pivot bolts, and pivoting the generator to set the correct tension before retightening the bolts.

On all later models the generator or alternator top support stay has the nut welded to it, so that the unit is held in one fixed position and a spring-loaded jockey pulley automatically sets the correct driving belt tension.

4:6 The water pump

The water pumps on all the models covered by this manual are of similar construction and design though the details vary slightly, and the pumps fitted to the 4.2 litre models have a higher pumping capacity than those fitted to 3.8 litre models. The latest type of pump fitted to the 4.2 litre model is shown in **FIG 4:4**, and allowing for the minor differences this figure can be used for all models.

Removing the pump:

1 Drain the cooling system and disconnect the battery.
2 Disconnect the electrical cables to the thermostatic switch and disconnect the water hoses to the header tank. Undo the nuts securing the header tank support bracket to the subframe and remove the header tank, collecting the mounting rubbers.
3 Slacken the bottom securing bolts on the alternator or generator and remove the top bolt. Press the alternator or generator towards the cylinder block, and if a jockey pulley is fitted, hold it back by hand to slacken the belt. Remove the belt from the water pump pulley.
4 Disconnect all the water hoses to the pump. Remove the four setscrews 14 and washers 15 to free the pump pulley 13 from the pump. Undo all the nuts, bolts and setscrews securing the pump to the engine and lift out the pump.

Replacing the pump is the reversal of the removal procedure. Use a new gasket 9 and smear both sides lightly with non-setting jointing compound.

Dismantling the pump:

For guidance a sectioned view of the pump is shown in **FIG 4:5**.

1 Use a suitable extractor to remove the pulley carrier 9 from the front of the pump. Slacken the locknut 8 and remove the lockscrew 7.
2 Withdraw the spindle and impeller assembly from the back of the pump. **The parts must not be pushed out using the end of the spindle otherwise the bearings will be damaged.** Use a tube (of $1\frac{3}{32}$ inch (27.77 mm) external diameter and an internal diameter of $\frac{31}{32}$ inch (24.61 mm)) to press against the outer sleeve of the bearing assembly and so remove the parts.
3 Use a press to separate the impeller 1 from the spindle 4 and then remove the seal 2 from the back of the impeller and the spinner 3 from the spindle. The spindle assembly 4 cannot be dismantled any further.

Examining the parts:

Wash all the parts, except the spindle assembly 4, to remove dirt or sediment. Wipe the outside of the spindle assembly. If the spindle assembly runs roughly or feels worn it must be renewed completely. The assembly is sealed and lubricated for life. Clean away rust or scale from the spindle using fine emerycloth and protect the bearings from the ingress of rust or dirt.

·015 ± ·003
(·381 ± ·07 MM)

Renew the seal 2 if the carbon face is worn or scored. Renew the impeller if the sealing face is scored or worn or the impeller is no longer a tight fit on the spindle.

The pump body 6 will have to be renewed if there are signs of wear in the bearing bore.

Reassembling:

Refit the spindle assembly into the pump housing, ensuring that the locating hole aligns with the lockscrew 7. Replace the lockscrew 7 and the locknut 8. Refit the spinner 3 and the seal 2. Use a press and a mandrel to refit the spindle down into the impeller. Press on until the spindle end is flush with the face of the impeller and check the gap, shown in **FIG 4:5**, using feeler gauges.

In a similar manner press on the pulley carrier 9 until its face is also flush with the end of the spindle.

4:7 The thermostat

The method of fitting the thermostat on 3.8 litre models is shown in **FIG 4:6** and the mounting on 4.2 litre models in **FIG 4:7**.

Before removing the thermostat drain the cooling system so that the level is below the thermostat. Remove the nuts and washers securing the cover. Lift it off the studs to break the seal and swing it out of the way, still attached to the water hose. Remove the gasket and withdraw the thermostat.

Replacing the thermostat is the reversal of the removal procedure but use a new gasket and make sure all the parts of the old gasket are removed.

The thermostatic switch is secured to the header tank by three setscrews and the joint is sealed with a gasket.

Test the thermostat by suspending it in water. Heat the water, stirring it to ensure an even temperature, and measure the temperature with an accurate thermometer. Note the temperature at which the thermostat valve starts opening. If the valve does not start to open at the correct temperature, or sticks in the open position, then the thermostat is defective and will have to be renewed. The correct opening temperature for the C.12867/2 thermostat is 165°F (73.9°C) and the correct temperature for the C.20766/2 thermostat is 159°F (70.5°C).

The thermostatic switch may also be tested in a similar manner. Connect the terminal through a low-wattage 12-volt test bulb to one terminal of the battery and connect the other battery terminal to the body of the switch. Immerse the temperature sensitive bulb only in the water. As the water is heated the light should come on at approximately 80°C for 3.8 litre models and 86°C for 4.2 litre models. Allow the water to cool and note the temperature at which the light goes out again. For 3.8 litre models this temperature should be approximately 72°C, whilst the correct temperature for 4.2 litre models is 74°C. Renew the switch if it does not open and close at the correct limits.

4:8 Frost precautions

Antifreeze should always be used in very cold weather otherwise there is a danger of the bottom half of the radiator freezing, even when the engine is running. Draining the cooling system overnight is not an adequate frost precaution as some water will always remain in the heater.

The cooling system contains aluminium parts, so ensure that the antifreeze used is of the inhibited Ethylene Glycol base type. Use the quantity recommended by the makers for the degree of protection required.

Before adding antifreeze drain and flush the cooling system. Leave the heater control on hot and make sure the drain taps are closed. Add the antifreeze first and then fill up to the normal running level with soft, clean water. Replace the filler cap and run the engine until it is hot so as to thoroughly mix the antifreeze. When the engine has cooled remove the cap and top up if required.

On later models fitted with an expansion tank the tank should be half-filled with a mixture of antifreeze and water.

To prevent the dilution of the antifreeze already in the system always top up with a mixture of antifreeze and water.

4:9 Fault diagnosis

(a) Internal water leakage

1 Cracked cylinder head
2 Loose cylinder head nuts
3 Faulty head gasket

(b) Poor circulation

1 Radiator core blocked
2 Engine water passages restricted by deposits
3 Low water level
4 Loose fan belt (earlier models only)
5 Defective fan belt
6 Perished or collapsed water hoses

(c) Corrosion

1 Impurities in the water
2 Infrequent draining and flushing

(d) Overheating

1 Check (b)
2 Sludge in crankcase
3 Incorrect ignition timing
4 Weak mixture
5 Defective thermostatic switch
6 Defective cooling fan motor
7 Low oil level in sump
8 Tight engine
9 Choked exhaust system
10 Binding brakes
11 Slipping clutch
12 Incorrect valve timing (if this is excessively wrong, damage will be caused to the engine before overheating problems are apparent)

NOTES

CHAPTER 5

THE CLUTCH

5:1 Description

All the models use a clutch consisting of a single dry disc operating between a pressure plate in the clutch and the rear face of the engine flywheel. The parts are contained in a cover which is bolted to, and revolves with, the flywheel. Internal springs in the clutch press the pressure plate firmly forwards to grip the driven plate by its friction surfaces. As the pressure plate is also revolving with the engine the driven plate therefore rotates. The input shaft to the gearbox is splined to the centre of the driven plate, so that the drive is taken from the engine to the gearbox. The earliest models of clutch fitted to the 3.8 litre models used coil springs for moving the pressure plate forwards, but all later models were fitted with a diaphragm type spring.

The clutch release mechanism is shown in **FIG 5:1**. When the pedal 62 is pressed, hydraulic pressure is generated in the master cylinder 32 and this pressure is passed to the slave cylinder 13 by the metal pipes and flexible hose. The hydraulic pressure pushes out the pushrod 23 which is connected to the operating fork 10. The operating fork carries a carbon-faced release bearing. When the pushrod 23 moves, the fork 10 pivots and the release bearing is pressed into contact with the release mechanism in the clutch itself. Lever action draws back the pressure plate, freeing the driven plate. The driven plate and the gearbox input shaft are then free to revolve separately, or come to a stop, without transmitting any drive even though the flywheel continues to turn.

The clutch slave cylinder has been modified from time to time. The earliest models were fitted with a slave cylinder that required adjustment as the clutch wore. This slave cylinder was then replaced with a hydrostatic model, which once set, required no further adjustment until the clutch was renewed. This was later replaced by the original slave cylinder on which regular adjustments are required. The two types of slave cylinder are easily differentiated as the hydrostatic model does not have a return spring fitted to it.

5:2 Routine maintenance

1 At regular intervals check the fluid level in the master cylinder reservoir. The level should not be allowed to fall below the 'Fluid Level' mark. Wipe the top of the reservoir before removing the cap to ensure that no dirt falls into the reservoir. Ideally use only Castrol/

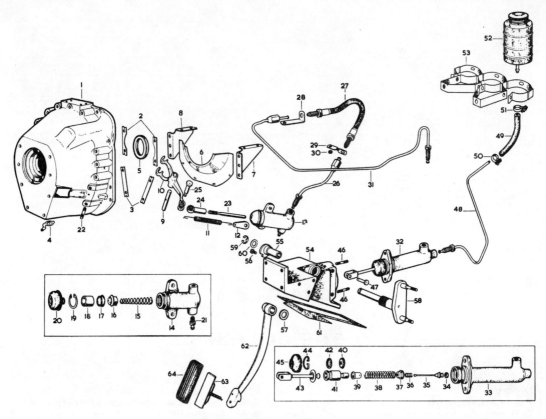

FIG 5:1   Clutch operating system

Key to Fig 5:1   1 Clutch housing   2 Locking plate   3 Locking plate   4 Timing aperture cover   5 Oil seal
6 Coverplate   7 Support bracket   8 Support bracket   9 Shaft   10 Operating fork   11 Return spring
12 Anchor plate   13 Slave cylinder   14 Slave cylinder body   15 Spring   16 Cup filler   17 Seal   18 Piston
19 Circlip   20 Rubber dust cover   21 Bleeder screw   22 Stud   23 Operating rod   24 Adjuster assembly
25 Pivot pin   26 Hydraulic pipe   27 Flexible hydraulic pipe   28 Bracket   29 Bracket   30 Distance piece
31 Hydraulic pipe   32 Master cylinder   33 Master cylinder body   34 Seal   35 Valve   36 Spring   37 Spring support
38 Main spring   39 Spring support   40 Cup seal   41 Piston   42 Static seal   43 Pushrod   44 Circlip
45 Dust cover   46 Stud   47 Clevis pin   48 Hydraulic pipe   49 Flexible pipe   50 Hose clip   51 Hose clip
52 Reservoir   53 Mounting bracket   54 Clutch pedal housing   55 Bush   56 Setscrew   57 Fibre washer
58 Pedal shaft   59 Circlip   60 Washer   61 Gasket   62 Pedal   63 Pedal pad   64 Pedal pad cover

Girling Crimson Clutch and Brake Fluid to specification
SAE.J1703A. As an alternative Lockheed Super Heavy
Duty Brake fluid may be used. If neither of these
fluids is obtainable ensure that the fluid used con-
forms to the SAE.J1703A specification. It is dangerous
to use a fluid that does not meet this specification as
it may rot the seals in the system, causing total clutch
failure.

2 On adjustable slave cylinders (fitted with a return
spring) the clearance should be checked every 2500
miles, as shown in **FIG 5 : 2**. Remove the return spring
and move the pushrod in and out through the free play.
If the play is excessive, slacken the arrowed locknut
and turn the pushrod to vary the adjustment. Screwing
the rod into the fork end will increase the travel, and
screwing it out will decrease the travel. Set the travel
to the dimension shown in the figure, tighten the
locknut and replace the return spring.

3 At intervals of five years the system should be stripped
down and seals and hydraulic fluid renewed. **This
must also be done if the incorrect hydraulic
fluid has been used.** Gummy or old hydraulic fluid
may be removed from the system by pumping it out
through the bleed nipple on the slave cylinder and
pumping through at least a quart of methylated
spirits (denatured alcohol) before refilling the system
with fresh hydraulic fluid.

5 : 3 Servicing the master cylinder

A sectioned view of the clutch master cylinder is shown
in **FIG 5 : 3**. The clutch pedal is connected directly to the
pushrod, so that when the pedal is depressed the pushrod
moves the piston down the bore of the cylinder. Fluid in
front of the piston will be forced out of the outlet on the
side of the cylinder, along the pipes and from there to

operate the slave cylinder. Fluid leakage past the piston is prevented by the cup seal and the sealing ring. When the clutch pedal is released the return spring moves the piston back up the bore of the cylinder, allowing the fluid to return from the slave cylinder. As the piston nears the very end of its stroke the head of the valve stem connects with the spring support and the valve stem opens the recuperation valve against the pressure of the weak valve spring. This valve opens the port to the reservoir ensuring that the clutch system returns to atmospheric pressure and any fluid losses are replenished. As soon as the piston moves in on the pressure stroke the weak valve spring shuts off this interconnection and the build up of pressure ensures that it stays shut until it is opened again on the return stroke of the piston.

Removing the master cylinder:

1 Drain the clutch fluid reservoir 52. **Take care not to allow fluid to drip onto paintwork otherwise the paint will soften and spoil very rapidly.**

2 Undo the unions securing the pipes 31 and 48 to the master cylinder and withdraw the pipes carefully, in order not to bend or distort them.

3 Working inside the car remove the splitpin and withdraw the clevis pin 47. From under the bonnet remove the two nuts securing the master cylinder to the studs 46 and lift out the master cylinder.

Replacing the master cylinder is the reversal of the removal procedure. Ensure that the flexible pipe 49 is not twisted or kinked, preventing the flow of fluid. After refitting the master cylinder the clutch system must be filled with fluid and bled to remove any trapped air.

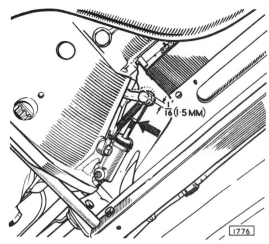

FIG 5:2   Adjusting clutch operating rod

Dismantling the master cylinder:

The parts of the master cylinder are shown in the lower inset in **FIG 5:1**.

1 Gently press in the pushrod 43 to relieve the pressure from the return spring 38. Use a pair of long-nosed pliers and remove the circlip 44 after pulling back the dust cover 45. The dust cover, pushrod and its stop plate can now be removed.

2 Carefully shake out the internal parts of the master cylinder. If stubborn, they may be dislodged by gentle

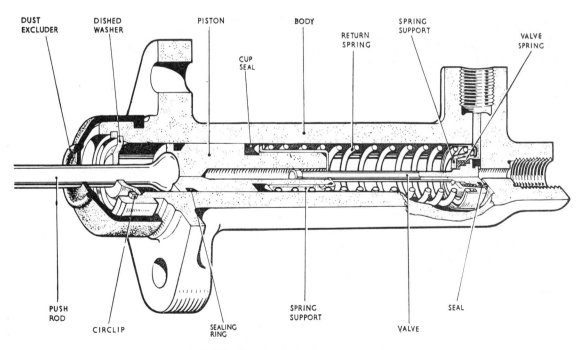

FIG 5:3   Sectioned clutch master cylinder

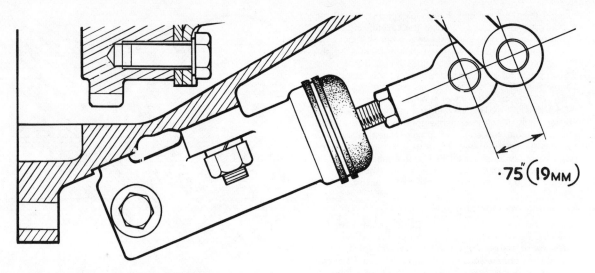

FIG 5:4   Setting dimension for Hydrostatic clutch slave cylinder. Note the absence of a return spring

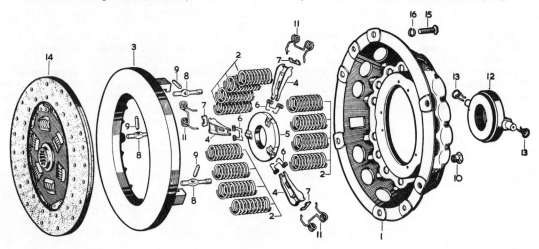

FIG 5:5   Coil spring operated clutch

Key to Fig 5:5   1 Cover   2 Thrust spring   3 Pressure plate   4 Release lever   5 Release lever plate
6 Release lever retainer   7 Release lever strut   8 Release lever eyebolt   9 Eyebolt pin   10 Adjustment nut
11 Anti-rattle spring   12 Release bearing and cup assembly   13 Release bearing retainer   14 Drive plate assembly
15 Securing bolt   16 Spring washer

air pressure at the outlet. The spring support 39 has a little tongue spring which locks into the groove on the piston 41. Part the coils of the spring 38 and use a small screwdriver to lift the tongue to free the spring support from the piston. Use the fingers to remove the seals 40 and 42 from the piston 41.

3 The spring support 39 has a larger hole offset in the end so compress the spring 38 and pass the head of the valve 35 through the offset hole to free the spring support 39. Remove the spring 38, spring support 37 and valve spring 36. Use the fingers to remove the seal 34 from the end of the valve 35.

4 Examine the bore of the cylinder and the working surface of the piston. If either are pitted, worn or

scored they must be renewed. **The interior of the bore must be polished and smooth.**

Reassembling the master cylinder:

The parts are reassembled in the reverse order of dismantling with attention to the following points:

1 Renew all the seals unless the old ones are in perfect condition.
2 Clean the parts, using methylated spirits or clean hydraulic fluid only.
3 As the parts are reassembled dip them in clean hydraulic fluid for lubrication. Use the fingers only to refit the seals and work them around to make sure they are properly seated.

4 Take great care when refitting the internal parts of the master cylinder not to damage or bend back the lips of the seals.

5:4 Servicing the slave cylinder

The parts of the slave cylinder are shown in **FIG 5:1**.

Removing the slave cylinder:

Disconnect the supply pipe 26. Pull the rubber dust cover 20 back off the body and take out the two bolts securing the cylinder to the bellhousing. Remove the cylinder, leaving the operating rod 23 and adjuster 24 still attached to the operating fork 10.

The slave cylinder is replaced in the reverse order of removal but the system will have to be topped up and bled after refitting.

Dismantling the slave cylinder:

Remove the circlip 19 and use gentle air pressure at the outlet to blow out the internal parts. Examine the internal surface of the bore. **It should be smooth and polished**. Pitting, roughness or wear means that the assembly will have to be renewed.

Reassembling is the reversal of the dismantling process. Lubricate the parts with clean hydraulic fluid and take great care when refitting the seal 17 to ensure that the lips are not turned back or the seal in any way damaged.

Setting the slave cylinder:

The type fitted with a return spring should be set as detailed in operation 2 of **Section 5:2**.

The hydrostatic model should be set as shown in **FIG 5:4**. This operation need only be carried out when the slave cylinder has been removed or a new clutch unit fitted.

1 Remove the clevis pin securing the adjuster to the operating fork. Move the operating fork away from the slave cylinder until a definite resistance is felt. Wire the operating fork into this position.

2 Slacken the locknut on the adjuster. Press the pushrod into the slave cylinder to the limit of its travel. Turn the adjuster until the dimension between the hole centres is .75 inch (19 mm) as shown in the figure. Since the holes are of the same diameter it will be easier to measure between the front edges of the holes rather than try to estimate their centres.

3 When the distance is correct refit the clevis pin and tighten the locknut. Bleed the clutch system normally.

5:5 Bleeding the hydraulic system

Bleeding is not required as regular maintenance but it must be carried out if the system has been dismantled or if the level in the reservoir has fallen so low that air has been drawn into the master cylinder.

It is advisable to discard all fluid that has been drained or bled from the system. Only if the fluid is perfectly clean from draining should it be re-used, and even then it should be stored in a sealed clean container for 24 hours to allow it to de-aerate before using again. **Never return straight back to the reservoir fluid that has been bled through the system.**

Before commencing bleeding fill the master cylinder

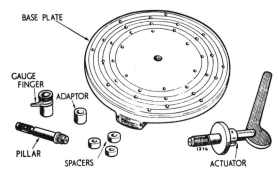

FIG 5:6 Churchill special tool

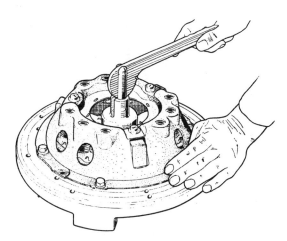

FIG 5:7 Actuating arm in position

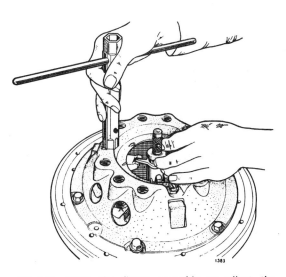

FIG 5:8 Using the finger assembly to adjust the release levers

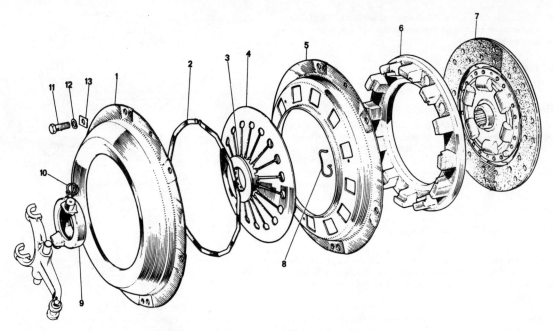

FIG 5:9 Laycock diaphragm-spring clutch details

Key to Fig 5:9   1 Cover   2 Spring retaining ring   3 Release ring   4 Diaphragm spring   5 Driving plate
6 Pressure plate   7 Driven plate assembly   8 Clip   9 Release bearing   10 Clip   11 Bolt   12 Spring washer
13 Balance weight

reservoir right up to the top. Fluid will be used throughout the operation so the master cylinder must be constantly refilled, otherwise the level in the reservoir may drop so low that air is again drawn into the system.

Attach a length of plastic or rubber small-bore tube to the bleed nipple on the slave cylinder and immerse the free end in a little clean fluid in a clean glass container. Unscrew the bleed nipple one complete turn and have a second operator depress the clutch pedal. **Tighten the bleed nipple before the pedal reaches the end of its stroke and allow the pedal to return unassisted.** On the first few strokes air will come out of the free end of the tube. Carry on bleeding until only clean fluid with no air bubbles is ejected from the tube.

Remove the bleed tube and top up the reservoir to the correct level.

5:6 Clutch driven plate condition

To examine the clutch, the engine and gearbox unit will have to be removed from the car. Separate the gearbox from the engine and remove the clutch as described in **Section 1:9, Chapter 1.**

The lining material is secured to the driven plate by rivets. If the lining has worn down nearly flush with the rivet heads, then the driven plate must be renewed irrespective of any other considerations. Check the whole driven plate for loose rivets and ensure that the cushioning springs are held securely in place with no slack. Examine the splines in the centre, not only for wear but to make sure that the metal is not cracking or damaged in any other way. Faults of this nature will also require renewal of the driven plate assembly.

Examine the friction lining surface. **For maximum efficiency they should be light coloured with a polished glaze through which the grain of the material is clearly visible.** A small quantity of oil will produce a smearing on the surface, while more oil will produce a dark glazed deposit hiding the grain of the friction material. A large amount of oil will be obvious from the free oil in the housing and the oil soaked appearance of the friction linings. Whatever the quantity of oil reaching the clutch, the source must be found and the fault rectified. Provided that the grain of the friction material can still be seen clearly the driven plate may be used again. If the grain is obscured by the deposit the driven plate should be renewed as the deposit cannot be removed and will always be a source of slip, drag or fierceness in the clutch.

5:7 Coil spring operated clutch

This type of clutch was only fitted to the earliest 3.8 litre models and the components are shown in **FIG 5:5.** Before removing the clutch from the flywheel check that the balance marks B on the flywheel and the flange of the clutch cover are aligned. Note the position of any balance weights if they are fitted. It is possible to use a press to dismantle and reassemble the clutch but accurate assembly is difficult. The Churchill special tool shown in **FIG 5:6** should be used.

Dismantling the clutch assembly:

1 Lay the baseplate of the special tool on a flat surface and lay the spacers in the correct positions. Place the

clutch assembly in position on top of the baseplate, ensuring that the release levers are as near as possible to the spacers.

2 Screw the actuating arm into position on the base plate as shown in **FIG 5:7** and press down the handle to compress the clutch. Mark the parts indelibly to ensure that they will be reassembled in the same relative positions. Screw the cover 1 to the base plate with the setscrews provided. Remove the actuating arm.

3 Use a socket spanner to undo and remove the three adjusting nuts 10. Progressively and evenly slacken the bolts securing the cover to the base plate, allowing the twelve coil springs to expand. When the bolts are removed lift off the cover 1 and take out the springs 2, storing them in the correct order for reassembly.

4 If required dismantle the clutch disengaging mechanism, carefully storing the parts in the correct order for reassembly. Wash the metal parts in clean fuel to remove dirt and dust. Examine the working face of the pressure plate 2. Light 'blueing' patches are acceptable but if the surface is burnt, scored or has fine hairline cracks the plate should be renewed.

Reassembling the clutch :

1 Lay the pressure plate back into position on the base plate of the special tool. Reassemble the clutch release mechanism if it has been dismantled. Very lightly lubricate the bearing surfaces with either Lockheed Expander Lubricant or Duckhams Keenol K.O.12.

2 Replace the twelve springs 2. Refit the cover 1 and clamp it down using the actuator arm. Secure the cover into place using the bolts provided. Refit the three adjusting nuts 10 and screw them into place until the top of the nut is level with the top of the eye bolt. Work the actuating arm several times to settle the components and remove the actuating arm from the base plate.

FIG 5:10 Balance marks on clutch and flywheel. Note the balance weight under securing bolt and the stamped numerals

3 Screw the pillar, correct adaptor and finger gauge into the central hole in the base plate. Turn the finger on the gauge so that it is over a release lever. Use a spanner to turn the appropriate adjusting nut 10 until the release lever just contacts the underside of the finger, as shown in **FIG 5:8**. Repeat the operation on the other two release levers. Remove the gauge finger and pillar.

4 Replace the actuating arm and operate it at least six times to resettle the components. Remove the actuating arm and again replace the pillar, adaptor and finger gauge. Check the release levers for position and finally adjust the nuts 10 if required. Lock the adjusting nuts 10 by peening the cylindrical portion into the slot

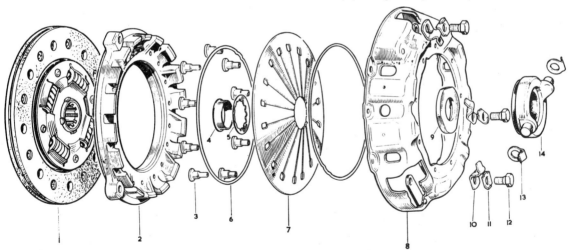

FIG 5:11   Borg and Beck diaphragm-spring clutch

Key to Fig 5:11   1 Driven plate   2 Pressure plate   3 Rivet   4 Centre sleeve   5 Belleville washer
6 Fulcrum ring   7 Diaphragm spring   8 Cover pressing   9 Release plate   10 Retainer   11 Tabwasher   12 Setscrew
13 Retainer   14 Release bearing

in the eye bolt, using a small blunt chisel and hammer.

5 If a new pressure plate 2 has been fitted, the clutch assembly must be rebalanced. Specialized equipment is required for this operation and this will have to be carried out by a suitably equipped garage.

6 The height of the release levers can be set without using the special tool, though the method is not as accurate. Mount the clutch on the flywheel or a suitable flat surface. Use a press to actuate the clutch. The driven plate should be in position. Adjust the nuts 10 until the face of the tip of each lever is 2.45 inch (62.23 mm) from the face of the flywheel. Operate the clutch, using a press, and recheck the settings. Release the clamping pressure and turn the driven plate through 90 deg. to compensate for any inaccuracies in the driven plate, and again recheck the distance from the lever to the flywheel. Lock the adjusting nuts as described in operation 4.

5 : 8 Laycock diaphragm spring clutch

This type of clutch was fitted to the later models of the 3.8 litre and to the earlier models of the 4.2 litre. The details of the assembly are shown in **FIG 5 : 9**. Normally if the unit is defective it should be replaced with a new complete assembly, but it may be dismantled as follows.

1 Remove the cover from the flywheel by progressively and evenly slackening the securing bolts. Lift off the cover 1, the remainder of the clutch assembly and the driven plate 7.

2 Remove the retaining ring 2 and lift out the diaphragm spring 4. Free the pressure plate 6 from the driving plate 5 by removing the spring clips 8.

3 Examine the surface of the pressure plate 6 for signs of excess heat or fine hairline cracks. Check that there is not an excessive clearance between the lugs on the pressure plate 6 and the slots in the driving plate 5.

Reassemble the clutch in the reverse order of dismantling. Lubricate the sides of the pressure plate lugs, all the fulcrum points where the diaphragm spring fits and also the finger tips of the diaphragm spring, with moly-disulphide or zinc based grease. **Do not overlubricate, a light smear is sufficient.** The pressure plate, driving plate and cover are marked on their flanges to ensure that the parts are reassembled in their correct positions so that the unit is correctly balanced on reassembly. Fit the retaining ring 2 with the cranked ends of the ring uppermost and the twelve crowns fitting into the grooves in the twelve lugs on the pressure plate. **Make sure the retaining ring is fully seated into the grooves.**

When refitting the clutch to the engine use a mandrel, or old input shaft from the gearbox, to centralize the driven plate while progressively tightening the securing bolts. The balance mark B on the clutch should align with the balance mark B on the flywheel, as shown in **FIG 5 : 10**. Note also that balance weights are fitted under the securing bolts. These are stamped with numbers 1 to 3, No. 3 being the heaviest, and both the flywheel and clutch cover should be stamped with numbers indicating the positions of the balance weights.

5 : 9 Borg and Beck diaphragm spring clutch

This type of clutch is fitted to later models of the 4.2 litre. The components of this clutch are shown in **FIG 5 : 11**, but it should be noted that the parts are riveted together. The clutch is removed and replaced in the same manner as the Laycock diaphragm spring clutch and is fitted with similar balance weights and markings.

If the clutch is defective it should be replaced with a new unit. In some overseas areas complete clutch units may not be readily available, in which case the clutch may be dismantled and new parts fitted. Special tools are required for the operation, and a special tool must be made for clamping the clutch. After reassembly the clutch must also be rebalanced on specialized equipment so it is best to leave the task to the local agents.

5 : 10 Clutch release bearing

All the models of the E type Jaguar are fitted with a release bearing which consists of a special graphite ring shrunk into a metal housing. It is essential that the clutch slave cylinder is correctly adjusted and that the car is not driven with a foot resting on the clutch pedal, otherwise the release bearing will be in constant contact with the clutch and suffer excess wear as a result.

The release bearing can only be examined when the gearbox has been removed from the engine. Check that the carbon face is neither chipped nor scored. The release bearing must also be renewed if the wear is such that the thrust face of the carbon ring is close to the metal housing.

5 : 11 Fault diagnosis

(a) Drag or spin

1 Oil or grease on driven plate linings
2 Leaking master cylinder, slave cylinder or pipe connections
3 Driven plate hub binding on splines
4 Distorted driven plate
5 Warped or damaged pressure plate
6 Broken drive plate linings
7 Air in the clutch hydraulic system

(b) Fierceness or snatch

1 Check 1, 2, 4 and 5 in (a)
2 Worn clutch linings

(c) Slip

1 Check 1 in (a) and 2 in (b)
2 Seized piston in clutch slave cylinder

(d) Judder

1 Check 1 and 4 in (a)
2 Contact area of driven plate linings not evenly distributed
3 Faulty engine mountings or stabilizer

(e) Tick or knock

1 Badly worn driven plate hub splines
2 Worn release bearing

CHAPTER 6

THE GEARBOX

6:1 Description

The gearbox fitted to the 3.8 litre models is different from the type fitted to the 4.8 litre models. All the gearboxes are fourspeed, and while the 4.2 litre version has constant-mesh gears with synchromesh on all four forward speeds, only the top three speeds on the 3.8 are so made and the first-speed gears are spur-cut and are slid into mesh. The reverse gears on both types of gearbox have spur teeth and are not meshed when not in use.

On the 3.8 litre model the gearlever moves an intermediate selector shaft which in turn moves the striker shafts to select the gears. On the 4.2 litre model the intermediate selector shaft is omitted and the gearlever moves the selector shaft of each gear directly.

On the 4.2 litre model the gears are pressure fed with oil from an oil pump unit mounted at the rear of the mainshaft. The pressure of the oil is approximately 5 lb/sq in (.35 kg/sq cm). The 3.8 litre model has no oil pump fitted and the parts are lubricated either by dipping into the oil bath or by the oil splash thrown up by the gears.

A sectional view of the gearbox fitted to the 3.8 litre is shown in **FIG 6:1** and a similar view of the gearbox on the 4.2 litre in **FIG 6:2**.

6:2 Routine maintenance

At regular intervals, of approximately 2500 miles, check the oil level in the gearbox. Lift the trim and remove the access panel arrowed in **FIG 6:3**. The combined filler and level plug on the side of the gearbox housing is accessible under this cover. The oil should be level with the bottom of the filler hole.

At longer intervals, approximately every 10,000 miles, drain the oil out through the drain plug fitted underneath the gearbox. The oil will drain faster when it is hot, so the car should be taken for a reasonably long run before draining. Refill the gearbox to the correct level with fresh oil. The 3.8 litre gearbox uses SAE.30 engine oil but the 4.2 litre gearbox must be refilled using the correct hypoid type oil.

6:3 Removing the gearbox

The gearbox cannot be removed while the engine is still fitted to the car. Remove the engine and gearbox unit from the car as described in **Chapter 1, Section 1:2** before removing the gearbox.

Remove the bolts and take off the front cover from the

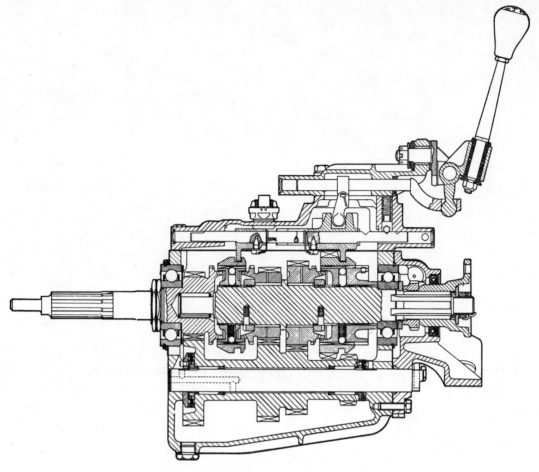

FIG 6:1 Sectioned view 3.8 litre gearbox

bottom of the bellhousing. Undo all the bolts and nuts securing the bellhousing to the engine and withdraw the gearbox from the engine. **Support the gearbox weight during this operation to prevent it resting on the input shaft.** If the weight of the gearbox is allowed to rest on the input shaft damage to the clutch can easily result.

Replace the gearbox in the reverse order of dismantling. If the clutch has been removed, **the driven plate must be centralized using a mandrel when refitting the clutch** otherwise the input shaft of the gearbox will not align with the splines in the hub. **Take care not to let the weight of the gearbox hang on the input shaft when mating the gearbox to the engine.**

PART I THE 3.8 LITRE GEARBOX

A sectional view of this gearbox is shown in **FIG 6:1**. The fixed components are shown in **FIG 6:4** and the moving components in **FIG 6:5**.

6:4 The top cover and gear selector mechanism

The components of this are shown in **FIG 6:4**. The

assembly is secured to the gearbox casing by ten setscrews and spring washers. The two long setscrews are at the rear and the two short setscrews at the front. When removing the top cover assembly it will have to be lifted clear of the locating dowels. Leave the selectors in neutral.

If the assembly is dismantled take great care not to lose any springs, balls or plungers. When removing the striking rod assemblies the centre first/second speed striker shaft 40 should be removed first, while ensuring that the other two shafts are in the neutral position, and the interlock balls 53 carefully removed. Wire-lock all dowel screws into place after reassembly.

Welch plugs:

Remove these by using a drift from the inside. If the inside is inaccessible, flatten them from the outside using a hammer and punch.

Clean out the recess for the plug before fitting a new one. Press the new plug into place, by hand, with the convex face outwards. Secure it in position by tapping on the outer face until the plug is a tight fit. If a plug leaks, do not flatten it any more but remove it and use a little jointing compound around the edges.

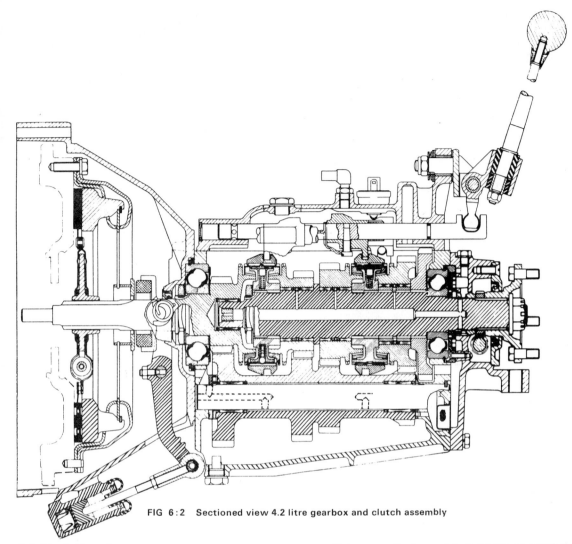

FIG 6:2 Sectioned view 4.2 litre gearbox and clutch assembly

6:5 The bellhousing

Remove the clutch slave cylinder from the housing, if this has not been done already, by removing the two securing bolts and withdrawing the clevis pin securing it to the operating fork.

Remove the clutch release bearing from the operating fork by withdrawing the two securing spring clips.

Slacken the locknut and remove the Allen-headed screw securing the operating fork to the pivot shaft. Withdraw the pivot shaft downwards and remove the operating fork.

Cut the lockwire and free the locktabs on the eight bellhousing securing bolts. Remove the bolts and lift off the bellhousing.

6:6 Dismantling the gearbox

1 Remove the locking screw 18 and washer 19 so as to allow the speedometer drive gear 17 to be withdrawn. Lift off the gasket 13 and prise out the fibre disc 12 which covers the forward hole for the countershaft.

2 Engage both first and top gear to lock the gearbox. Referring to **FIG 6:5**, withdraw and discard the splitpin 4. Undo the nut 2 and remove it with the washer 3. Pull off the flange 1.

3 Refer to **FIG 6:4**. Remove the seven setscrews securing the rear end cover 14 to the case 1. Leave the locking plate 4 in place and draw the rear cover back from the case so that the reverse spindle and countershaft are drawn out with the cover. From the front of the gearbox, through the hole where the fibre disc 12 was removed, insert a dummy countershaft, of dimensions as shown in **FIG 6:6**. This dummy shaft must be kept in contact with the proper countershaft until the countershaft is free, leaving the countershaft gears suspended on the dummy countershaft.

4 Remove the speedometer driving gear 6 and washer 7 from the back of the mainshaft 5. Draw out the dummy countershaft and allow the countershaft gears to fall to the bottom of the casing.

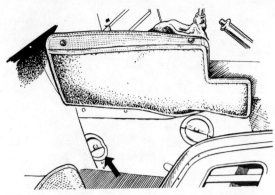

FIG 6:3 Access plate to gearbox filler and level plug

5 Disengage the gears that were selected and rotate the input shaft 22 until the cutaway portions of the driving gear are facing the top and bottom of the casing. Use a rawhide hammer to tap the mainshaft forwards into the gearbox. This action will drive out the input shaft assembly and its front bearing from the front of the gearbox. When the front bearing is free of the casing withdraw the input shaft assembly. Carry on tapping until the mainshaft is free from the rear bearing. Use a steel drift to drive the rear bearing evenly out of the back of the casing. Lift the front end of the mainshaft assembly and manoeuvre it out of the top aperture.

6 Move the reverse gear back as far as it will go to clear the first-speed gear. Lift out the countershaft gear assembly, taking care not to lose any of the needle rollers fitted to the bearings, and not forgetting the thrust washers fitted at either end of the assembly.

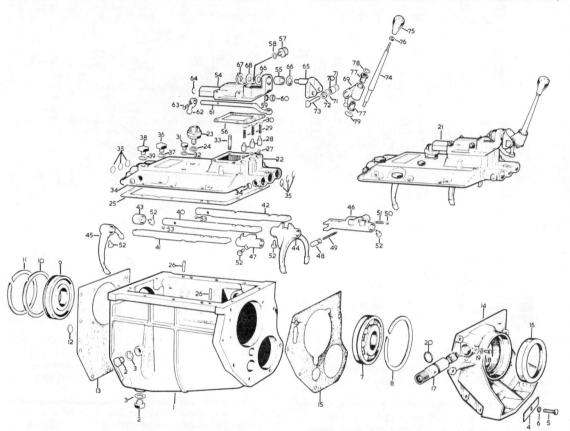

FIG 6:4   3.8 litre gearbox fixed parts details

Key to Fig 6:4   1 Gearbox case   2 Drain plug and oil filler plug   3 Fibre washer   4 Locking plate   5 Setscrew
6 Spring washer   7 Ballbearing   8 Circlip   9 Ballbearing   10 Collar   11 Circlip   12 Fibre washer   13 Gasket
14 Rear end cover   15 Gasket   16 Oil seal   17 Speedometer drive gear   18 Locking screw   19 Washer   20 O-ring
21 Remote control assembly   22 Top cover   23 Switch   24 Gasket   25 Gasket   26 Dowel   27 Ball   28 Plunger
29 Spring   30 Shims   31 Plug   32 Washer   33 Stud   34 Welch washer.   35 Welch washer   36 Plug
37 Fibre washer   38 Plug   39 Copper washer   40 Striking rod assembly—1st and 2nd gears
41 Striking rod assembly—3rd and top gears   42 Striking rod—reverse gear   43 Stop   44 Changespeed fork—1st and 2nd gears
45 Changespeed fork—3rd and top gears   46 Changespeed fork—reverse gear   47 Selector—3rd and top gears   48 Plunger
49 Spring   50 Ball   51 Spring   52 Dowel screw   53 Ball   54 Housing   55 Bush   56 Gasket   57 Breather
58 Fibre washer   59 O-ring   60 Retaining clip   61 Selector shaft   62 Selector finger   63 Screw   64 Welch washer
65 Pivot jaw   66 Washer   67 Spring washer   68 D-washer   69 Selector lever   70 Bush   71 Washer   72 Spring washer
73 Pivot pin   74 Gearlever   75 Knob   76 Nut   77 Bush   78 Washer   79 Washer

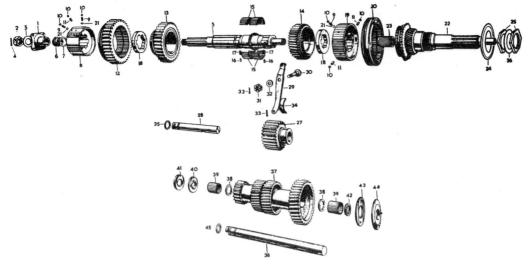

FIG 6:5   3.8 litre gearbox moving parts details

Key to Fig 6:5   1 Flange   2 Nut   3 Washer   4 Splitpin   5 Mainshaft   6 Speedometer driving gear
7 Distance piece   8 2nd gear synchronizing sleeve   9 Spring   10 Ball   11 Plunger   12 1st speed gear   13 2nd speed gear
14 3rd speed gear   15 Needle roller   16 Plunger   17 Spring   18 Thrust washer   19 Synchronizing sleeve
20 Operating sleeve   21 Shim   22 Input shaft   23 Roller bearing   24 Oil thrower   25 Locknut   26 Tabwasher
27 Reverse gear   28 Reverse spindle   29 Lever   30 Fulcrum pin   31 Slotted nut   32 Plain washer   33 Splitpin
34 Reverse slipper   35 Sealing ring   36 Countershaft   37 Gear unit on countershaft   38 Retaining ring   39 Needle roller
40 Thrust washer   41 Thrust washer   42 Retaining ring   43 Thrust washer   44 Thrust washer   45 Sealing ring

7 Push the reverse gear 27 back into the casing and lift it out. Note that this gear has a renewable bush pressed into it.

Dismantling the mainshaft:

As the parts are removed, wash them in clean fuel and lay them out in the correct order on a clean piece of paper. Use small tins or jars to contain the small plungers, balls and springs and to keep them identified with their correct associated parts. Examine the gears for damaged, worn or missing teeth. Renew any gears necessary. Examine the shafts and bushes for chatter marks, scuffing or wear. Refer to **FIG 6:5**.

1 Withdraw the synchronizing sleeve 19 and operating sleeve 20 assembly from the front of the mainshaft. Wrap the assembly in a piece of cloth and press the operating sleeve 20 off the synchronizing sleeve 19. Unwrap the parts and collect the six synchronizing springs 9, balls 10 and any shims 21. Remove the interlock plungers 11 and balls 10 from the synchronizing sleeve 19.

2 Remove the first-speed gear 12 and second-speed synchronizing sleeve 8 assembly from the rear of the mainshaft and dismantle the parts inside a piece of cloth as already described.

3 Press in the plunger 16 locking the third-speed gear thrust washer 18, as shown in **FIG 6:7**, and rotate the washer until the splines align and the washer can be removed up the splines. Remove the plunger 16 and the spring 17 under it. Remove the third-speed gear 14 taking care not to lose any of the needle rollers 15 fitted underneath the gear.

4 In a similar manner to operation 3 remove the other thrust washer 18, second-speed gear 13 and other plunger 16 and spring 17. Draw these parts off from the rear of the mainshaft.

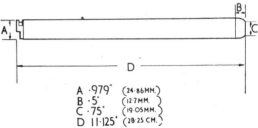

A ·979" (24·86MM.)
B ·5" (12·7MM.)
C ·75" (19·05MM.)
D 11·125" (28·25 CM.)

FIG 6:6   Dummy countershaft dimensions

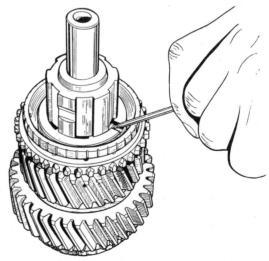

FIG 6:7   Depressing the third-speed thrust washer locking plunger

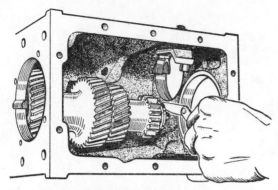

FIG 6:8　Checking the countershaft assembly end float

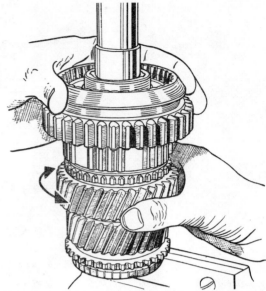

FIG 6:10　Checking first- and second-speed interlock plunger

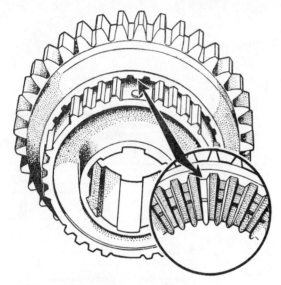

FIG 6:9　Relieved tooth on internal splines of first-speed gear aligned with stop on second-speed synchro-sleeve

Dismantling the input shaft assembly:

Free the tabwasher 26 and unscrew both locknuts 25. Remove the front bearing and then the oil thrower 24. Refer to **FIG 6:4**. The circlip 11 and collar 10 can be removed from the front bearing 9. Similarly the circlip 8 can be removed from the rear bearing 7.

6:7 Reassembling the gearbox

Refit the countershaft gear assembly, using the thrust washers and the dummy countershaft. Measure the end float of the countershaft assembly, using feeler gauges as shown in **FIG 6:8**. The end float should be .002 to .004 inch (.05 to .10 mm) Various thicknesses of thrust washer are supplied (see Technical Data for details), and these should be selectively fitted to give the correct end float.

Remove the dummy countershaft and keep the gears in place with a thin rod instead. Refit the reverse gear so that the bush is in the slipper of the selector and the gear is as far rearwards as possible.

Reassembling the mainshaft:

1　Fit forty-one needle rollers in place behind the shoulder of the mainshaft, securing them in place with grease. Slide the second-speed gear 13 into place on the rollers so that the synchronizing cone is at the rear. Fit a spring 17 and plunger 16 into place. Slide the thrust washer 18 up the splines and into place. Turn the second-speed gear 13 until the large hole in the synchronizing cone is over the plunger 16, and use a steel rod to press in the plunger. Rotate the thrust washer into the locked position with the cutaway portion in line with the plunger 16.

2　In a similar manner refit the remaining forty-one rollers 15, third-speed gear 13 (so that its synchronizing cone faces forwards) and the thrust washer 18.

3　Check the end float of both gears, using feeler gauges. If the end float is not correct between .002 and .004 inch (.05 to .10 mm), new thrust washers 18 will have to be selectively fitted to bring the end float within correct limits. The thicknesses of the thrust washers available are given in Technical Data.

4　Fit the six sets of springs 9, balls 10 and any shims 21 to the six blind holes in the second gear synchronizing sleeve 8. Compress the springs by fitting a hose clip around the sleeve 8. Slide the sleeve 8 into place in the first-speed gear 12 until the balls are heard and felt to click into place in the internal groove. When reassembling these parts the relieved tooth in the internal splines of the gear 12 must be aligned with the stop in the sleeve, as shown in **FIG 6:9**. Use a spring balance and adaptor to check that the load required to disengage the synchronizing sleeve from the neutral position is 62 to 68 lbs (28 to 31 Kg). If the load varies from the correct figures, shims 21 must be removed or replaced under the springs 10 to set the correct load.

FIG 6:11 Relieved tooth correctly aligned with inter-lock hole

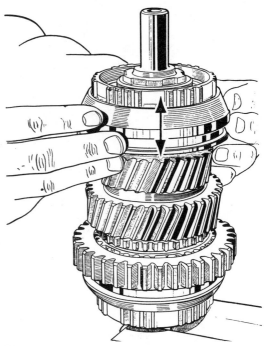

FIG 6:13 Checking third-speed interlock plunger with third-speed engaged

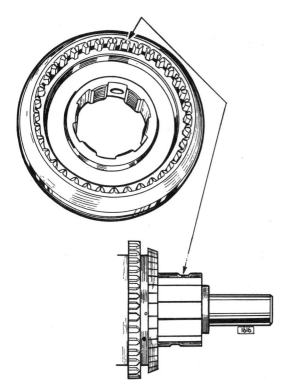

FIG 6:12 Wide chamfer at front and relieved tooth aligned with foremost groove in mainshaft

5 Fit the parts assembled in operation 4 onto the mainshaft. Check that the assembly slides freely on the splines, without the ball 10 and plunger 11 fitted. If the assembly does not slide freely remove the assembly, check the splines for burrs and try again mating the parts onto different splines. When the assembly does slide freely, mark a pair of mating splines to ensure reassembly in the same relative position and remove the assembly.

6 Fit the ball 10 and plunger 11 and refit the second gear assembly back onto the mainshaft so that the marked splines are aligned. Slide the outer operating sleeve into the first gear position as shown in **FIG 6:10**, and rotate the second-speed gear. If the synchro cones are felt to rub, a longer plunger 11 must be fitted. These are available in .490, .495 and .500 inch (12.4, 12.52 and 12.65 mm) lengths.

7 Refit the balls, springs and shims to the synchronizing sleeve 19 and then refit the assembly into the operating sleeve 20. The wide chamfer of the operating sleeve must be fitted to the same side as the large boss on the synchro sleeve, and the relieved tooth in the operating sleeve must align with the hole for the interlock ball and plunger as shown in **FIG 6:11**. Check that the load to move the parts from the neutral position is 52 to 58 lbs (24 to 26 kg) and adjust the amount of shims 21 to bring the load within the correct limits.

8 Fit the assembled top/third synchromesh unit to the mainshaft so that the widest face of the chamfer on the operating sleeve 20 is forwards, and the relieved tooth in the operating ring 20 aligns with the forward groove in the mainshaft, as shown in **FIG 6:12**.

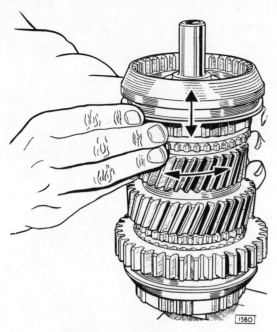

FIG 6:14 Checking fourth-speed (top) interlock plunger with the operating sleeve in top gear position

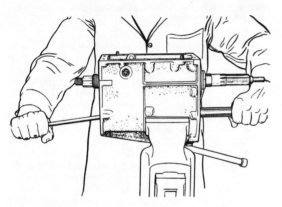

FIG 6:15 Lifting the countershaft assembly into mesh and inserting the dummy countershaft

Check that the sleeve slides freely on the mainshaft splines in this position. Remove the assembly and clean off any burrs if the sleeve did not slide freely. Fit the two sets of balls 10 and plungers 11 and refit the assembly to the mainshaft. **It is essential that the assembly is fitted as instructed, otherwise full engagement of top and third gears will be prevented.**

9 Slide the operating sleeve 20 into the third gear position as shown in FIG 6:13. Move the assembly up and down as shown and it should move $\frac{3}{32}$ inch (2.5 mm) without any drag being felt. If drag is felt a shorter third-speed plunger 11 should be fitted. This is the plunger furthest away from the relieved tooth on the operating sleeve.

10 Move the operating sleeve into the top-speed position, as shown in FIG 6:14. It should be possible to move the synchronization assembly up and down approximately $\frac{3}{16}$ inch (4.5 mm) without any drag being felt. If the assembly does not move freely a shorter top-speed plunger must be fitted. Press lightly down on the assembly and rotate the third-speed gear. If the synchronizing cones bind then a longer top gear plunger must be fitted. The top gear plunger is the one nearest to the relieved tooth in the operating sleeve.

Refitting the gears to the casing:

1 Reassemble the input shaft assembly in the reverse order of dismantling.

2 Lower the mainshaft assembly through the top aperture in the gearbox, passing the mainshaft through the bearing hole in the rear of the casing.

3 Insert the input shaft assembly into the front of the gearbox with the cutaway portions of the toothed driving member facing the top and bottom of the casing, after fitting a new front gasket. Tap the input shaft assembly into place until the circlip and collar on the front bearing are tight against the front of the casing.

4 Align the mainshaft in position and drive the rear bearing back into place until the circlip on the bearing is tight against the rear face of the casing.

5 Lift the countershaft gear assembly by using the thin rod until the gears mesh with those on the mainshaft. Insert the dummy countershaft from the front end of the casing to hold the gears in position as shown in FIG 6:15.

Refit the speedometer drive gear in the reverse order of dismantling and refit the rear end cover, using a new gasket. The countershaft and reverse spindle are replaced fitted to the rear end cover, using the countershaft to push out the dummy countershaft through the front of the casing. Fit a new fibre disc to the hole. Refit the remainder of the parts in the reverse order of dismantling.

PART II THE 4.2 LITRE GEARBOX

A sectional view of this gearbox is shown in FIG 6:2.

6:8 The top cover and gear selector mechanism

A plan view of the cover is shown in FIG 6:16 and a view from the underside of the cover with all the parts correctly fitted is shown in FIG 6:17.

Removal:

Set the gearlever to the neutral position. Remove the eight setscrews and two nuts securing the cover. Lift off the cover, noting that it is aligned by two dowels. Remove the old gasket.

The top cover is replaced in the reverse order of removal.

Dismantling:

1 Unscrew the self-locking nut securing the gearlever pivot to the cover. Remove the double coil spring washer, flat washer and fibre washer. Withdraw the gearlever and replace the washers and nut to prevent loss of the parts.

2 Cut the locking wire and unscrew the fork securing screws.

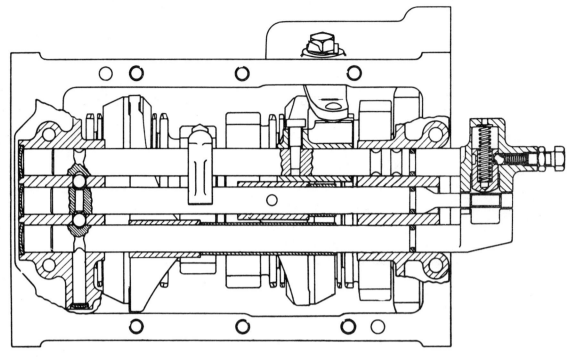

FIG 6:16 Plan view of gearbox showing selector arrangements

3 Withdraw the third/top selector rod first, collecting the selector fork, spacing tube and interlock ball. Similarly remove the reverse selector rod, and finally the first/second selector rod, noting the loose interlock plunger in it.

4 Reassembly is the reversal of the dismantling procedure, but taking care to fit the interlock balls and plunger. Fit new O-ring seals.

Setting the reverse plunger :

This is fitted to the reverse selector rod to prevent the inadvertent selection of reverse gear. Refit the parts to the selector rod, leaving the adjusting screw slack. Press the plunger in as far as possible and screw in the adjusting screw until the ball prevents the plunger from moving out. Slowly slacken the adjusting screw until the plunger is just released and the ball seats in the annular groove in the plunger. Hold the adjusting screw in this position and tighten the locknut to secure it.

6:9 Dismantling the gearbox

1 The clutch bellhousing is removed in a similar manner to the one fitted to the 3.8 litre model (see **Section 6:5**).

2 The rear end cover differs from the one fitted to the 3.8 litre model in that it contains the oil pump. Remove the cover, after taking out the speedometer driving gear, and withdraw from the end of the mainshaft the speedometer drive gear, key, and key for the oil pump drive. The oil pump, shown in **FIG 6:18**, is secured by three setscrews and staked in to the metal of the rear cover. If it is necessary to remove the oil pump,

break the staking and remove the securing setscrews. The pump can then be driven out of the cover by evenly screwing two of the setscrews into the threaded holes provided in the pump. Mark the gears with marking ink to ensure that they will be correctly replaced in the cover.

3 On this model the countershaft remains in the gearbox after the removal of the rear end cover. Remove the blanking fibre plug from the front of the casing. Drive out the countershaft from the front end of the casing. The rear thrust washer for the countershaft is pegged to the casing and **it is essential that this drops round in a clockwise direction,** viewed from the rear of the casing, otherwise it will foul on the reverse gear when removing the mainshaft. Either rock the gearbox or use a bent piece of wire to ensure that the washer moves in the right direction.

4 Rotate the input shaft until the cutaway portions on the gear face the top and bottom of the casing. Ease the assembly forwards, using two levers as shown in **FIG 6:19**, until the front bearing is free out of the casing and the assembly can be removed. The assembly is dismantled in a similar manner to the one fitted to the 3.8 litre model.

5 Use a rawhide hammer to tap the end of the mainshaft forwards into the gearbox. It is essential to hold the reverse gear in tight contact with the first gear during this operation, otherwise the gears will slip and the needle rollers fall out. Set the mainshaft so that a cutaway portion on the synchronizing hub aligns with the countershaft as shown in **FIG 6:20**.

6 Drive out the rear bearing from the rear face of the

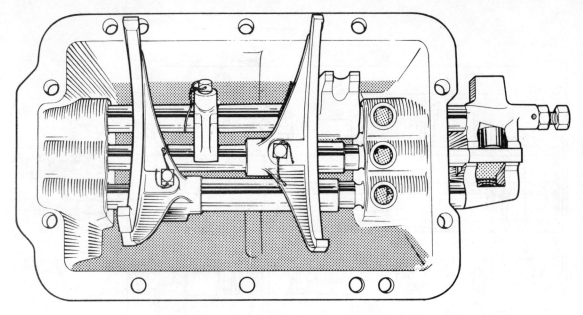

FIG 6:17 View of the underside of the top cover

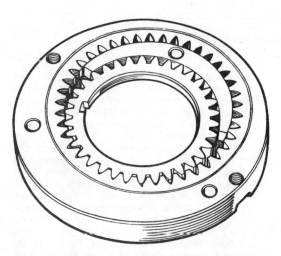

FIG 6:18 The oil pump

FIG 6:19 Easing input shaft assembly forward

casing. **Once the bearing is removed slide a hose clip onto the mainshaft and tighten the hose clip so that it secures the reverse gear tightly against the first gear.** Lift the front end of the mainshaft assembly out of the top aperture and then manoeuvre the assembly out of the casing.

7 Lift out the countershaft gear unit and collect the needle bearings and retaining rings. Withdraw the reverse idler shaft and lift out the gear.

Dismantling the mainshaft:

The needle rollers under the gears are graded for size and must be kept in their original sets.

1 Remove the hose clip holding the reverse gear in place,

and slide off the reverse gear. Withdraw the first-speed gear from the mainshaft and collect the 120 needle rollers, spacer and sleeve.

2 Withdraw the first/second synchronization assembly and collect the two loose synchro-rings. Withdraw the second-speed gear and collect the 106 needle rollers. Leave the spacer on the mainshaft.

3 Free the tabwasher and remove the large nut securing the third/top synchronizing assembly to the mainshaft. Withdraw the synchronizing assembly and collect the two loose synchro-rings.

4 Withdraw the third-speed gear and collect the 106 needle rollers and spacer.

5 Dismantle each synchronizing assembly by pressing

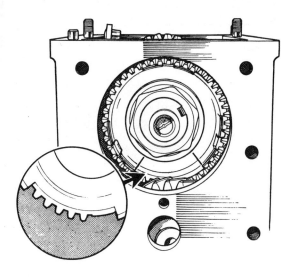

FIG 6:20 Correct position of cutaway for removing mainshaft assembly

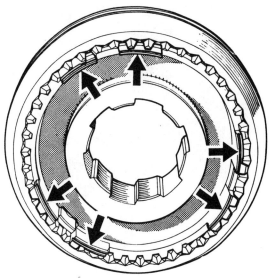

FIG 6:21 Identification grooves on third/top synchronizing assembly

the parts apart while they are surrounded by a piece of clean cloth to catch the springs and plungers. Keep the parts separated so as to avoid interchanging parts between the two assemblies. The top/third synchronizing assembly can be readily identified from the other similar assembly by the groove machined on the edge of the top/third synchronizing hub, as shown in **FIG 6:21**.

6:10 Reassembling the gearbox

Both synchronizing assemblies are identical except for the groove shown in **FIG 6:21**, and they are reassembled in exactly the same manner:

1 They must be assembled so that the wide boss of the hub is on the opposite side to the wide chamfer on the operating sleeve, and the three balls and springs are in line with the teeth on the operating sleeve which have three grooves (the rest of the teeth having only one groove).

2 Lay the operating sleeve on a flat surface and lay in the hub with a packing piece under it so that the holes for the detent balls are exactly level with the top face of the operating sleeve, as shown in **FIG 6:22**. Fit the balls, thrust members, plungers and springs in the relative positions shown in **FIG 6:23** and retain them in place with grease.

3 Compress the springs using a large hose clip or piston ring clamp, and carefully pressing the parts together lift them off the packing piece. Press the hub inwards slightly and use a screwdriver to push the thrust members down until they click into place in the neutral groove, as shown in **FIG 6:24**. Lay the assembly back on a flat surface and use a soft-faced hammer to tap the hub down until the balls are heard and felt to engage in the neutral groove. This is the centre groove so the balls must be tapped through and past the outer groove.

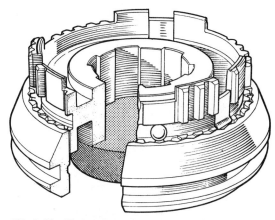

FIG 6:22 Fitting the spring, plungers, thrust members and balls

Refitting the countershaft gear cluster:

1 Fit a retaining ring to the front end of the cluster and fit in the 29 needle rollers, locating them with grease. Fit the inner thrust washer so that the peg on it locates in the groove on the gear cluster. Fit a retaining ring then 29 needle rollers followed by another retaining ring to the rear of the gear cluster.

2 Refit the reverse idler gear, lever and idler shaft. Fit the pegged rear washer to the casing and hold it in position with grease. Fit the front outer thrust washer to the front of the gear cluster and hold this in place with grease also. Carefully, so as not to move the washers, lower the assembly into the casing and secure it in place either on a dummy countershaft or the actual countershaft.

3 Measure the end float of the assembly using feeler gauges, as shown in **FIG 6:25**. If the end float is not correct it must be adjusted by fitting new outer thrust

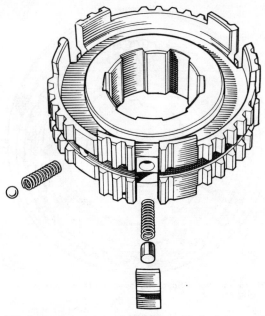

FIG 6:23 Relative positions of detent ball, plunger and thrust member

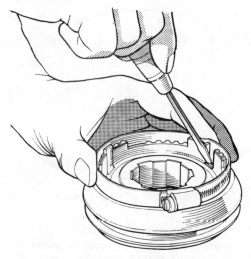

FIG 6:24 Pushing down the thrust members

washers (see Technical Data for thicknesses available).

Refitting the gears in the casing:

The mainshaft assembly is assembled in the reverse order of dismantling. The end float of the gears should be checked. If they vary from the correct dimensions given in Technical Data the only cure is fitting new parts. If new gears are fitted it should be noted that E type input shaft, countershaft and third-speed gear have a groove machined around the periphery of the gear. This is to distinguish the gears from similar but different ratio gears fitted to some other Jaguar cars.

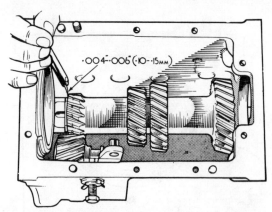

FIG 6:25 Checking the end float on countershaft assembly. Note the peripheral groove on end gear of cluster indicating an E type gear cluster

1 Remove the countershaft supporting the gear cluster by pushing it out with a thin rod and leaving the rod in place.
2 Replace the mainshaft assembly in the reverse order of removal, making sure that the parts are prevented from sliding apart by a small hose clip. Tap the input shaft assembly back into position, after fitting a new front gasket. Align the mainshaft, remove the hose clip and drive in the rear bearing, taking care to keep the reverse gear pressed firmly forward during this operation.
3 Lever the countershaft gear cluster up using the thin rod and rotate the mainshaft and pinion until all the gears are meshed. Carefully replace the countershaft to hold the gear cluster in position.

The remainder of the parts can now be refitted in the reverse order of dismantling. If the oil pump has been removed it should be refitted, using the three setscrews and staking the cover to hold it in place. Lubricate the gears with clean oil. After refitting the gearbox to the car drive the car in top gear as soon as possible to prime the gearbox oil pump.

6:11 Fault diagnosis

(a) Jumping out of gear

1 Broken spring behind striking rod locating ball
2 Excessively worn locating groove in striking rod
3 Worn coupling dogs
4 Selector fork to striking rod dowel screw loose

(b) Noisy gearbox

1 Insufficient oil
2 Excessive end float in countershaft gear assembly
3 Worn or damaged bearings or gear teeth

(c) Difficulty in engaging gear

1 Incorrect clutch pedal adjustment
2 Worn synchromesh assemblies

(d) Oil leaks

1 Damaged gaskets
2 Worn or damaged oil seals
3 Damaged cover faces

CHAPTER 7

THE AUTOMATIC TRANSMISSION

7:1 Description

A Borg-Warner Model 8 automatic transmission unit may be fitted as an optional extra in place of the conventional clutch and manually operated gearbox. The automatic transmission consists of two main parts; a torque converter and an epicyclic automatic three-speed gearbox.

The combination of these two assemblies eliminates the need for a clutch pedal and the manual gearchange from the conventional clutch/gearbox arrangement. A selector lever is fitted so that a degree of control over the gearbox can be exercised, but the gearbox is basically designed to ensure that, under any condition of load or throttle opening, the correct gear ratio is automatically provided to give the correct output torque with the engine operating in its most efficient condition.

The torque converter:

The torque converter provides a smooth transfer of power through the use of a fluid medium, combined with an infinitely variable torque multiplication between the ratio of 2:1 and 1:1.

The torque converter consists of three main components; the impeller connected to the engine, the turbine connected to the input shaft of the gearbox, and a stator between these two.

The impeller rotates with the engine and transmits energy to the fluid within the unit. This energy is directed as a flow of fluid towards the curved blades of the turbine. With the turbine held stationary the fluid is redirected back towards the impeller via the stator. The stator vanes are set to direct the fluid so that it enters the impeller at the most efficient angle to assist the engine in driving the impeller. A rotary flow of fluid through the unit is set up and the net result is that with the turbine stationary a torque multiplication of up to 2:1 is available at the correct engine speed.

The torque multiplication lessens as the turbine moves, because less energy in the fluid is passed back to the impeller. The reduction in torque multiplication continues with increasing turbine speed until the turbine and impeller are rotating at similar speeds, the torque ratio then being 1:1.

Once the torque converter has been assembled at the factory the outside parts are locked together by welding. **The unit cannot be dismantled and any fault will require the fitting of a new unit.**

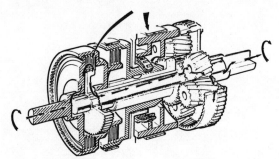

FIG 7:1 Mechanical power flow—first gear (L) selected

Hydraulically controlled transmission unit:

The unit incorporates two oil pumps. One pump is driven by the input shaft and supplies the lubrication and pressure required by the gearbox when the car is stationary or travelling slowly. The other pump, at the rear of the unit, is driven by the output shaft and is capable of supplying all the hydraulic requirements above a speed of approximately 20 mile/hr (32 kilometres/hr).

The unit consists of a series of epicyclic gears, the gears being brought into operation by the hydraulic pressure acting on a clutch and individual brake bands. The mechanical power flow for the different gears is shown in **FIGS 7:1, 7:2, 7:3, 7:4 and 7:5**.

Forward or reverse gears are selected manually at the selector lever. Movement in the lever is transmitted mechanically to a hydraulic valve, which directs the hydraulic pressure to operate the band brakes on the appropriate planetary gears. In the case of normal drive being selected the gear ratios will be automatically selected by the operation of a governor valve. This valve operates in relation to the engine speed and the throttle position.

Certain operations are beyond the scope of the average owner and he is strongly advised to take the car to a suitable specialist if the tests and adjustments outlined in this chapter are insufficient to produce a correct and satisfactory working of the unit.

7:2 Operation

Though owning a car fitted with automatic transmission, the owner may still not be fully sure of the exact function of the different selector lever positions or the limitations of the system.

The selector lever can be set in one of six positions, some of which are gated to prevent accidental selection. The positions are in order P–R–N–D2–D1–L. It should be noted that the starter motor will only operate when the selector is in the P or N position. This is a safety precaution to ensure that the car will not suddenly move off as soon as the engine is started.

P position:

In this position the gearbox is internally locked when the car is stationary and this prevents the car from rolling.

It is only a safety precaution and the handbrake should always be engaged if the car is left unattended.

R position:

This is equivalent to the normal reverse on a manually operated gearbox, the speed of the car being controlled by the throttle pedal.

N position:

This is equivalent to the normal neutral position on a manually operated gearbox. **If the car is to be stationary with the engine running for some time, this position should be selected.**

D2 position:

This is the normal selection for ordinary forward driving where the conditions are straightforward. Only the two top gears will be selected, but with the torque multiplication of the torque converter the performance will be perfectly satisfactory.

D1 position:

The gearbox will select the appropriate gear as required throughout the whole range of the gearbox. This selection should be used when making hill starts or when high acceleration is required, as the first gear is also used.

L position:

The gearbox will automatically shift downwards at the appropriate speeds but once in first gear it will be

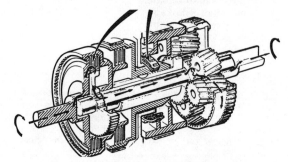

FIG 7:2 Mechanical power flow—first gear (D1) selected

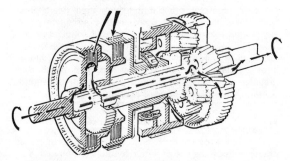

FIG 7:3 Mechanical power flow—second gear (L or D) selected

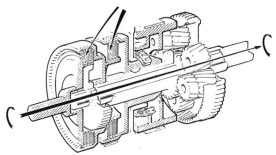

FIG 7:4 Mechanical power flow—third gear (D) selected

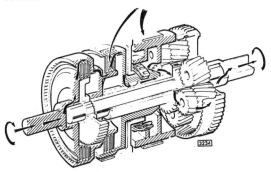

FIG 7:5 Mechanical power flow—reverse (R) selected

locked in this and not change up automatically into second. **Care must be taken as the throttle controls the engine speed and it is possible to over-rev the engine.** This selection may be used to provide engine braking, especially down long steep hills, and it is safe to select it at any speed as the gearbox will not shift down until the road speed is low enough for this to be done safely. Similarly this selection should be used for climbing long hills or on full acceleration but care must be taken not to allow the engine to overspeed.

Towing:

This is possible provided the road speed is between 20 and 30 mile/hr. If the speed drops below 20 mile/hr the rear oil pump may not be able to provide sufficient oil.

Starting:

In the event of a flat battery the engine may be started by towing the car. Select **N** until the car reaches a minimum speed of 20 mile/hr (32 kilometre/hr) and then select a forward gear. It is advisable for the car to be either run down hill or pushed, because when being towed there is the danger of the engine suddenly starting and the car catching up on the towing car.

Rocking:

If the car is stuck in mud or snow it will often be found helpful to rock the car between reverse and forward gear so as to free it. Use a little throttle and move the selector lever between R and D positions so that the gearbox will automatically reverse direction, rocking the car.

Kick-down:

Depending on the speed of the engine, the gearbox will automatically downshift gear when the accelerator pedal is pressed past the full throttle position. This ensures that full acceleration is always available for over-taking or any other requirement.

7:3 Routine maintenance

Cleanliness is absolutely essential in all operations involving the automatic gearbox and it is necessary even when checking or topping up the gearbox oil level. The torque converter produces heat, so the cover and the stone guards on the cover should always be kept clean and free from blockage or a layer of dirt (which will act as a heat insulator). This is particularly important in areas which have a high ambient air temperature.

The oil level in the automatic transmission must be checked with the car on level ground, the engine idling and the transmission oil at its normal working temperature. If any of these precautions are ignored then the level will be incorrect.

The level should be checked every 3000 miles. Drive the car until the transmission is hot and then stop on level ground. Set the selector to the P position and set the handbrake firmly on. Leave the engine at its normal idling

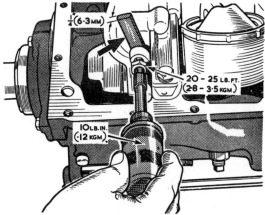

FIG 7:6 Front band adjustment

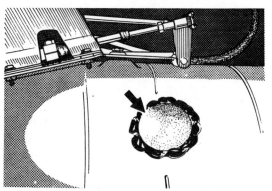

FIG 7:7 Rear band adjustment access point

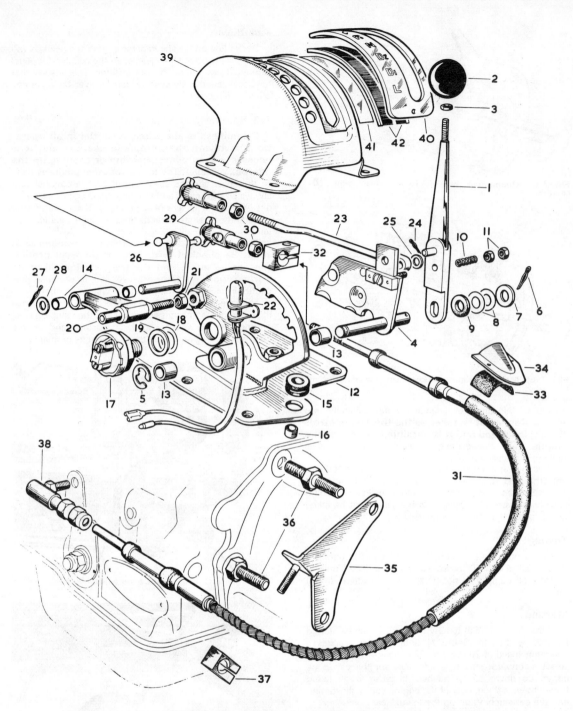

FIG 7:8 Transmission selector mechanism details

Key to Fig 7:8 1 Selector lever assembly   2 Knob   3 Nut   4 Cam plate assembly   5 Circlip   6 Splitpin
7 Washer   8 Shim   9 Rubber washer   10 Spring   11 Nut   12 Mounting plate and selector gate assembly
13 Bush   14 Bush   15 Grommet   16 Distance tube   17 Reverse lamp switch   18 Shim   19 Shim
20 Starter cut-out switch   21 Nut   22 Lamp assembly   23 Operating rod assembly   24 Splitpin   25 Washer
26 Transfer lever assembly   27 Splitpin   28 Washer   29 Ball joint   30 Nut   31 Gear control cable assembly
32 Clamp   33 Pad   34 Plate   35 Abutment bracket   36 Stud   37 Clamp   38 Adjustable ball joint
39 Cover assembly   40 Indicator plate   41 Light filter   42 Seal

76

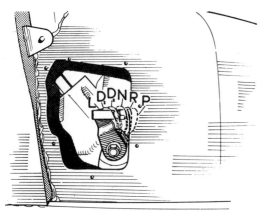

FIG 7:9 Transmission manual selector lever positions

speed. Use a clean cloth and wipe the dipstick top and tube clear of any dirt. Withdraw the dipstick, situated just in front of the bulkhead in the engine compartment, and wipe the whole length of it clean. Re-insert the dipstick fully into position and withdraw it again immediately. Top up as required to bring the level to the 'Full' mark on the dipstick. The difference between the 'Full' and 'Low' marks on the dipstick represents approximately 1½ Imperial pints (2 US pints, or .75 litres). **Do not overfill the transmission. Use only the correct type of oil, Automatic Transmission Fluid type 'A' or type 'A' suffix 'A' (AQ-ATF).**

The total capacity of the transmission from dry (including cooler) is 16 Imperial pints (19 US pints, or 9 litres).

Draining:

This will be necessary for adjusting the front brake band. Remove the filler connection and catch the oil as it runs out in a container. Remove the oil pan. Examine the dregs of oil in the oil pan. Some particles are normally found there, but a large amount indicates that further examination should be carried out. **A large amount of metal particles or friction material will necessitate the car being taken to a suitably equipped garage.**

Brake band adjustment:

Both the front and the rear bands should be adjusted every 21,000 miles. The correct procedure must be used and if a torque wrench is not available the car should be taken to a garage for the adjustments.

The transmission must be drained and the oil pan removed to adjust the front brake band. Loosen the adjusting screw locknut, shown in **FIG 7:6**, apply the lever and check that the adjusting screw turns freely. Fit a ¼ inch (6.3 mm) thick piece of steel between the adjusting screw and the servo piston pin, as shown. Tighten the adjusting screw to a torque load of 10 lb in (.12 kg m) and hold it in this position while tightening the locknut to a torque of 20 to 25 lb ft (2.76 to 3.46 kg m). Remove the spacer, replace the oil pan and refill the transmission. Pour in about ten pints of oil and then start the engine before pouring in any more oil. Top up finally when the oil is hot.

The rear brake band can be adjusted without removing the oil pan. The access cover is shown in **FIG 7:7**. Slacken the locknut and unscrew it two or three turns. Check that the adjusting nut turns freely in the case. Tighten the adjusting screw to a load of 10 lb ft (1.382 kg m) and then unscrew it precisely one and a half turns. Hold the adjusting screw in this position and tighten the locknut to a load of 35 to 40 lb ft (4.84 to 5.53 kg m).

7:4 The selector linkage

The details of this are shown in **FIG 7:8**. To adjust the cable, gain access by removing the transmission tunnel cover assembly and the carpet at the side of the transmission tunnel. Lift off the rubberized felt and take off the coverplate on the lefthand side of the transmission cover. Loosen the locknut on the adjuster ball joint 38 and slacken the cable 31. Free the ball joint from the lever on the transmission. Set the selector control to the L position and also set the lever on the transmission to the L position. The various positions of the lever on the transmission are shown in **FIG 7:9**. Turn the adjuster 38 until the end of the cable fits freely into the lever on the transmission. Reconnect the cable and move the selector to each position in turn, checking in each case that the transmission lever locates positively in the transmission detents without the gate in the selector moving the transmission lever out of position. When satisfied tighten the locknut on the cable and recheck before replacing the covers and carpets.

7:5 The kick-down cable

This cable must be correctly adjusted as it indicates the position of the throttles in the transmission unit and therefore controls not only the shift positions but the shift quality.

Before commencing adjustments the car should be road tested on a flat road.

1 Set the selector to either the D1 or D2 position, and with the least possible throttle opening the 2 to 3 upshift should occur at 1100 to 1200 rev/min. A 'run up' of 200 to 400 rev/min indicates a low pressure.

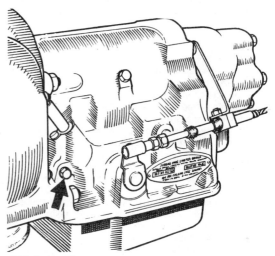

FIG 7:10 The transmission pressure take-off point

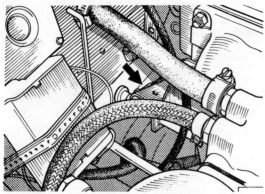

FIG 7:11 Kick-down cable adjustment point

2 Set the selector to D1 and accelerate hard. The 2 to 3 upshift should occur smoothly. Allow the car to decelerate with closed throttle and check that the 2 to 1 downshift is also smooth. If the upshift is jerky or the downshift is sharp then this indicates a high pressure.

The cable should be set as follows, if the road test indicates that the setting is incorrect.

1 Run the car until the transmission has reached its normal operating temperature. Switch off the engine and fit a 0–200 lb/sq in (0–14 kg/sq cm) pressure gauge in place of the plug arrowed in **FIG 7:10**.
2 Start the engine and firmly apply the handbrake. As an added precaution the rear wheels can be chocked. Select D1 or D2 and increase the engine idling speed to exactly 1250 rev/min. The pressure reading on the gauge should be 72.5 ± 2.5 lb/sq in (5.097 ± .175 kg/sq cm).
3 Stop the engine and if the pressure is incorrect adjust the cable at the fork end shown in **FIG 7:11**. Release the fork end locknut, remove the splitpin and withdraw the fork end clevis pin. Turn the fork end in a clockwise direction to lower the pressure and in an anticlockwise direction to raise the pressure. One full turn will vary the pressure by 9 lb/sq in (.63 kg/sq cm) but only slight adjustment should be necessary.
4 Refit the clevis pin, splitpin and locknut. Start the engine, checking that the throttle butterflies are fully closed, and again check the pressure at precisely 1250 rev/min.
5 If after several attempts it is found impossible to stabilize the pressure it is likely that the cable itself is defective and is either binding or has kinked, preventing free movement. The cable should be renewed if this is the case.
6 Remove the pressure gauge and refit the sealing plug. Reset the engine idling speed.

Renewing the cable :

1 Disconnect the cable at the fork end and remove the cable retaining clip.
2 From inside the car remove the trim, carpets and underfelt from the transmission cover, and take off the access panel on the lefthand side. This cover is secured by six drive screws.
3 Remove the Allen-headed screw and washer securing the cable outer cover. Withdraw the outer cable. Use a

small screwdriver to spring open the clip securing the inner cable to the control rod operating the kick-down cam in the transmission.

4 The new cable is fitted in the reverse order of removing the old cable. Adjust the cable so that there is $3\frac{5}{16}$ inch (84.1 mm) between the centre line of the clevis and the outer end of the cable. Set the correct adjustments as described earlier.

7:6 The governor

This can be inspected or removed without taking off the oil pan. The parts are shown in **FIGS 7:12 and 7:13**.

1 Remove the inspection cover and gasket to expose the governor. The output shaft will have to be turned so that the governor head is exposed in the aperture.
2 Check the freedom of the valve by pushing and pulling on the weight 135.
3 If required the governor can be removed by undoing the two screws securing it in place. **Take great care not to drop the securing screws down into the casing.** Dismantle the unit and clean all the parts in clean fuel.
4 **It is essential that the two screws securing the plate 139 and the two screws securing the governor in place are tight and correctly torque loaded otherwise the governor will fail to operate.** Tighten the plate securing screws to a load of 20 to 30 lb in (.24 to 36 kg m) and tighten the two screws securing the governor to a load of 50 to 60 lb in (.60 to .72 kg m).
5 Replace the inspection cover, using a new gasket, and tighten the securing screws to a load of 50 to 60 lb in (.60 to .72 kg m).

7:7 Stall speed test

This test provides a rapid check on the condition of the complete transmission system. The test, as the name implies, involves checking the maximum speed of the engine with the turbine of the converter held stationary. **A great deal of heat is produced in the torque converter during this test and for this reason the transmission should not be stalled for more than 10 seconds at each test and the total tests should be limited to one minute at stall in each half-hour period.**

The engine condition will also affect this test. A drop of 300 rev/min from the normal stall speed usually indicates that the engine is in poor condition, and not developing full power.

Run the car until both the transmission and engine have reached their normal operating temperatures. Set the handbrake, chock the wheels and apply the footbrake. Select L or R position and fully depress the throttle pedal. Within 10 seconds note the engine maximum rev/min and allow the engine to slow down again. Select N and allow the engine to idle in order to disperse the heat.

The normal maximum rev/min should be 1600 to 1700.

The stator of the torque converter is fitted with a one way clutch and if this slips the torque multiplication effect cannot occur, as the stator rotates in the opposite direction to the turbine. If on stall test the engine runs below a maximum of 1000 rev/min, then this clutch is slipping. This will be further confirmed by the car having poor acceleration from standstill and failing to drive away on steep hills. At high speeds the converter acts as a fluid flywheel and if the stator clutch sticks in the locked position then maximum speed will be reduced and acceleration in third gear above 30 mile/hr (48 kilometre/hr) will be substandard. The torque converter cannot be rectified and a new unit must be fitted.

A stall speed higher than normal (over 2100 rev/min) indicates that either the converter is not receiving its full supply of fluid or the clutches in the gearbox are slipping.

Clutch and band checks:

These can be checked without removing the transmission unit. Apply the handbrake and start the engine. Select each gear in turn and check that there is drive. If a clutch or brake band functions in one selector then it is reasonable to assume that the element is satisfactory. If the clutch or band fails in two separate selection positions then it is reasonable to assume that it is faulty.

7:8 Pressure test

If a suitable pressure gauge is available these tests should be carried out in conjunction with the stall speed test outlined in **Section 7:7. The time limit of 10 seconds must be observed to prevent the torque converter from overheating.** As all the gears will be checked and this will entail more heating in the transmission, the outside of the unit should be cleaned to remove any heat insulating dirt and the stone guards cleaned to ensure that they are not blocked and allow free flow to the cooling air. The pressures given are only for the normal operating temperature range 150 to 185°F (65.5 to 85°C) and if the unit overheats it should be allowed to cool before carrying on with the tests. The correct pressures are as follows:

Selector position	Control pressure* Idle rev/min	Control pressure* Stall rev/min
D2	50 to 60	150 to 185
D1	50 to 60	150 to 185
L	50 to 60	150 to 185
R	50 to 60	190 to 210
N	55 to 60	—

*Pressure in lbs/sq in

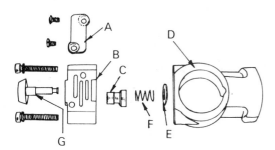

FIG 7:12 Governor details

Key to Fig 7:12
A Governor body coverplate
B Governor body   **C** Valve   **D** Counterweight
E Spring retainer   **F** Spring   **G** Weight

A low pressure indicates a leak in the circuit tested, while low pressure in all the selector positions indicates leakage, faulty pump or incorrect pressure regulation.

High pressures in all the selector positions indicate faulty pressure regulation, incorrect cable adjustment or stuck valves.

7:9 Road test

This section is given so that the owner can check the correct function of the automatic transmission system and can diagnose faults.

1 Check the movement of the selector control, ensuring that it moves through the gates and that it is trapped by the gate in the P position. Try the starter motor in every selection and ensure that it only operates in the P or N position.

2 With the engine running, apply the handbrake and check that there is drive in the R, L, D1 and D2 positions. Select L and carry out a stall speed check as detailed in **Section 7:7**

3 Let the engine idle or increase the speed very slightly. A gear whine indicates dragging front clutch plates, with the selector in N. If the car also tends to creep forward with the handbrake off this is a confirmation of dragging front clutch plates. Rev the engine between idle and 2000 rev/min. A high-pitched whine indicates a faulty front pump, a dirty oil screen above the oil pan, or a blocked suction pipe to the pump.

4 Select D1 and accelerate away with the minimum throttle opening and check that the 1 to 2 and 2 to 3 upshifts take place. The correct speeds are given in Technical Data but the changes may be so smooth as to be unnoticeable. Check that they have occurred by selecting L and feeling the changes as the gearbox shifts down on deceleration.

5 Accelerate up to just over 30 mile/hr (48 kilometre/hr). Select N and switch off the ignition, allowing the car to coast. At 30 mile/hr switch on the ignition and select L. The engine should start. If the engine is not driven by the rear wheels and fails to start, the rear oil pump is defective.

6 Carry out acceleration tests. Accelerate with the throttle wide open but with the accelerator pedal not through the detent position, and check the shift up speeds. Repeat the test with the accelerator pedal through the detent position and again check the shift up speeds. The correct speeds are given in Technical Data.

7 Drive at 26 mile/hr in third gear and then accelerate with the accelerator in the full-throttle position. The car should accelerate away in third gear without shifting down to second. Repeat the test, driving at a steady 30 mile/hr but depressing the accelerator pedal to the kick-down position. The car should downshift into second before accelerating away.

8 Drive at a steady 40 mile/hr (64 kilometre/hr), release the accelerator and select L. Check both downshifts and ensure that engine braking takes place. Stop the car and, with L still selected, accelerate at full-throttle to 20 mile/hr (32 kilometre/hr) taking care not to over-rev. There should be no slip, clutch break-away or upshifts.

9 Stop the car, select R and accelerate in reverse, using full throttle if possible. Take care not to over-rev and check that there is no slip or clutch break-away noise.

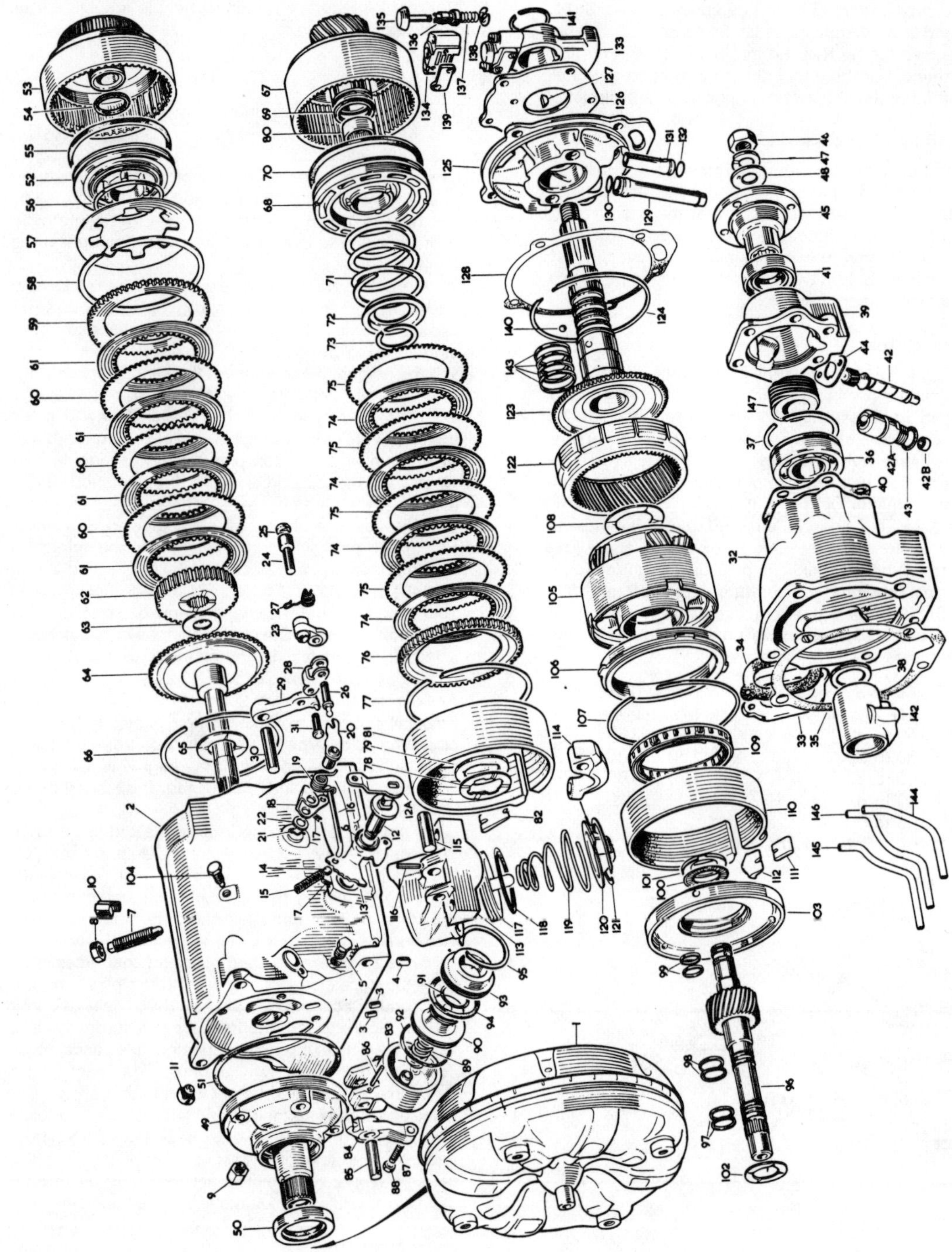

FIG 7:13   Transmission details

10 Stop the car facing downhill on a gradient and, with the brakes on, select P. Release the brakes and check that the car is held stationary. Before selecting another gear and driving off re-apply the brakes. Repeat the test with the car facing up the gradient.

It must be stressed that to be fully effective the road test must be carried out on a private road where the legal speed limit of 70 miles per hour does not apply, as the kick-down acceleration tests will involve road speeds of over 90 mile/hr (145 kilometre/hr) It also goes without saying that a good road surface must be used and a very competent driver employed.

Many race circuits allow high-speed testing for a moderate fee, and this might solve all the problems raised above.

7:10 Servicing the automatic transmission system

Apart from the operations given in this chapter, the car should always be taken to a suitable specialist for any work involving dismantling the gearbox. If the torque converter is faulty, a new unit must be fitted, and this is within the scope of the average owner. Any defect in the hydraulic system also entails taking the car to a suitably equipped specialist. The system is controlled by several accurately set valves and, because of the complexity, no details of the system have been given in this manual. Instead the full tests are given so that the owner can himself diagnose faults and condition, therefore knowing reasonably well what to expect when the unit is stripped down at a garage. The tests, though full, are not exhaustive and one symptom may be caused by more than one defect which will only be discovered on strip down.

The details of the gearbox are shown in **FIG 7:13** but apart from the governor parts and identification of connections this figure is for interest and guidance only.

The rear suction tube screen can be removed and cleaned after the oil pan has been removed. Undo the retaining clip and lift out the screen, as shown in **FIG 7:14**. Wash the screen in clean fuel and allow it to dry before replacing.

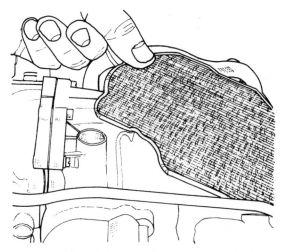

FIG 7:14 Removing the screen from the rear pump suction tube. The unit has been removed from the car and is therefore inverted in this figure

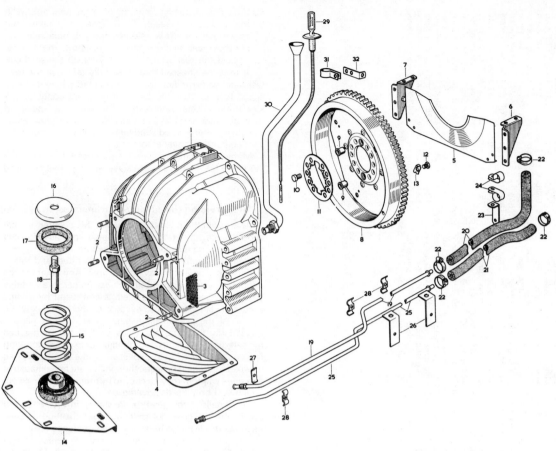

FIG 7:15   Converter housing details

Key to Fig 7:15   1 Converter housing   2 Stud   3 Stoneguard assembly   4 Bottom cover   5 Front cover
6 Righthand support bracket   7 Lefthand support bracket   8 Drive plate assembly   9 Dowel   10 Setscrew   11 Plate
12 Setscrew   13 Tabwasher   14 Supporting bracket   15 Coil spring   16 Retainer   17 Rubber spring seat
18 Pin assembly   19 Oil outlet pipe   20 Flexible hose   21 Flexible hose   22 Clip   23 Bracket   24 Clip
25 Oil return pipe   26 Bracket   27 Clamp   28 Clip   29 Transmission dipstick assembly   30 Tube assembly
31 Clip   32 Strut

7:11 Removing the transmission unit

The unit cannot be removed while the engine is still fitted to the car. Remove the engine and transmission unit complete from the car as instructed in **Chapter 1, Section 1:2**. Drain the oil from the transmission unit and remove the bolts securing the gearbox to the converter housing shown in **FIG 7:15**. Disconnect the kick-down linkage at the operating shaft and withdraw the unit.

Refitting the unit is the reversal of the removal procedure. Ensure that converter lugs are properly aligned with the front pump drive gear when refitting the unit to the converter housing, otherwise parts will be damaged in the effort to force them together. After the engine/transmission unit has been refitted to the car it is essential that the engine rear stabilizer is correctly adjusted and that the kick-down cable is also correctly adjusted.

Removing torque converter and flywheel:

1 Remove the cover 5 from the front of the housing 1. Remove the starter motor. Undo the setscrews securing the converter housing 1 to the engine and carefully lift off the housing.

2 Free the tabs on the lockwashers 13 and remove the bolts 12 in turn. These are accessible through the starter motor mounting hole after turning the engine to line up each bolt in turn. Lift out the torque converter. The flywheel can then be removed normally by undoing the lockwasher and setscrews securing it to the crankshaft.

The parts are replaced in the reverse order of dismantling. The maximum allowable runout readings for the housing bore or face relative to the crankshaft centre line are .010 inch (.25 mm) but it is desirable that neither exceeds .006 inch (.015 mm).

7:12 Fault diagnosis

(a) Transmission overheats

1 Stone guards on converter housing blocked
2 Converter housing covered with dirt
3 Oil cooler core blocked
4 Air passages in oil cooler core blocked
5 Rear brake band incorrectly adjusted
6 Front brake band incorrectly adjusted
7 Stator one-way clutch locked in engaged condition

(b) Excessive noisy operation

1 Low fluid level

(c) Incorrect shift speeds

1 Kick-down cable incorrectly adjusted, or damaged
2 Selector cable incorrectly adjusted, or damaged
3 Governor sticking or incorrectly assembled

(d) Poor acceleration

1 Check 5, 6 and 7 in (a)
2 Stator one-way clutch slipping

(e) Jumps in engagement

1 Check 5 and 6 in (a) and 2 in (c)
2 Incorrect engine idle speed

(f) Car does not hold in P position

1 Check 2 in (c)

(g) Incorrect stall speed

1 Check 5 and 6 in (a); 1 and 2 in (c) and also check (b)

(h) Reverse slips or chatters

1 Check 5 in (a) and 1 in (c)

(i) Car creeps

1 Check 2 in (e)

The above diagnosis is not fully comprehensive and only covers the more common faults. Only the faults which can be cured by the owner have been presented and if the fault persists after the adjustments have been carried out a specialist should be consulted.

NOTES

CHAPTER 8

THE PROPELLER SHAFT, REAR AXLE, REAR SUSPENSION

8:1 Description

Drive is taken from the output shaft of the gearbox to the differential of the rear axle by a propeller shaft. The propeller shaft has universal joints at either end and a sliding joint allowing it to take up any angular mis-alignment as well as contracting or extending slightly as the car flexes.

The differential is mounted in a substantial crossmember bolted to the car. Drive from the differential is taken to the wheel hubs by two universally jointed halfshafts. It should be noted that the rear disc brakes are mounted inboard, one on either side of the differential. The wheel carrier is secured to the differential by the halfshaft, and a lower link, pivotted at the wheel carrier and crossmember, provides the other location in a lateral direction for the wheels. A sectioned view of the suspension is shown in **FIG 8:1**. Longitudinal support is supplied by two substantial radius arms pivotting in rubber bushes.

The load on the rear suspension is taken by two coil springs acting on either side, a total of four for the complete suspension, and they are damped by concentrically mounted telescopic dampers, one damper to each spring.

8:2 Routine maintenance

Propeller shaft:

All the models have a grease nipple fitted to each universal joint at either end of the shaft. Earlier models also have a grease nipple fitted to the sliding joint. All the nipples should be greased at 2500 mile intervals. The rear universal joint nipple and sliding joint nipple are accessible from underneath the car. The front universal grease nipple is only accessible after removing the rear access plate from the transmission tunnel (see **Chapter 6 FIG 6:3**). Rotate the propeller shaft until the nipple is aligned with the access hole. Take care not to get grease or dirt on the trim or upholstery.

Halfshafts:

Earlier models are fitted with a grease nipple on each universal joint. These are omitted on later models but are fitted to the latest models covered by this manual. They should be greased every 2500 miles. Push the car until the nipples are accessible from underneath the rear of the car. On the 4.2 litre models access to the outer joint nipples is made by removing the sealing plugs from the joint covers.

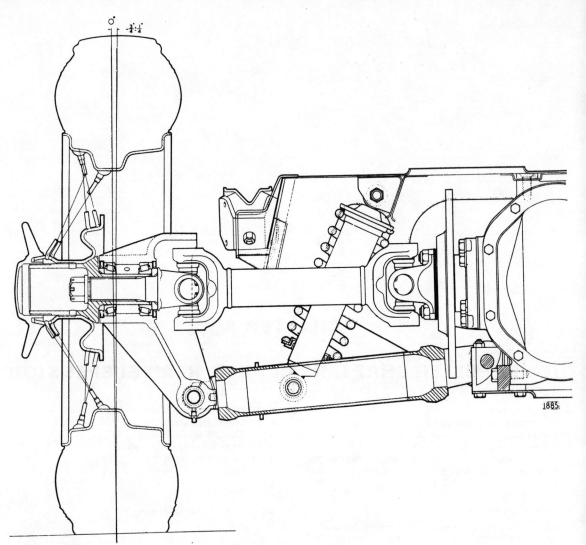

FIG 8:1   Sectioned view of the rear suspension

Rear suspension:

Each lower wishbone arm is fitted with three grease nipples, arrowed in **FIG 8:2**. These should be greased every 5000 miles.

Differential unit:

This is filled with hypoid oil to the bottom of the hole for the combined filler and level plug arrowed in **FIG 8:3**. The level should be checked every 2500 miles and topped up if required.

Different brands of oil have different additives which may not mix satisfactorily. If the brand of oil in the unit is not known it is safer to drain the unit and refill rather than topping up with an incompatible oil.

The drain plug is at the bottom of the unit and can be reached through the aperture in the bottom tie plate. Drain the oil when it is hot as it will flow more easily.

Rear wheel bearings:

These should be lubricated every 10,000 miles. Jack up the rear of the car and remove the road wheels. Remove the plug arrowed in **FIG 8:4** and carefully inject grease. Do not pump the grease in under high pressure or overfill, otherwise the grease may escape past the oil seal.

When carrying out lubrication operations cleanliness is essential. Wipe grease nipples before fitting the grease gun. Similarly remove any dirt before unscrewing or prising out sealing plugs. Wipe away surplus grease or oil after lubrication to prevent road dirt sticking to it. If grease is hard to force through a nipple the nipple should be removed and checked by pumping grease through it. Damaged grease nipples should be renewed.

8:3 Removing the rear suspension

The suspension and rear axle assembly can be removed from the car as a unit. A large number of operations on the unit can only be performed after it has been removed from the car, and, unless otherwise stated in the relevant sections, the unit should be removed and the work carried out on the bench.

1 Remove the exhaust tail pipes by undoing the clamp bolts securing them to the silencer and removing the nuts and bolts securing them to the mounting point under the rear of the body.

2 Detach the radius arms at the front end. Jack up the rear of the car, using a slab of wood at least an inch thick between the jack and the tie plate under the differential. Use a trolley jack. Lower the car back onto stands, again using wood to protect the car, with the stands placed forward of the radius arm mounting posts. Leave the trolley jack in position.

3 Remove the rear road wheels. Disconnect the anti-roll bar links. Disconnect the flexible brake pipe at the connection on the body. Disconnect both the inner and outer cables of the handbrake at the rear suspension.

4 Remove the bolts and self-locking nuts securing each front mounting rubber to the car frame. Note the quantity and position of any shims fitted. Remove the two bolts and three self-locking nuts securing each rear mounting rubber to the suspension crossmember.

5 If required, lower the suspension slightly and disconnect the propeller shaft from the pinion flange on the differential by removing the four bolts and self-locking nuts.

6 Lower the suspension unit on the jack, checking that all connections are undone, and withdraw the unit as shown in **FIG 8:5**.

Refitting is the reversal of the removal procedure. Check the mounting rubbers for deterioration and renew them if necessary. If the rubbers have been removed it is essential that they are refitted as shown in **FIG 8:6**. The brake system will have to be bled and the handbrake adjusted after the suspension assembly has been refitted.

8:4 The propeller shaft

This cannot be removed from the car without taking out either the engine or the rear suspension unit. As it is easier to remove the rear suspension, it is suggested that this should be done rather than take out the engine. Disconnecting the rear end of the propeller shaft has already been dealt with in **Section 8:3**. The front end is disconnected from the gearbox flange by removing the four locknuts and tapping out the bolts. To gain access to the front universal joint, so as to be able to disconnect it, the radio panel, gearbox tunnel trim, tunnel cover and plastic gearbox cowl must all be taken out.

A 'clonk' from the transmission on taking up drive or overrun can be caused by a defective propeller shaft. The noise will be more pronounced when changing from forward direction to reverse or vice-versa. This can easily be checked on a car fitted with automatic transmission by moving the selector from forward to reverse and then back again with the engine running a little faster than idle.

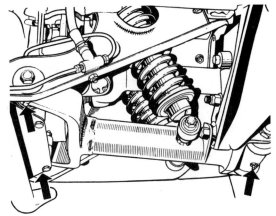

FIG 8:2 Rear suspension lower wishbone grease nipples

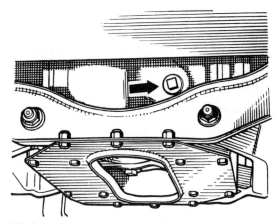

FIG 8:3 Rear axle combined filler and level plug. For illustrative purposes only the exhaust pipes have been removed

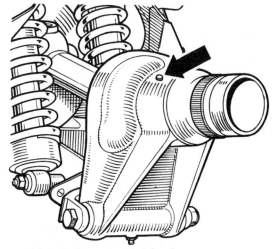

FIG 8:4 Rear wheel hub bearing grease cap

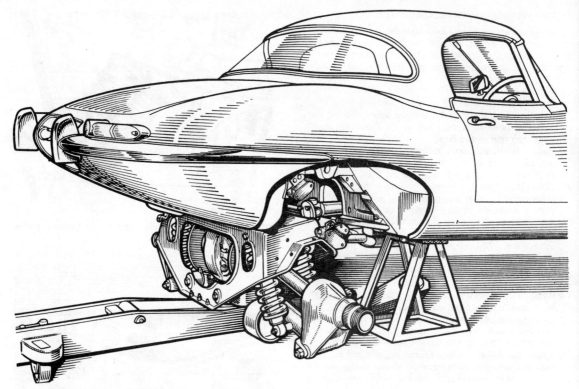

FIG 8:5   Removing the rear suspension assembly from the car

It is difficult to check the propeller shaft by hand, as the universal joints are virtually inaccessible. Rotate the shaft backwards and forwards smartly by hand to check for excessive rotational play. Lift the shaft up by hand as near to the ends as possible. Excess play indicates worn thrust faces.

Dismantling the propeller shaft :

The details of the earlier type of propeller shaft are shown in **FIG 8 : 7**. Later types are similar but the sliding joint cannot and should not be dismantled as it is lubricated and sealed for 'life'. No grease nipple is fitted to the later type of propeller shafts and this provides a quick method of identification.

After long service the sliding joint splines may wear. If the circumferential movement, measured on the outside diameter of the splines, exceeds .004 inch (.1 mm) the complete propeller shaft should be renewed.

As a universal joint rotates there are slight angular variations in output throughout the cycle. When correctly assembled, the variations in one joint are cancelled out by the variations in the other end joint, while if they are assembled out of phase the variations will augment each other, causing vibration. If the sliding joint is dismantled (early types only) then it must be reassembled so that universal joints are in the angular plane as shown in **FIG 8 : 7**. Arrows are stamped on the sleeve yoke 3 and mainshaft to facilitate correct reassembly. Check that these are present and are not covered with dirt.

1 On the early types, unscrew the metal dust cover 4 by hand and slide off the sliding yoke 3.
2 Clean enamel, dirt and rust from the recesses holding the eight snap rings. Remove the snap rings by pinching together the ends with a suitable pair of pliers, prising them out with a screwdriver if necessary. Lightly tap the bearing cups inwards to free snap rings which are tight.
3 Hold the shaft with a lug uppermost as shown in **FIG 8 : 8**. Tap the yoke arm with a soft-faced hammer and

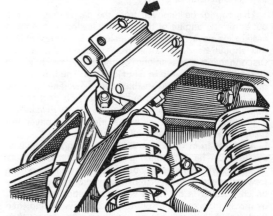

FIG 8:6   Correct position of the chamfer on the rear suspension mounting rubbers

FIG 8:7 Propeller shaft details (early type)

Key to Fig 8:7

3 Sleeve yoke	1 Flange yoke	2 Journal assembly
6 Cork washer	4 Dust cap	5 Steel washer
9 Grease nipple	7 Bolt	8 Self-locking nut

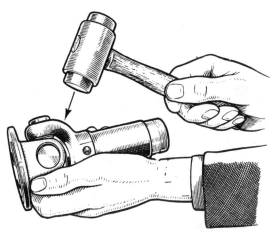

FIG 8:8 Tapping the yoke to remove a bearing

the bearing cup should start to emerge as shown. Carry on tapping until enough of the bearing cup has emerged to allow it to be gripped and withdrawn. If the bearing cup cannot be removed by this method use a small round bar as a drift and drive them out as shown in **FIG 8:9**. The cork seal and retaining ring will be damaged by this method, and though they should normally be renewed on reassembly, they must be renewed after this operation.

4 Turn the shaft over and remove the opposite bearing cup in a similar manner. Rest the exposed trunnions on two wood or lead blocks and tap the yoke with a soft-faced hammer to remove the remaining two bearings on that universal joint. In a similar manner dismantle the other universal joint.

Examination of the parts:

The splined sliding joint has already been dealt with earlier.

1 The bearing races and spider trunnions are the parts most likely to show wear. Renew the parts with a complete kit, do not renew parts individually.

2 It is essential that the bearing cups are a light drive fit into the holes in the yokes. After long service or inadequate lubrication of the bearings it is possible that the holes in the yokes will be worn oval. The flange yokes 1 are easily renewable. If the holes in the fixed yokes are worn the complete propeller shaft should be renewed. Only in extreme emergency should a worn yoke be cut off and a new one welded in its place, as not only will the balance of the propeller shaft be lost but the alignment may also be disturbed.

Reassembling the propeller shaft:

1 Use a hollow snug-fitting drift to fit new cork seals and retaining rings to the spider trunnions.

2 Replace the needle bearings in the bearing cups, using grease to retain them in place. The needles must exactly fill the cups, leaving no gaps. Universals not fitted with grease nipples must be packed with grease on assembly.

3 Insert the spider into a flange yoke. Place a bearing cup and needles into place and drive it in, using a soft-nosed drift of diameter just smaller then the bearing cup. Fit all three bearing cups in a similar manner and then lock them into place with the snap rings. The cups must be a light drive fit and if one suddenly stops moving take it out and check that a

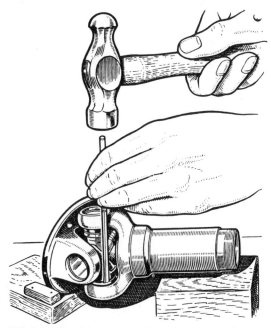

FIG 8:9 Tapping out a bearing using a small diameter drift

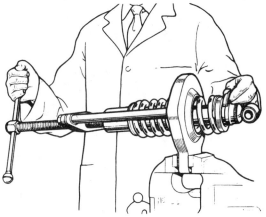

FIG 8:10 Removing a road spring from the damper

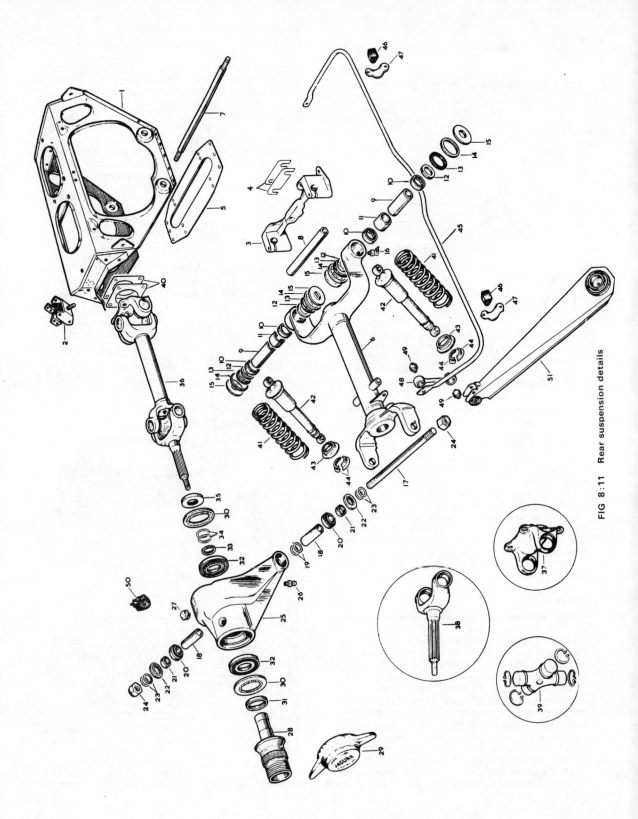

FIG 8:11 Rear suspension details

Key to Fig 8:11
1 Rear suspension crossmember 2 Rubber mounting 3 Inner fulcrum mounting bracket 4 Shims 5 Tie plate 6 Wishbone
7 Inner fulcrum shaft 8 Distance tube 9 Bearing tube 10 Needle bearings 11 Spacing collar 12 Inner thrust washer 13 Sealing ring
14 Sealing ring retainer 15 Outer thrust washer 16 Grease nipple 17 Outer fulcrum shaft 18 Distance tube 19 Shims 20 Bearing 21 Oil seal track 22 Oil seal
23 Shims 24 Self-locking nut 25 Hub carrier 26 Grease nipple 27 Grease retainer cap 28 Rear hub 29 Hub cap 30 Oil seal 31 Oil seal track
32 Outer bearing 33 Spacer 34 Shims (early cars only) 35 Oil seal track 36 Halfshaft 37 Flange yoke 38 Splined yoke 39 Journal assembly
40 Shim 41 Coil spring 42 Shock absorber 43 Seat 44 Retaining collet 45 Anti-roll bar 46 Rubber bush 47 Bracket 48 Link 49 Rubber bush
50 Bump stop 51 Radius arm

needle roller has not become displaced. The needles are very hard and brittle so a displaced needle can easily be snapped.

4 In a similar manner refit the remaining four bearing cups to the other universal joint. Check that the universal joints move freely, tapping them with a wooden mallet to relieve any bearing pressure if they are tight.

5 On the early types of propeller shaft grease the splines and fit the sliding yoke onto the shaft so that the arrows are aligned. Use a new cork seal 6 and tighten the dust cap 4 handtight only.

8:5 Road spring and hydraulic damper assembly

These parts can be removed from the suspension with the suspension assembly still fitted to the car.

1 Chock the front wheels, jack up the rear of the car and place it on stands. Remove the appropriate rear road wheel.

2 Remove the two self-locking nuts and washers securing the dampers to the lower wishbone. Support the suspension under the wheel carrier and use a long rod to drift out the hydraulic damper mounting pin.

3 Remove the self-locking nut from the bolt securing the top of the damper. Support the damper and spring assembly and withdraw the securing bolt. Lift out the damper and spring assembly. In a similar manner remove the remaining damper.

The damper and spring assemblies are refitted in the reverse order of dismantling.

Dampers:

Remove the spring and damper assembly as just described. Use a suitable press (Churchill tool No. J.11 with SL.14 as shown in **FIG 8:10**) and compress the road spring so that the split collets can be removed. Ease the pressure on the spring and withdraw the damper. On earlier models an aluminium pad is fitted to either end of the spring.

Refit the spring to the damper in the reverse order of removal. On earlier models fit the aluminium pad with the machined recess to the shrouded end of the damper. Make sure the pads and split collets are securely and squarely in place before releasing the pressure on the road spring.

Testing the dampers:

Remove the damper as instructed. Examine the body and the operating rod. If the body is dented or damaged, or the rod bent, the damper must be renewed. Mount the damper vertically in a vice, with the shroud uppermost and using lead or wood to protect it. Pump the damper through about half its full range of movement for several strokes to allow the internal air to pass to the top of the damper. Finish by extending the damper through its full range of movement for several strokes. There should be appreciable and constant resistance to motion in both directions. Pockets of no resistance, low resistance in either direction or such a high resistance that the damper can hardly be moved necessitate fitting a new damper. The dampers are sealed units and once defective cannot be repaired.

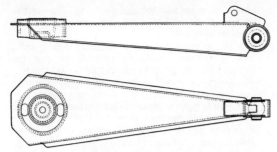

FIG 8:12 Correct positions of mounting rubbers in radius arm

Road springs:

When they have been removed from the dampers, clean off dirt and rust. Examine each spring visually to ensure that there are no cracks or other damage. Measure the free length and compare it to the dimension given in Technical Data. If the spring is short it should be renewed as it will have weakened with service.

8:6 Wheel hub assembly

The details of these parts and the remainder of the rear suspension are shown in **FIG 8:11**.

It is essential that the rear hubs 28 are refitted to the same side as they were originally removed from. If they are incorrectly fitted, then there is a danger of the hub cap 29 working loose, allowing the rear wheels to become loose with consequent wear on the splines, dangerous handling or, even worse, the loss of a wheel.

1 Remove one of the self-locking nuts 24. Support the hub carrier and wishbone 6. Use a rod to drift out the fulcrum shaft 17. Remove the oil seal track 21, oil seals 22 and shims 23. Remove the inner races of the bearings 20 and withdraw the spacers 18 and the shims 19.

2 After the nut has been removed the radius arms may also be removed. The radius arms 51 are fitted with renewable rubber bushes and if these are perished new ones should be fitted as shown in **FIG 8:12**. The bush that fits to the suspension should be pressed in so that there is an equal clearance on either side of it.

3 Turn the hub until the splitpin is accessible through the hole through the splines, and remove the splitpin locking the castellated nut. Remove the castellated nut and plain washer. Use an extractor, Churchill tool No. J.7, to withdraw the hub and hub carrier assembly from the splines on the halfshaft.

4 Remove the oil seal 35, shims 34 (if fitted) and the spacer 33. Mount the hub carrier assembly with the hub downwards and use a press to press out the hub. Prise out the oil seal and remove the inner race from inside the hub carrier. Use an extractor to withdraw the other inner race from the hub. Remove the oil seal and oil seal track assembly from the hub.

5 If required the bearing outer races can be drifted evenly out of the hub carrier.

Use newspaper and rags to remove the excess dirt and grease and then remove the remainder by brushing with paraffin. Clean all the bearings separately in clean fuel.

Examine the faces of the races and ensure that they are bright and polished. Similarly check the rollers. Corrosion, pitting or wear means that the bearings will have to be renewed as a pair. Fit the inner race back into the outer and rotate the inner race while pressing the parts firmly together, without lubrication. Any roughness in the running will then be apparent. Renew all seals on assembly and any other parts that are worn.

Refitting the hub to the carrier:

1 Drive the outer races squarely back into the recesses in the hub carrier, if they have been removed. Ensure that the outer oil seal assembly is correctly in position on the hub and press an inner race into position on the hub.

2 Use a special collar (Churchill tool No. J.15) and press the other inner race into position with the parts reassembled as shown in **FIG 8:13**. The inner race is pressed into position until the special collar just contacts the inner face of the hub.

3 Mount a DTI (Dial Test Indicator) on the hub carrier and measure the end float of the hub. On assembly a spacer 33 should be fitted so as to give the correct end float of .004 ± .002 inch (.102 ± .051 mm). The spacers 33 are supplied in thicknesses of .109 inch (2.77 mm) increasing in steps of .003 inch up to .151 inch (3.87 mm). To assist in identification they are lettered from A (the thinnest) to R (the thickest) but letters I, N and O are not used.

For example, if the measured end float is .025 inch (.64 mm), subtract the nominal end float (.004 inch)

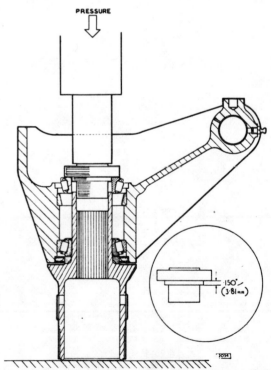

FIG 8:13 Pressing in the hub bearing inner race using the special collar Churchill tool No. J.15

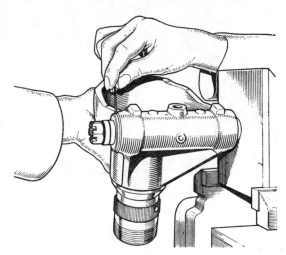

FIG 8:14 Using a simple jig to set the hub carrier bearings

from this, giving a figure of .021 inch (.53 mm). The thickness of the special collar is .150 inch (3.81 mm) and therefore the thickness of the spacer required is .150 —.021 inch = .129 inch (3.28 mm). The nearest size spacer to this is .130 inch (3.30 mm) thick which is graded H. Therefore, in this hypothetical case an H spacer should be fitted.

4 With the hub replaced in the carrier, align the hub so that the access hole through the splines is in line with the splitpin hole in the threaded portion of the half-shaft. With the oil seals and spacer in position press the hub on to the halfshaft by hand. When sufficient of the threaded portion has emerged through the hub, refit the plain washer and castellated nut. Draw the hub fully into place by tightening the castellated nut to a torque of 140 lb ft (19.3 kg m). Check that the end float is within the correct limits and secure the castellated nut with a new splitpin. **Before fitting the hub carrier and hub assembly back to the halfshaft the correct clearance for the outer wishbone should be set.** Pack the hub bearings with grease before final reassembly.

Reassembling the wishbone outer pivot :

1 Replace the tapered outer races for the bearings if they have been removed. Fit the spacers 18 and a known amount of shims 19 into place. The bearings are preloaded but for measurement of the correct quantity of shimming required use an excess of shims to ensure that there is end float.

2 Make up a jig, consisting simply of a piece of plate steel approximately 7 x 4 x $\frac{3}{8}$ inch (18 x 10 x 1 cm) with a hole drilled and tapped through the centre to take the thread of the fulcrum shaft 17.

3 Screw the fulcrum shaft 17 into the plate and fit the hub carrier to the shaft using all the parts, including the excess shims 19 but excluding the oil seals 22. Fit a large flat washer (an outer thrust washer 15 from the inner wishbone fork is ideal) against the outside of the assembly and then use sufficient ordinary

washers to pack out with and prevent the nut becoming threadbound. Fit a castellated nut 24 and tighten it to a torque of 55 lb ft (7.60 kg m).

4 Press the hub carrier firmly towards the metal plate and turn the carrier about the shaft to settle the bearings. Still pressing the carrier, measure the gap between the large washer and the machined face of the hub carrier, as shown in **FIG 8:14**. Pull the assembly away from the metal plate and again rotate it to settle the bearings. Still pulling firmly again measure the gap between the washer and the carrier. The difference between the two measurements will represent the end float with the excess shims fitted. Remove sufficient shims to give a preload of .000 to .002 inch (.00 to .05 mm). The shims are supplied in thicknesses .004 inch (.101 mm) and .007 inch (.17 mm) and a diameter of $1\frac{1}{8}$ inch (28.67 mm). As an aid a section through the parts is shown in **FIG 8:15**.

5 Refit the halfshaft as previously instructed and use a dummy shaft, Churchill tool No. J.14, through the pivot of the hub carrier to keep the parts in place and to facilitate reassembly.

6 Offer up the wishbone to the hub carrier and when aligned press out the dummy shaft so that the pivot shaft 17 replaces it. Keep the two in firm contact during this operation to ensure that the internal shims are kept in position as the shafts slide through. Measure with feeler gauges the gaps on either side between oil seal tracks 21 and sides of the fork of the wishbone. Fit shims 23 (supplied .004 inch x $\frac{7}{8}$ inch diameter) to centralize the hub carrier in the fork and prevent the fork ends from being nipped in when the nuts are tightened. Use the dummy shaft to drive out the pivot shaft 17 if the carrier has to be removed from the fork.

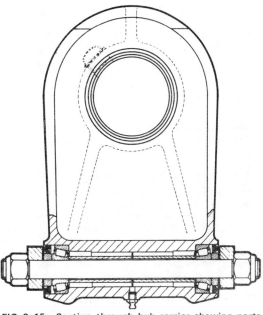

FIG 8:15 Section through hub carrier showing parts correctly assembled

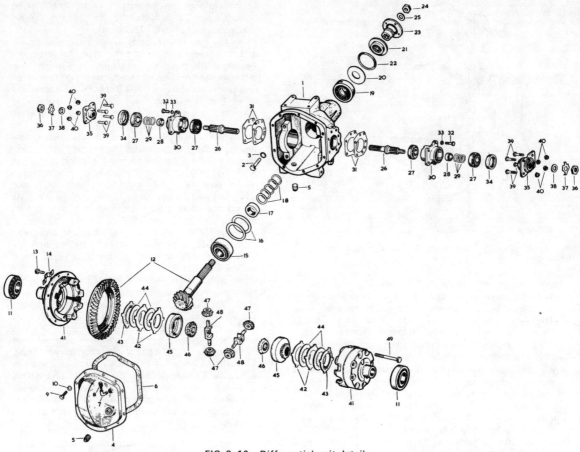

FIG 8:16   Differential unit details

Key to Fig 8:16   1 Gear carrier   2 Setscrew   3 Lockwasher   4 Cover   5 Plug   6 Gasket   7 Elbow
8 Breather   9 Setscrew   10 Spring washer   11 Roller bearing   12 Crownwheel and pinion   13 Setscrew
14 Locking plate   15 Roller bearing   16 Shim   17 Distance piece   18 Shim   19 Roller bearing   20 Oil thrower
21 Oil seal   22 Gasket   23 Companion flange   24 Nut   25 Washer   26 Output shaft   27 Roller bearing
28 Distance piece   29 Shim   30 Bearing housing   31 Shim   32 Bolt   33 Spring washer   34 Oil seal
35 Flange   36 Nut   37 Tabwasher   38 Washer   39 Bolt   40 Self-locking nut   41 Differential case
42 Flat friction plate   43 Dished friction plate   44 Friction plate   45 Side gear ring   46 Side gear   47 Pinion mate gear
48 Shaft   49 Bolt

7 Pack the bearings 20 with grease before final reassembly and tighten the nuts 24 to a torque of 55 lb ft
(7.60 kg m).

8:7 Wishbone inner pivot assembly

Refer to **FIG 8:11**. Before these can be dismantled the
appropriate spring and damper assemblies must be
removed (see **Section 8:5**). The wishbone should also
be disconnected from the hub carrier (see previous
section), but a dummy shaft can be used and the parts
secured in place with masking tape or similar so that
they will not be lost or displaced otherwise the owner
may have to begin setting the clearances from scratch.

Dismantling and removing the wishbone:

1 Remove the tie plate 5 by undoing the eight bolts
securing it to the inner fulcrum mounting brackets 3

and the six sets of nuts and bolts securing it to the
crossmember 1.
2 Remove one of the self-locking nuts securing the inner
fulcrum shaft 7 and use a long rod to drift out the
shaft. Lift out the wishbone 6 and collect the sets of
thrust washers, sealing rings and sealing ring retainers
parts 12, 13, 14 and 15.
3 If required, the bearings 10 can be removed. Use
suitable drifts to remove the bearing tube 9 and then
tap out the bearings.

Refitting the wishbone:

1 If the needle roller bearings 10 have been removed,
press one bearing into position in each fork so that the
engraving on the bearing faces outwards. Insert into
each fork the spacer collar 11 and press the remaining

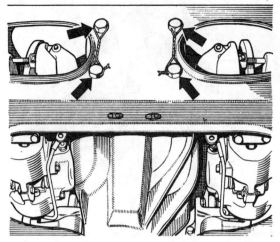

FIG 8:17 Top differential casing mounting bolts

bearings 10 into position. Pack the bearings with grease and fit into place the bearing tubes 9.

2 Smear the thrust washers, sealing rings and retaining rings with grease and use the grease to hold them on either side of each fork on the wishbone. They are fitted in the order of part numbers in the index so that the inner thrust washers 12 are placed in position first then in order 13, 14 and 15.

3 Offer up the wishbone carefully into position, taking care not to displace the parts held in by grease. Make sure the mounting for the radius arm faces the front of the car. Align the holes and spacers and carefully tap a dummy shaft J.14 through each side of the crossmember and wishbone.

4 Grease the fulcrum shaft 7 and gently tap it into position, driving each dummy shaft in turn out in front of it. The dummy shafts are fitted first to facilitate reassembly and to prevent the thrust washers from being pushed out of alignment. Secure the shaft in place by tightening the self-locking nuts to a torque of 55 lb ft (7.60 kg m).

5 Replace the tie plate 5 and reconnect the wishbone outer end to the hub carrier as described earlier.

8:8 The halfshafts

These are removed by first taking off the hub and hub carrier assembly (see **Section 8:6**). Remove the front spring and damper assembly (see **Section 8:5**). Undo the steel locknuts securing the halfshaft inner universal to the inboard disc brake. Remove the halfshaft, noting carefully the number of shims between it and the disc brake.

Replace the halfshaft in the reverse order of dismantling. **If a new halfshaft is fitted the camber of the rear wheels will have to be readjusted,** as it is controlled by the exact length of the halfshaft and the number of shims fitted between it and the disc brake.

Ensure that the steel-type locknuts are used to secure the halfshaft universal to the disc brake. Nylon fitted locknuts will have the nylon melted out by the heat from the brake, possibly causing them to come loose.

The halfshaft universal joints are serviced in exactly the same manner as the universal joints fitted to the propeller shaft (see **Section 8:4**). Some universal joints may not be fitted with grease nipples and these should be well packed with grease on reassembly.

8:9 The differential unit

All the models covered by this manual use a Thornton 'Powr-Lok' type differential. A conventional differential always drives the wheel which is easiest to turn, so that if one wheel spins on ice or mud the other wheel stays stationary with hardly any torque driving it. This also occurs if a wheel loses contact with the ground under cornering or acceleration. The wheel in the air spins, drive is lost until the wheel regains contact with the ground and usually the snatch as the spinning wheel hits the ground causes the car to swerve or veer.

The 'Powr-Lok' differential contains clutches which lock together, tending to stop the differential rotating and ensuring that many times the torque of the spinning wheel is applied to the other wheel. Drive is therefore possible even when one wheel is standing on a patch of ice. **It should be noted that, if the car is tested in gear with only one wheel jacked up, the car will drive itself off the stand or jack. Both wheels must be off the ground to prevent drive.**

A detailed view of the unit is shown in **FIG 8:16** but it should not be dismantled if faulty. Jaguars operate an exchange scheme and this should be used. Special tools and experience are both required to make the accurate settings which the unit requires and if, due to local conditions, the exchange scheme does not operate, the services of a suitably equipped agent should be enlisted instead of the owner trying to service the unit himself.

Several different ratios are available, and the ratio varies from model to model. The full list is given in Technical Data. A tag stamped with the ratio of the particular unit is attached by one of the rear cover securing screws, so quick identification of the ratio is possible.

Removing the unit:

1 Remove the road spring and damper assemblies (see **Section 8:5**). Remove the wheel hub and hub carrier assemblies (see **Section 8:6**). Remove the lower

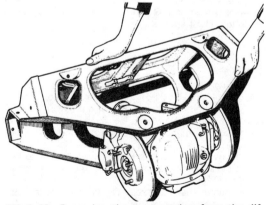

FIG 8:18 Removing the crossmember from the differential unit

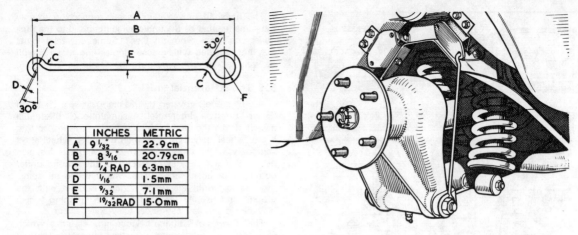

	INCHES	METRIC
A	9¹/₃₂"	22·9 cm
B	8³/₁₆"	20·79 cm
C	¹/₄" RAD	6·3 mm
D	¹/₁₆"	1·5 mm
E	9/₃₂"	7·1 mm
F	¹⁹/₃₂"RAD	15·0 mm

FIG 8:19 Details and position of link for holding suspension while setting or checking rear wheel camber

wishbones (see **Section 8:7**) and the halfshafts (see **Section 8:8**).

2 Remove the two bolts securing the handbrake compensator and then remove the compensator. Disconnect the two hydraulic pipes to the disc brake.

3 Break the locking wire and remove the two bolts securing the wishbone inner fulcrum brackets to the differential casing. Withdraw the brackets and any shims fitted between them and the differential case.

4 Make sure that the differential is drained of oil and then turn the assembly over. Break the locking wire and undo the four bolts shown in **FIG 8:17**. Remove the crossmember by tilting it forward over the nose of the differential as shown in **FIG 8:18**.

5 Free whatever has been used to lock the disc brake caliper bolts. Earlier models use locking wire but this was later changed to lockwashers. Remove the bolts and withdraw the brake caliper, carefully noting the positions of all shims. Remove the brake disc.

The differential unit is replaced in the reverse order of dismantling. The refitting of the various components is given in the relevant sections. It should be noted that the four bolts securing the differential casing to the crossmember (shown in **FIG 8:17**) should be torque loaded to 75 lb ft (10.4 kg m).

Oil leaks:

If the unit leaks oil first check that the breather 8 on the rear cover 4 is not blocked, as if it is, a build up of pressure can occur internally, forcing the oil out. Overfilling can also be a cause of oil leaks, so check that the level is correct and no higher than the lowest point of the filler hole.

If the pinion oil seal 21 is leaking it is advisable to take the unit to a suitably equipped garage as it will have to be dismantled.

The output shafts and seals can be removed after the disc brakes have been removed.

1 Remove the five bolts 32 and washers 33. Tap on the.

driving flange with a soft-faced hammer to draw the output shaft assembly out of the casing 1.

2 Remove the drive flange 35 by drawing it off after removing the nut 36, tabwasher 37 and plain washer 38.

3 Press the output shaft 26, complete with the inner race from bearing 27, distance piece 28 and shims 29, from the housing 30. Prise out the oil seal 34 and discard it. If the bearings 27 are worn drift out the old outer races from the bearing housing and press the new ones into place.

4 Reassemble the parts in the reverse order of dismantling but leave out the oil seal 34 and do not lock the nut 36 with the tabwasher 37. Use a DTI to measure the end float of the output shaft within the assembly. The correct end float should be .001 to .003 inch (.025 to .076 mm) and if it is incorrect the shims 29 will have to be adjusted to suit. Dismantle the parts and add shims 29 to increase the end float or take away shims to decrease the end float.

5 When the correct end float has been attained, refit a new oil seal 34 and finally assemble the parts, locking the nut 36. Refit the shims 31 back to the housing and enter the output shaft into the differential assembly. When aligned tap the complete assembly back into place and secure it with the five bolts.

8:10 Rear wheel camber angle

This requires specialist equipment to check. As the camber varies with the suspension height, the rear suspension must be locked in the midway position for checking the camber. Make up two hooks and fit them to the rear suspension as shown in **FIG 8:19** to set it in the correct position.

The correct reading for the camber should be $-\frac{3}{4} \pm \frac{1}{4}$ deg. The camber is varied by removing or replacing shims between the inner universal joint on the halfshaft and the disc of the rear brake. One shim .020 inch (.5 mm) thick will alter the camber by approximately $\frac{1}{4}$ deg. **Remove the setting link after adjusting or checking.**

8:11 Fault diagnosis

(a) Noisy axle

1 Insufficient or incorrect lubrication
2 Worn bearings
3 Worn gears

(b) Vibration

1 Propeller shaft out of balance
2 Worn universal joint bearings
3 Propeller shaft universal joints assembled 'out of phase'

(c) Rattles

1 Radius arm rubbers worn or perished
2 Anti-roll bar rubbers worn or perished

(d) 'Settling'

1 Weak or broken coil spring
2 Damaged or perished suspension mounting rubbers

NOTES

CHAPTER 9

THE FRONT SUSPENSION AND HUBS

9:1 Description

The front wheels are independently mounted using unequal length wishbones. A torsion bar provides the springing and load taking member for each front suspension assembly. Each torsion bar is splined at either end, one end being fitted into a bracket anchored to the frame of the car whilst the other is fitted to the lower wishbone of the suspension assembly. As the suspension moves it twists the torsion bar and the reaction from this provides the force required to take the load. A telescopic damper, fitted between the lower wishbone and a bracket on the frame, provides the control required to prevent undamped oscillations. The two lower wishbones of the suspension are connected by an anti-roll bar. On sharp cornering the weight of the car is transferred to the outside wheels, causing the body to roll as the suspension rises with the extra load. The anti-roll bar evens the load between the front wheels and therefore helps keep the body level.

A vertical stub axle carrier pivots in two ball joints at the outer ends of the wishbones to provide the movement required for steering. This carrier has bolted to it a stub axle about which the wheel hub rotates on two tapered bearings. The stub axle carrier also has the mounting points for the front brake caliper. The details of the suspension unit are shown in **FIG 9:1**. The suspension assembly cannot be removed as a complete unit from the car and parts should be dismantled from it as required. **FIG 9:8** gives a sectioned view of the suspension.

Jacking-up:

The need for the complete reliability of any stands or supports used to hold up the car cannot be overstressed.

Before jacking the car up under the frame or putting it on stands, undo the cable clips from the front crossmember and insert into the channel a block of hardwood measuring $16 \times 1 \times 1\frac{1}{8}$ inch (40.6 x 2.54 x 2.86 cm). Make sure that the pad of the jack rests against the wood, as shown in **FIG 9:2**. The normal position of chassis stands is also shown in this figure.

9:2 Routine maintenance

1 At 2500 mile intervals grease the ball joints through the nipples provided. The two nipples on each suspension, shown in **FIG 9:3**, are accessible from underneath the front of the car.

2 The front wheel bearings should be greased every 10,000 miles. It is recommended that the front hubs

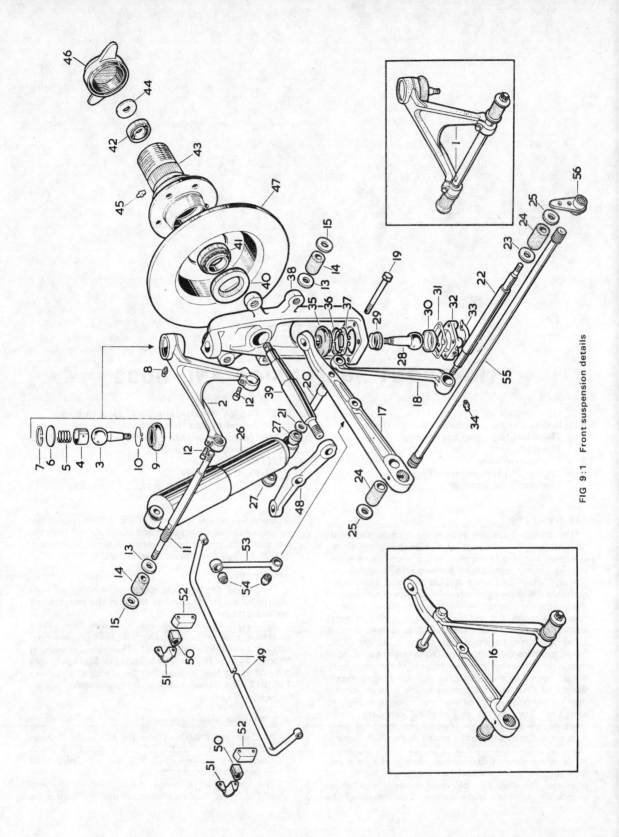

FIG 9:1 Front suspension details

Key to Fig 9:1   1 Righthand upper wishbone assembly   2 Righthand upper wishbone   3 Upper wishbone ballpin   4 Ballpin socket   5 Spring   6 Top cover   7 Circlip   8 Grease nipple   9 Rubber gaiter   10 Clip   11 Upper wishbone fulcrum shaft   12 Pinch bolt   13 Distance washer   14 Upper wishbone rubber bush   15 Special washer   16 Righthand lower wishbone assembly   17 Righthand front lower wishbone lever   18 Righthand rear lower wishbone lever   19 Bolt   20 Sleeve   21 Washer   22 Lower wishbone fulcrum shaft   23 Distance washer   24 Lower wishbone rubber bush   25 Special washer   26 Front shock absorber   27 Shock absorber, bottom bush   28 Lower wishbone ballpin   29 Ballpin spigot   30 Morganite socket   31 Shims   32 Lower ballpin cap   33 Tabwashers   34 Grease nipple   35 Rubber gaiter   36 Gaiter retainer   37 Clip   38 Stub axle   39 Stub axle carrier   40 Oil seal   41 Inner bearing   42 Outer bearing   43 Righthand front hub   44 D-washer   45 Grease nipple   46 Hub cap   47 Brake disc   48 Steering arm   49 Anti-roll bar   50 Rubber bush   51 Bracket   52 Distance piece   53 Anti-roll bar link   54 Rubber bush   55 Torsion bar   56 Rear end torsion bar bracket

be removed and the old grease cleaned out so that the condition of the bearings can be inspected. The bearings can then be packed with grease on reassembly.

Instead of dismantling, they can be lubricated through the grease nipple shown in **FIG 9:4**, accessible after the front wheel has been removed. When greasing by this method, check by looking down the bore of the splined hub and stop greasing when grease appears past the outer hub bearing.

9:3 The front hubs and brake discs

The details of these are shown in **FIG 9:5**.

Removal:

1 Securely jack up the front of the car and remove the road wheel. Cut the wire locking and remove the two bolts securing the brake caliper to the stub axle carrier. Note carefully the position of any shims fitted and remove the brake caliper. Wire it safely out of the way without straining the flexible hose. If the hose will not allow the caliper to be removed, the hose will have to be disconnected at the frame connection and the brake system bled after reassembly (see **Chapter 11**).

2 Turn the hub 5 until the splitpin 2 is accessible through the holes in the hub. Remove the splitpin. Unscrew the castellated nut 1 and withdraw the washer 3. The hub can now be drawn off the stub axle 9. Collect the inner race of the front bearing 4.

3 Extract the oil seal 8 and remove the inner race of the bearing 7. If required, the outer races of both bearings can be drifted out of the hub, and the disc 6 separated from it by undoing the nuts 12 and tapping out the bolts 11.

Examining the hub parts:

The brake disc will be dealt with in **Chapter 11**. Use newspaper and rags to remove most of the grease and dirt and then brush with paraffin or petrol to clean off the remainder. Wash the disc in either methylated spirits

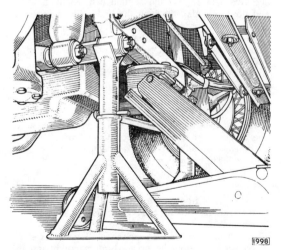

FIG 9:2   Correct position of axle stand; note the piece of hardwood fitted into the front crossmember for the jack pad to operate against

JAG/E

101

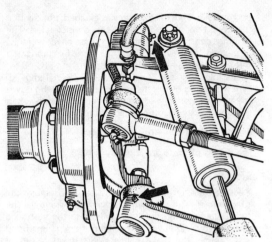

FIG 9:3 The ball joint grease nipples

or trichlorethylene to remove all traces of grease or finger marks. Wash the bearings separately in clean solvent. Examine the bearing surfaces and make sure that they are clean, bright and polished. Signs of pitting, wear or corrosion will require both bearings to be renewed as a set.

Reassembly:

If both hubs have been removed it is essential that they are replaced on their correct sides. The hub caps are labelled and the threads are different, so that righthand hub caps are tightened anticlockwise and lefthand hub caps tightened clockwise.

Replace the parts in the reverse order of dismantling. The nut 1 should be tightened so that the hub has an end float of .003 to .005 inch (.07 to .13 mm) as measured with a DTI. If a DTI is not available tighten the nut until all the end float is taken up and the bearings drag slightly on rotation. Slacken back the nut between one and two flats so that the splitpin can be fitted. If the end float exceeds .005 inch the brake disc may rub in contact with the brakes, causing dragging. Refit the brake caliper, ensuring that the correct shims are replaced, and if in doubt check the position as described in **Chapter 11.**

Make sure that the bearings are lubricated before replacing the road wheel.

9:4 The dampers

The damper mounting points can be seen in **FIG 9:8.** The dampers are sealed telescopic units which cannot be repaired or adjusted when defective. No provision is made for topping them up.

Removal:

1 Jack up the front of the car and place it on stands so that the appropriate road wheel is just clear of the ground.
2 If required, remove the road wheel. Remove the splitpins and nuts from the top and bottom mounting bolts. Support the suspension on a block of wood and withdraw the top mounting bolt from the bracket

on the chassis. **The suspension should not be allowed to drop beyond its full rebound position otherwise the ball joints on the stub axle carrier may be damaged.**

3 Partially compress the damper to clear the top from the frame bracket and draw the damper off the mounting on the lower wishbone.

Examine the damper body for signs of physical damage and renew the unit if the body is dented or the rod bent. A new damper should be mounted vertically in a vice, using lead or wood protection, and pumped for several short strokes to bleed any air trapped in the pressure chamber up to the top of the unit. Keep the damper vertical until it is refitted. Test the damper by moving it through several full strokes. There should be appreciable and constant resistance in both directions. The damper must be renewed if the resistance is weak, excessive or completely missing for part of a stroke.

The damper is replaced in the reverse order of dismantling. Do not tighten the nuts on the mounting bolts until the car has been lowered back to the ground. This is to ensure that the rubber bushes are set to their normal working position, as otherwise they will be under continuous strain, leading to early failure. If the mounting rubbers are worn or perished they should be renewed otherwise there will be a constant rattle from the suspension.

9:5 The anti-roll bar

The details of this are shown in **FIG 9:1.** Remove the bolts securing the brackets 51 and distance pieces 52 to the car frame. Remove the self-locking nuts and tap out the bolts securing the links 53 to the lower wishbones 17 and lift out the anti-roll bar. The links can be detached from the anti-roll bar 49 by removing the self-locking nuts and bolts.

Examine the rubbers 50, which are split to facilitate removal and replacement, and the rubber bushes 54. Renew any that are worn or perished. The rubber bushes 54 are a press fit in the links 53.

Refit the anti-roll bar in the reverse order of removal. The nuts should all be left slack until the full weight of the car is on the suspension to allow the bushes and rubbers to take up their normal working positions.

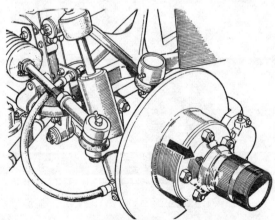

FIG 9:4 The front hub grease nipple

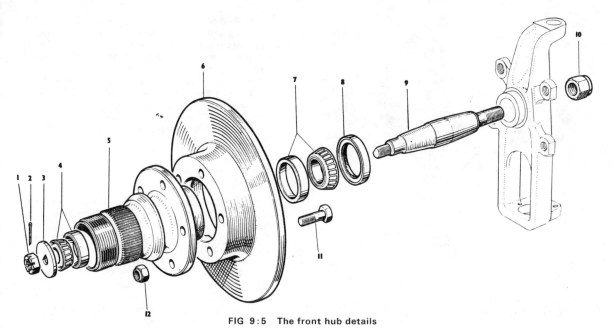

FIG 9:5 The front hub details

9:6 Separating tapers on ball joints

Ball joints are used to allow two parts to swivel. A tapered pin with a ball head is free to rotate in a socket about the ball, in one member. The tapered end of the pin fits into an accurately machined mating taper on the other member and is held there by a nut and washer, which pulls the tapers together more tightly.

Once the securing nut and washer have been removed there remains the difficulty of separating the two tapers. They can be separated by hammering on the end of the pin, but even with an old nut fitted on the pin the threads are still likely to become riveted over or damaged. Extractors are made for this purpose but may not be readily available. Instead, use a wedge to pull the members firmly apart. A screwdriver can sometimes be used. Lay a block of metal against one side of the tapered eye and hammer on the opposite side, effectively pinching the tapers. Preferably use a copper-faced hammer to prevent damage. The tapers will quickly free and can then be pulled apart easily.

9:7 The upper wishbones

The details of these are shown in **FIG 9:1**, and the wishbone fitted to its fulcrum shaft and supporting brackets is shown in **FIG 9:6**.

Removal:

1 Jack up the front of the car and place it on stands as described in **Chapter 1, Section 1:1**. Separate the top ball joint from the stub axle carrier as described in **Section 9:5**. When the ball joint has been separated tie the stub axle carrier to the frame to prevent it falling outwards and either straining the brake flexible hose or damaging the bottom ball joint.

2 Remove the two sets of bolts, nuts and lockwashers securing the fulcrum shaft rear carrier bracket to the frame. Remove, carefully noting the position and quantity, the shims 12 (see **FIG 9:6**) from between the bracket and the frame. A stiffening piece is also fitted behind the frame and this should be collected as well.

3 Remove the three setscrews, securing the fulcrum shaft front carrier bracket to the frame and lift out the wishbone assembly, carefully noting the position and quantity of the shims 13 (see **FIG 9:6**).

4 The brackets, washers and rubber bushes can be removed after taking out the splitpins and unscrewing the nuts. If required slacken the two clamp bolts on the wishbone and turn the fulcrum shaft in a clockwise direction, viewed from the rear, until the threaded portion is clear of the wishbone and the shaft can be removed.

The parts are replaced in the reverse order of dismantling. Finally tighten and splitpin the castellated nuts after the weight of the car is on the suspension. The shims behind the pivot brackets control the camber of the wheels and turning the fulcrum shaft in the wishbone controls the castor angle, so both the castor and camber angles should be checked using garage equipment.

The top ball joint:

The parts of this are shown in **FIG 9:6**. **The ball joint should never be moved far enough for the ballpin 6 to come into hard contact with the side of the socket.** If the top wishbone and stub axle carrier are removed together, they should both be supported without allowing the stub axle carrier to swing on the ball joint.

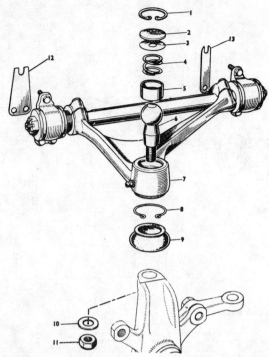

FIG 9:6   The upper wishbone and ball joint details

Key to Fig 9:6   1 Circlip   2 Top cover   3 Shims
4 Socket spring   5 Ballpin socket   6 Ballpin
7 Upper wishbone   8 Circlip   9 Rubber gaiter
10 Washer   11 Nut   12 Camber shims (front carrier
bracket)   13 Camber shims (rear carrier bracket)

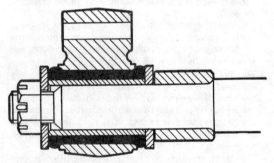

FIG 9:7   Section through lower wishbone pivot bracket

1 The upper wishbone need not be removed to service
the ball joint. Separate the tapers and support the
stub axle carrier.

2 Remove the circlip 8 and take off the rubber gaiter 9.
Renew the gaiter if it is split or otherwise damaged.

3 Hold the top cover 2 in place and remove the circlip 1.
Release the pressure and remove the top cover 2,
shims 3 and spring 4. Gently ease out socket 5 and
ballpin 6.

4 Use newspaper to remove the surplus grease and then
wash the parts in clean fuel. Also wash out the
mounting in the wishbone. Examine the socket 5 and

pin 6. If either are worn they must both be renewed.
Packing with extra shims will not cure wear.

5 Replace the parts in the reverse order of dismantling,
securing them in place with the circlip 1 and omitting
the spring. Dismantle and add shims until when
reassembled without the spring the ball is tight in its
socket. Remove shims to the thickness of .004 inch
(.10 mm) and reassemble the unit complete with the
spring. The ballpin should now move by hand. Grease
the unit through the grease nipple and reconnect it to
the stub axle carrier.

9:8 The lower wishbones and torsion bars

Removal :

1 Securely jack up the front of the car and remove the
road wheel. Disconnect the brake flexible hose at the
frame connection.

2 Disconnect the upper ball joint and tie the upper
wishbone up out of the way. Disconnect the steering
tie rod ball joint from the steering arm 48. Disconnect
the lower ball joint from the wishbone 17 and lift
away the stub axle carrier complete with hub and
brake caliper.

3 Place a jack under the lower wishbone and partially
take the weight of the car without lifting the car off the
stands. Remove the damper (see **Section 9:3**) and
lower the jack again.

4 Free the anti-roll bar from the lower wishbone by
removing the self-locking nut securing the link 53.
Remove the locking bolt holding the front of the
torsion bar to the wishbone 17. Remove the two bolts
securing the adjusting bracket 56 to the car. Slide the
bracket forward along the torsion bar until it is free
of the splines. Slide the torsion bar rearwards until the
front splines are clear of the wishbone and then
remove the torsion bar from the front of the car.

5 Undo the nuts and bolts holding the fulcrum shaft 22
brackets to the frame and remove the lower wishbone
assembly. A section through the bracket is shown in
FIG 9:7. Withdraw the splitpin and unscrew the
castellated nut. The brackets can now be slid off the
fulcrum shaft. If the rubber and steel bushes 24 are
worn press the old ones out of the brackets and press
new ones into place, using twelve parts of water to
one part of soft soap as lubricant, so that they protrude
evenly on both sides out of the bracket.

Refit the parts in the reverse order of dismantling,
after renewing any worn parts. Leave all fulcrum pin
castellated nuts slack and tighten and splitpin them when
the weight of the car is on the suspension, to ensure that
the rubber bushes are in their normal working positions.
Once reassembled, the brakes will have to be bled (see
Chapter 11) and the torsion bars adjusted as instructed
in the following section.

9:9 Adjusting the torsion bars

The torsion bar settings are checked by measuring the
standing height of the suspension. The standing height
should always be set correctly but it is even more important in the North American market as if the standing height
is incorrect the headlamps will not be at the correct level
and the car may not comply with the local regulations.

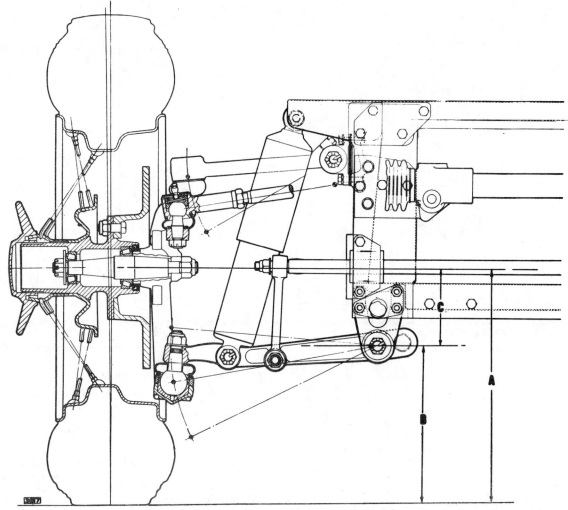

FIG 9:8 Checking the car standing height

Before checking the standing height the car must be filled with fuel oil and water. If the fuel tank is partially empty weights should be placed over the fuel tank to compensate for this. One Imperial gallon of fuel weighs 8 lbs (3.6 kg). Ensure that the tyres are inflated to the correct pressures. Finally place the car onto a long perfectly level surface with the wheels in the straight ahead position. Roll the car forward three lengths to ensure that the suspension has settled correctly.

The points for measurement are shown in **FIG 9:8**. On 4.2 litre cars measure the distance A from the ground to the wheel centre height and also measure the distance B from ground level to the centre line of the lower wishbone inner pivot points. Subtract B from A to obtain the dimension C. C should be $3\frac{1}{2} \pm \frac{1}{4}$ inch (88.9 $\pm$ 6.35 mm) for standard 4.2 litres and $3\frac{3}{4} \pm \frac{1}{4}$ inch (95.25 $\pm$ 6.35 mm) for 2 + 2 cars.

On 3.8 litre models and Series 2 4.2 litre models it is sufficient to measure the dimension B. For all Series 2

4.2 litre models the dimension B should be a minimum of 9 inches (22.86 cm). For all 3.8 litre models the dimension should be $8\frac{3}{4} \pm \frac{1}{4}$ inch (22.2 $\pm$ 6.35 cm).

Setting:

1 Jack up the front of the car, place it on stands and remove the road wheels. Remove the damper (see **Section 9:4**. Disconnect the upper wishbone ball joint and the steering tie rod ball joint (see **Section 9:6**) and tie the stub axle carrier in place. Disconnect the anti-roll bar link from the lower wishbone. Remove the two bolts securing the adjusting bracket at the rear of the torsion bar to the frame. Slacken the nuts on the lower wishbone inner pivots.

2 Make up a link and fit it between the damper mounting points, as shown in **FIG 9:9**. The dimensions for the link on all 3.8 litre models are also shown in **FIG 9:9**. On 4.2 litre models the dimensions for the distance

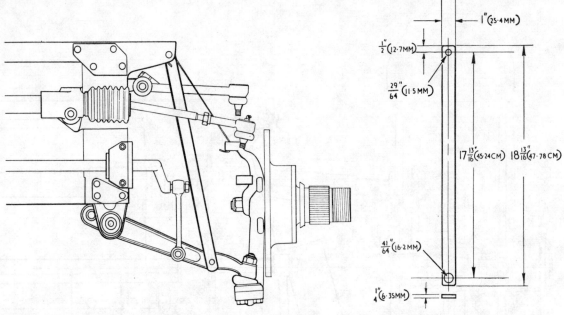

FIG 9:9 Torsion bar setting gauge for 3.8 litre models. The gauge for 4.2 litre models is similar except that the dimension between hole centres varies

between the hole centres varies depending on the type of model. The correct dimensions for all models covered by this manual are given in Technical Data.

3 Check the relative positions of the holes in the adjusting bracket and the holes in the frame. Mark the position of the adjusting bracket on the torsion bar splines and slide it forward to free it from the splines. Rotate it in the required direction and slide it back onto the splines. Repeat this process until the holes are accurately aligned.

4 There are 25 splines on the rear of the torsion bar and only 24 on the front. If the torsion bar is freed from the wishbone, after removing the locking bolt, it can be rotated to provide a very fine vernier adjustment.

5 Once the holes are aligned, secure the adjusting bracket to the frame. Reassemble the suspension in the reverse order of dismantling after removing the setting link. Replace the road wheels and lower the car back to the ground. Check the standing height as described earlier to ensure that the adjustment is correct.

Series 3:

On Series 3 models the distance between the ground and the lower surface of the front subframe lower cross-member should be measured as shown at **A** in **FIG 9:12**. This dimension should be $6\frac{1}{4} \pm \frac{1}{4}$ inch (15.9 $\pm$.64 cm).

If an adjustment should be required, slacken the locknut on the cam adjuster at the front of the lower wishbone and rotate the cam to obtain the correct height as shown in **FIG 9:13**. Tighten the locknut to 60 lb/ft and recheck the height.

9:10 The lower wishbone ball joint

The parts of this are shown in **FIG 9:10**. The parts should be serviced after the stub axle carrier has been removed or disconnected from the lower wishbone. Dismantle the unit by removing the circlip 4 and rubber gaiter 3, and then freeing the tabwashers 11 and removing the four setscrews 12.

Wash all the parts in clean fuel and examine the spigot 5, ballpin 6 and socket 7 for wear. **These must be renewed if worn and wear must not be taken up by removing shims 8.**

Reassemble the unit in the reverse order of dismantling, fitting shims 8 to give the correct clearance of .004 to .006 inch (.10 to .15 mm).

9:11 Suspension geometry

This must be checked or adjusted using accurate garage equipment. Before checking, the suspension must be set to its mid-laden position. Clip down the rear suspension with the hooks described in **Chapter 8, Section 8:10**. The front suspension must be held down by links, shown in **FIG 9:11**, between the damper mounting points.

Castor angle:

This is adjusted by turning the upper fulcrum shaft using the flats provided. Before the shaft can be turned both clamp bolts on the wishbone must be slackened, the splitpins removed and the nuts securing the rubber bushes also slackened. To increase positive castor angle, rotate the shaft in an anticlockwise direction when viewed from the front of the car. The correct castor angle

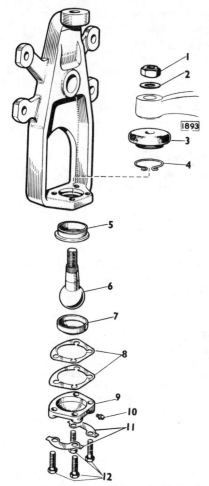

FIG 9:10 The lower wishbone ball joint details

Key to Fig 9:10   1 Nut   2 Washer   3 Rubber gaiter
4 Circlip   5 Spigot   6 Ballpin   7 Socket   8 Shims
9 Ballpin cap   10 Grease nipple   11 Tabwashers
12 Setscrews

should be $2 \pm \frac{1}{2}$ deg. positive, but both wheels must be
within $\frac{1}{2}$ deg. of each other. Tighten the clamp bolts and
securing nuts, and remove the links and hooks from
front and rear suspension. After the castor has been
readjusted the front wheel alignment should also be
checked.

Camber angle :

This is controlled by the number of shims fitted behind
the top fulcrum shaft brackets. The shims have slots for
the top bolts of both brackets so these need only be
slackened. The bottom bolts have to be removed when
fitting or removing shims. The correct camber angle is
$\frac{1}{4} \pm \frac{1}{2}$ deg. positive but the wheels must be within $\frac{1}{2}$ deg.
of each other. Remove or replace an equal thickness of
shims from behind each bracket otherwise the castor
angle will be varied. The addition of $\frac{1}{16}$ inch (1.6 mm) of
shim will increase a positive angle of camber (or decrease

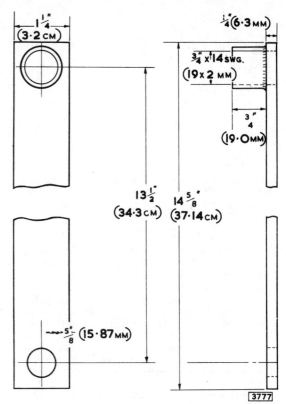

FIG 9:11   Details of link to be fitted between damper
mountings when checking suspension geometry

a negative angle) by approximately $\frac{1}{4}$ deg. Check the wheel
alignment (see **Chapter 10**) after altering the camber
angle.

**When the steering geometry has been checked
make sure all suspension holding hooks and links
have been removed.**

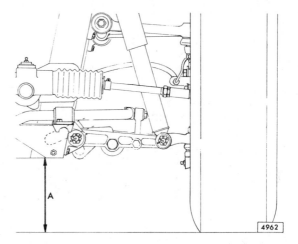

FIG 9:12   Measuring the front suspension riding height,
Series 3. Dimension **A** = 6.25 inch ± .25 inch

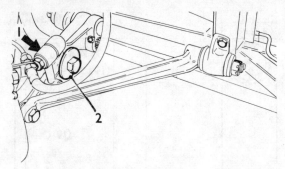

FIG 9:13 Adjusting the front suspension height with torsion bar cam adjuster

Key to Fig 9:13   1 Locknut   2 Rotating adjuster

9:12 Modifications

1 On series 2 4.2 litre models the swivel ball joints are fitted with a bleed hole covered by a nylon washer. The nylon washer will lift when sufficient grease pressure has been applied.

2 Pressed steel wheels are available as an optional extra on Series 2 4.2 litre models. The splitpin and nut retaining the hub to the stub axle is covered by a dust cap, which has to be prised off before the nut and splitpin are accessible. Sufficient lubrication of the bearings will be shown by grease exuding through the small centre hole in the dust cap.

3 Torsion bars of larger diameter were fitted to 4.2 litre models at the following and all subsequent chassis numbers:

FHC   IE. 35382 (LHD)
Open sports   IE. 17532 (LHD)
2+2   IE. 50875 (RHD)
2+2   IE. 77407 (LHD)

All models fitted with air conditioning are also fitted with these .780 to .784 (19.81 to 19.9 mm) torsion bars.

9:13 Fault diagnosis

(a) Wheel wobble

1 See **Chapter 10**
2 Worn hub bearings
3 Incorrectly adjusted or weak torsion bars
4 Uneven tyre wear
5 Worn suspension linkage
6 Loose wheel fixings

(b) Bottoming of suspension

1 Check 3 in (a)
2 Rebound rubbers worn or missing
3 Faulty dampers

(c) Excessive tyre wear

1 Check 5 in (a) also check 3 in (b)
2 Neglected lubrication of ball joints
3 See **Chapter 10**

(d) Rattles

1 Check 3 in (a) and also check 3 in (b)
2 Lubrication neglected
3 Damper mounting loose or bushes worn
4 Anti-roll bar mountings loose, bush worn
5 Suspension rubber bushes worn

(e) Excessive rolling

1 Check 3 in (a) and also check 3 in (b)
2 Anti-roll bar broken, mountings loose or bushes worn

CHAPTER 10

THE STEERING GEAR

10:1 Description

The steering wheel is connected to a rack and pinion steering unit by a system of shafts and universal joints. At either end of the steering unit is fitted a tie rod, which is connected by a ball joint to the steering arm on each stub axle carrier. When the steering wheel is turned the pinion rotates with it and drives the rack from side to side, taking with it the tie rods and thus steering the front wheels.

The steering rack is attached as a complete unit to the front crossmember of the chassis, between the radiator and the engine.

On later lefthand drive models a modified collapsible steering column is fitted. This is designed to comply with the USA safety regulations. The upper steering column and the lower steering column are both made of two separate sliding shafts. The two sliding shafts in each case are held together by nylon plugs. The outer portion of the upper column is also pierced in a lattice form. On a heavy frontal impact the nylon studs shear and allow the steering column to collapse progressively without causing injury to the driver. **If the nylon shear studs are damaged they cannot be repaired and a new unit must be fitted.**

Power assisted steering can be fitted as an optional extra to the Series 2 4.2 litre models.

10:2 Routine maintenance

There are three grease nipples fitted to the steering and they should be greased at 2500 mile intervals. The two grease nipples for the steering ball joints are items 31 in **FIG 10:1** and the grease nipple for the steering rack is item 12 in the same figure. Before commencing greasing check the rubber gaiters 32 and 36 both for security and for condition. Renew the gaiters if they are split, otherwise dirt can enter through the split and cause rapid and premature wear. Do not overlubricate. The bellows 26 must not become distended with grease.

PART I THE STEERING RACK

10:3 Steering rack removal

1 The steering rack cannot be removed until the radiator has been removed (see **Chapter 4**). Jack up the front of the car and place it on stands as described in **Chapter 9, Section 9:1**. Remove the front road wheels.

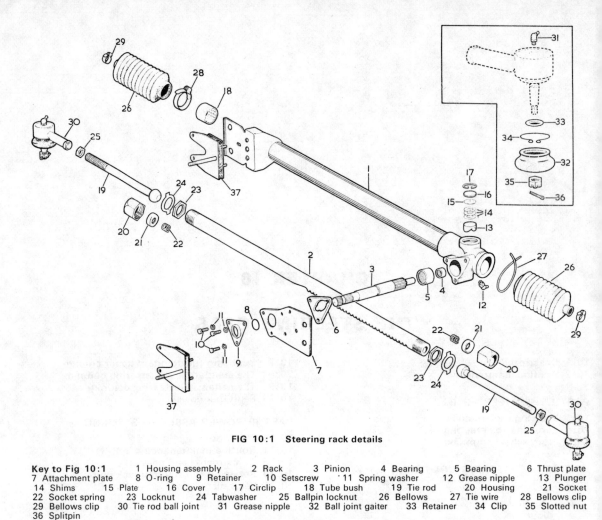

FIG 10:1 Steering rack details

Key to Fig 10:1   1 Housing assembly   2 Rack   3 Pinion   4 Bearing   5 Bearing   6 Thrust plate
7 Attachment plate   8 O-ring   9 Retainer   10 Setscrew   11 Spring washer   12 Grease nipple   13 Plunger
14 Shims   15 Plate   16 Cover   17 Circlip   18 Tube bush   19 Tie rod   20 Housing   21 Socket
22 Socket spring   23 Locknut   24 Tabwasher   25 Ballpin locknut   26 Bellows   27 Tie wire   28 Bellows clip
29 Bellows clip   30 Tie rod ball joint   31 Grease nipple   32 Ball joint gaiter   33 Retainer   34 Clip   35 Slotted nut
36 Splitpin

2 Disconnect the tie rod ball joints from the steering arms on the stub axle carriers, as described in **Chapter 9, Section 9:5**. Turn the steering until the Allen screw securing the lower steering column universal joint to the pinion 3 is accessible. Remove the Allen screw.

3 From the pinion side of the housing remove the two inner self-locking nuts, and the central bolt with the attached self-locking nut securing the housing to the rubber/steel bonded mounting 37. Remove the top and bottom outer self-locking nuts and withdraw the bolts, collecting the two spacer tubes fitted between the mounting bracket and the frame.

4 Undo the other end mounting in a similar manner but note that the two spacer tubes have been replaced by two adjusting nuts.

Replacing the unit:

This is the reversal of the removal procedure. When refitting the unit fully tighten all the nuts on the pinion side mounting, noting that this is the side with the spacer tubes fitted. Fully tighten the two inner and single central fixings. Tighten the two nuts securing the two outer bolts until the washers under the bolt heads can only just be rotated using the fingers. Hold these nuts in position and turn the inner locknuts towards the outer locknuts until all are tight.

Refill the cooling system after the radiator has been replaced, and check the wheel alignment after the wheels have been replaced and the car is back on the ground.

10:4 Servicing the steering rack

Refer to **FIG 10:1**.

Dismantling:

1 Slacken the locknuts 25 and unscrew both tie rod ball joints 30. Undo the locking wire 27 and all clips 28 and 29. Slide off both bellows 26.

2 Free the tabs on the washers 24 and slacken the locknuts 23. Remove the tie rods 19 by undoing the

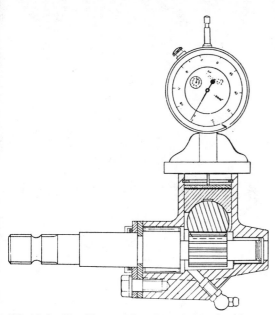

FIG 10:2 Checking end float in rack damping plunger

housing nuts 20. Remove the sockets 21, springs 22, washers 24 and locknuts 23.

3 Remove the three setscrews 10 and their washers 11. Lift off the retainer 9 and remove the O-ring 8. Lift off the attaching plate 7 and the thrust plate 6, then withdraw the pinion 3.

4 Remove the circlip 17 and withdraw the cover 16, Belleville washer 15, shims 14 and plunger 13. Withdraw the rack 2 from the housing.

Examining the parts:

1 Use newspapers and rags to remove the worst of the dirt and grease, then brush the parts with petrol or paraffin to remove the remainder. Dry the parts and examine them for wear.

2 **The tie rod ball joints cannot be dismantled and if they are worn they must be replaced with new assemblies.** The rubber gaiters 32 should be renewed separately if they are worn or split.

3 Examine the sockets 21 and balls on the tie rods 19. If they are excessively worn they must be renewed.

4 Examine the bellows 26 and renew them if they are split or wearing through.

5 If the bush 18 is worn it may be drifted out using a long rod through the housing. Thoroughly soak the new bush in oil for as many hours as possible, and press it into place using a stepped mandrel whose spigot is polished and of the same diameter as the rack 2. **Do not ream or bore the bush after it has been fitted.**

Reassembling:

1 Liberally grease the rack 2 and replace it in the housing 1. Grease the pinion 3 and replace it in the housing, securing it in place by replacing the thrust plate, mounting plate and cover in the reverse order of dismantling.

2 Insert the plunger 13 into position. Replace the cover 16 and circlip 17 but omit the shims 14 and Belleville washer 15. Mount a DTI so that the plunger presses vertically on the cover, as shown in **FIG 10:2**. Press the cover 16 firmly downwards so that the rack is fully engaged with the pinion. Set the DTI to zero. Press the rack firmly upwards so that all end float is eliminated and the cover is tight against the circlip. Note the reading on the DTI. Use a micrometer gauge to measure the thickness of the Belleville washer and subtract this thickness from the reading on the DTI. Select shims to make a pack of the correct end float thinner than the dimension calculated, so that the thickness of the shim pack is .006 to .010 inch (.15 to .25 mm) less than the DTI reading minus the thickness of the Belleville washer. Remove the circlip and cover, fit the shims and Belleville washer and then refit the cover and the circlip.

3 Screw the locknuts 23 back onto the rack 2 and fit on the washers 24. Slide the housing 20 followed by the bellows 26 down the tie rod and refit the locknut 25 and tie rod ball joint 30. Pull the bellows back up the tie rod so they are well clear of the inner ball joints.

4 Insert the springs 22 into the ends of the rack 2, and the sockets 21 into the housing 20. Attach the tie rod assembly to the rack using the housings. Suspend the tie rod ball joint by a spring balance, as shown in **FIG 10:3**. Adjust the housing 20 until the tie rod moves when a load of 7 lbs (3.18 kg) is applied at the spring balance. Hold the housing steady and tighten the locknut 23 up to it. Recheck that the tie rod moves at the correct load and lock the nuts by bending the tabs on the washer 24.

5 Apply grease generously to the ballhousing. Pull the bellows 26 into place and secure them with locking wire and the clips. Set the tie rod ball joints so that they are both screwed in an equal number of turns on the threads. Tighten the locknuts 25 only sufficiently to prevent the ball joints rotating under their own weight, as the front wheel alignment will have to be set once the unit has been refitted.

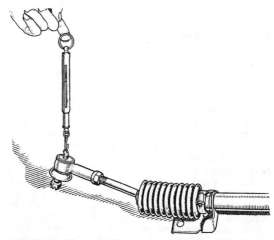

FIG 10:3 Checking the correct adjustment of the inner ball joint housing

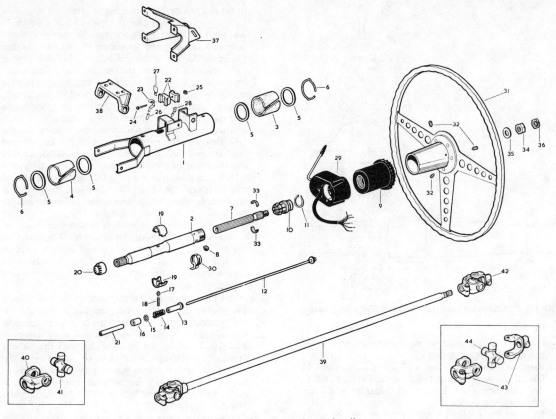

FIG 10:4 Steering column details

Key to Fig 10:4 1 Outer tube assembly 2 Inner column 3 Upper felt bearing 4 Lower felt bearing 5 Washer 6 Spring clip 7 Male inner column 8 Stop button 9 Locknut 10 Split collet 11 Circlip 12 Horn switch contact pin 13 Insulating bush 14 Spring 15 Washer 16 Insulating bush 17 Contact nipple 18 Spring 19 Rotor assembly 20 Slip ring 21 Insulating sleeve 22 Contact holder 23 Contact 24 Bolt 25 Nut 26 Insulating sleeve 27 Insulating strip 28 Earth contact 29 Direction indicator control assembly 30 Control striker 31 Steering wheel 32 Grub screw 33 Split cone 34 Nut 35 Washer 36 Locknut 37 Upper mounting bracket 38 Lower mounting bracket 39 Lower steering column 40 Lower universal joint yoke 41 Journal assembly 42 Upper universal joint assembly 43 Upper universal joint yoke 44 Journal assembly

10:5 Front wheel alignment

Ensure that the car is fully fuelled and has the correct quantities of oil and water. Place weights over the fuel tank to compensate for a partially filled fuel tank. (1 Imperial gallon of fuel weighs approximately 8 lbs [3.6 kg]). Stand the car on level ground with the front wheels in the straight-ahead position. Without turning the steering, push the car forwards for a few yards to settle the bearings and suspension. Measure, as accurately as possible, the distance between the front wheel rims at the front of the wheel and at wheel centre height. Mark the wheels with chalk as a guide and push the car forwards so that the wheels turn exactly half a revolution. This is to ensure that any inaccuracies in the wheel rims are accounted for. Measure, again as accurately as possible, the distance between the wheel rims at wheel centre height but at the rear of the front wheels. The difference between the two dimensions will be the amount of 'toe-in' present.

The correct toe-in for all models covered by this manual is $\frac{1}{16}$ to $\frac{1}{8}$ inch (1.6 to 3.2 mm). If the wheel alignment is incorrect the front tyres will wear unevenly, giving a feathered edge to the tread. Unless the error is very small both tie rods should be adjusted by the same amount so as to give the correct wheel alignment. Adjust by slackening the locknuts 25 and the small clips 29 securing the outer ends of the bellows 26 to the tie rods. Turn each tie rod 19 by an equal amount. Tighten the locknuts 25 and again check the track. When the adjustment is satisfactory check that the bellows 26 are not twisted and resecure them with the clips 29. Make sure the locknuts 25 are tight.

As the tyre wear will be greatly increased if the track is incorrect, the owner who has any doubts on the accuracy of his measurements is advised to take the car to a garage where there will be specialized equipment, for checking not only track but the rest of the steering and suspension geometry as well.

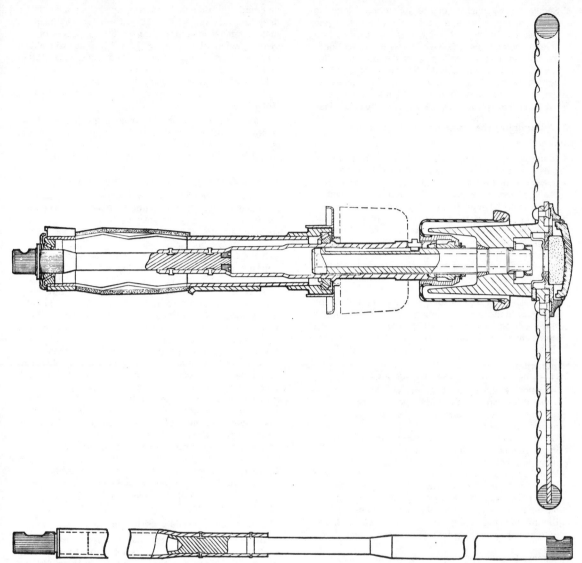

FIG 10:5   Sectioned view of upper and lower collapsible steering columns, showing the nylon shear studs. This type of steering column is only fitted to later lefthand drive 4.2 litre models, and those fitted with power-assisted steering

The wheel alignment for cars fitted with power assisted steering is dealt with separately in **Section 10:13**.

PART II THE STEERING COLUMN

The details of the standard steering column are shown in **FIG 10:4**, and a sectioned view of the collapsible steering column, fitted to later lefthand drive 4.2 litre models, is shown in **FIG 10:5**.

10:6 The steering wheel

The mounting for the steering wheel to the upper column is the same for both types of steering column.

Removal:

1 Undo the three grubscrews 32 from the steering wheel hub and remove the horn push assembly.
2 Slacken the locknut 36 and remove it and the nut 34 and plain washer 35. Remove the steering wheel 31 from the splines 7 with a sharp pull from behind the steering wheel. Collect the two halves of the split cone 33.

Replacement:

1 Set the front wheels in the straight-ahead position. Slacken the adjuster nut 9 and pull the inner column 7 out to its fullest extension. Tighten the locknut 9 to hold the column 7 in place.

2 Secure the two halves of the split cone 33 to the inner column 7 with a little grease, so that the narrowest diameter of the taper is towards the steering wheel. Fit the steering wheel back onto the splined inner column so that the bottom spoke is vertically downwards. Refit the washer 35 and fully tighten the nut 34 down onto the washer. Screw on the locknut 36 but do not overtighten it.

3 Refit the horn push with the Jaguar's head vertical.

10:7 Servicing the standard upper column

Removal:

1 Remove the steering wheel as described in the previous section. Isolate the battery and disconnect the wires to the direction indicator switch, labelling them to ensure correct reconnection on reassembly. Disconnect the horn push cable from the connector at the lower end of the upper column tube.

2 Undo the nut and remove the pinch bolt and washer securing the upper universal assembly 42 to inner column 2.

3 Remove the two sets of nuts, bolts and washers securing the outer tube assembly 1 to the lower mounting bracket 38. Remove the single long bolt, nut, washer and spacer tube securing the outer tube assembly to the upper mounting bracket 37. Withdraw the upper column assembly from the car, freeing the upper universal 42 from the splines on the inner column 2.

Dismantling:

1 Undo the spring clips holding the inner half of the indicator switch cover and remove it by pulling it towards the centre of the car. Remove the two screws securing the clamp and with the clamp taken off remove the switch.

2 Unscrew the telescopic adjusting nut 9 from the inner column 2. If required the collet 10 can be removed from the nut 9 after removing the circlip 11.

3 Withdraw the horn contact pin 12 and the top insulating bush 13 complete with spring 14 from the top of the column. Remove the direction indicator striker 30 after taking out the two securing screws. Remove the stop button 8 which is now exposed, and withdraw the splined column 7 from the inner column 2.

4 Remove the earthing contact 28 from the bracket on the outer column 1 and then remove the slip ring contact 23 from the contact holders 22. **Take care not to lose any of the insulating sleeves.**

5 Tap the inner column 2 upwards out of the outer sleeve 1. Compress the spring 6 and remove it from the top of the outer sleeve 1. The washers 5 and felt 4 can then be removed. Similarly remove the bottom felt bearing assembly.

6 If the slip ring 20 is badly worn or damaged it can be removed by prising up the slotted end and sliding it down the inner column 2 towards the splines. Light burn marks can be cleaned off using fine emerycloth. Take care of the plunger and spring exposed when the slip ring is removed.

Reassembling:

This is the reversal of the dismantling procedure. Renew the felt bushes 3 and 4 if they are worn or flattened. The direction indicator control switch 30 and direction indicator switch 29 must be reassembled so that the striker is central between the trip levers on the switch when the steering is in the straight-ahead position. The holes for the securing screws are slotted and if the parts are not correctly adjusted the indicators will cancel in different positions on either side.

Refitting:

This is the reversal of the removal procedure. If the steering wheel is fitted before the assembly is refitted take care to ensure that the steering wheel is in the straight-ahead position when the front wheels are.

10:8 The standard lower steering column

This can be removed after the upper steering column has been removed by taking out the Allen screw securing the lower universal joint yoke 40 to the pinion on the steering rack and then drawing the yoke off the splines on the rack pinion.

If the upper steering column is not to be dismantled, turn the steering wheel until the pinch bolt and nut securing the upper universal joint 42 to the inner column 2 can be removed. Remove the bonnet (see **Chapter 13**) and after draining the cooling system remove the radiator (see **Chapter 4**). Turn the steering wheel until the Allen screw securing the lower yoke 40 to the pinion on the rack can be reached and removed. Disconnect the electrical cables to the upper column and remove the nuts and bolts securing the outer sleeve assembly 1 to the upper and lower mounting brackets 37 and 38. Withdraw the upper steering column assembly sufficiently to allow the upper and lower universal joints to be drawn off the splines on the pinion and inner column. Withdraw the lower steering column through the front frame crossmembers above the anti-roll bar.

The universal joints are serviced in exactly the same manner as the propeller shaft universal joints (see **Chapter 8, Section 8:4**). No lubrication points are provided on these universal joints and they must be well packed with grease on reassembly.

10:9 The collapsible steering column

Under no circumstances must a hammer or mallet be used either to remove or to refit the universal joints to their mating splines. If the universal joints are difficult to refit, clean the splines using a fine triangular file to remove any burrs. Use penetrating oil to help loosen the splines if they are stiff to remove.

The nylon shear studs are designed to give on impact and this is the reason why excess force must not be used. **If the nylon studs have been sheared they cannot be repaired and a new unit must be fitted.**

Removal:

The upper column is removed in a similar manner to the standard type upper column. The ignition lock is fitted to the column and this must be removed by undoing the ring nut and detaching the lock from the mounting bracket. On cars fitted with air conditioning equipment the ignition lock is fitted to the evaporator unit and can therefore be left in place.

The lower column is detached after the upper column has been removed, and the lower universal joint has been disconnected from the pinion on the steering rack unit.

The complete steering column assembly is replaced in the reverse order of dismantling, but ensuring that the steering wheel is in the straight-ahead position at the same time as the front wheels.

The upper steering column uses sealed-for-life bearings and must not be dismantled further than removal of the steering column adjuster locknut, direction indicator switch and splined inner column as detailed in operations 1 to 3 under the heading 'Dismantling' in **Section 10 : 7**.

The pinch bolts on the universal joints should be tightened to a torque of 16 to 18 lb ft (2.2 to 2.5 kg m).

10 : 10 Fault diagnosis

This section on fault diagnosis covers only **Parts I and II** of this Chapter.

(a) Wheel wobble

1 Unbalanced wheels and tyres
2 Slack steering connections
3 Incorrect steering geometry
4 Incorrectly adjusted or weak torsion bars
5 Worn hub bearings
6 Excessive play in steering gear

(b) Wander

1 Check 2, 3 and 4 in (a)
2 Front suspension and rear suspension not in alignment
3 Uneven tyre pressures
4 Uneven tyre wear
5 Weak dampers

(c) Heavy steering

1 Check 3 in (a)
2 Very low tyre pressures
3 Neglected lubrication
4 Wheels out of track
5 Steering rack unit maladjusted
6 Steering column bushes or bearings tight

(d) Lost motion

1 Loose steering wheel
2 Worn splines throughout steering column
3 Worn universal joints on lower column

PART III POWER ASSISTED STEERING

10 : 11 Description

The system consists of three main components. A belt driven pump mounted on the lefthand side of the engine supplies the oil flow and pressure requirements. A reservoir contains the oil and this is mounted by brackets to the lefthand subframe. The rack and pinion unit is modified to take a valve and power steering equipment. All three are connected by flexible high-pressure rubber hoses.

When the engine is running there is a continuous flow of oil through the system and pressure only builds up when the steering is turned. A relief valve in the pump controls the maximum pressure, to prevent damage to the components. The rack and pinion unit has attached to it a rotary valve and a hydraulic cylinder, the piston of which is connected to the rack.

The valve rotor, which is also the input shaft to the steering gear, has three grooves machined in it. These three grooves lie between three grooves in the valve sleeve. The valve sleeve is positioned according to the piston in the cylinder so that when no load is applied to the steering wheel no pressure is supplied to the cylinder. When the steering wheel rotates the rotor is turned through a torsion bar. The manual effort is sufficient to twist the torsion bar, allowing the rotor to move relative to the sleeve. The relative movement allows oil under pressure to be passed to the correct side of the piston and move the steering in the required direction.

The steering column is of the collapsible type and serviced as described in **Section 10 : 9**.

10 : 12 Routine maintenance

1 Ensure that the oil level in the reservoir is always kept up. Carefully wipe the top free of dirt and remove the filler cap. Usually a dipstick is attached to the filler cap and the level should be kept up to the full mark on this.

2 The lubrication of the system is the same as that of the unassisted system. The grease nipple for the rack and pinion assembly is fitted to the rack adjuster pad and is accessible from underneath the front of the car at the driver's side.

3 The filter in the reservoir should be renewed without fail after every 20,000 miles. Clean the top and unscrew the bolt securing it to the body of the reservoir. Lift out the old filter from the reservoir and discard it. Fit the new filter and replace the cover and top up with oil before replacing the filler cap. If no dipstick is fitted to the filler cap top up to just above the top of the filter. **Do not use engine oil in the system.** The correct oil is the same as the oil used in automatic transmissions (Automatic Transmission Fluid Type A).

10 : 13 Adjustments and checks

The system parts do not need to be removed from the car for these checks.

Rack rattle :

This will be most apparent when travelling over rough roads. The rack internal clearance is adjusted as follows:

1 Slacken the locknut on the rack adjusting screw (identifiable by the grease nipple screwed into it) and screw the rack adjusting screw in until a firm resistance is felt.

2 Unscrew the adjusting screw $\frac{1}{16}$ of a turn or a maximum of $22\frac{1}{2}$ deg. Hold the adjusting screw in this position and tighten the locknut.

3 Grip the ballpin arm protruding from the pinion end of the rack unit and lift it in the direction of the adjusting screw. A spring return pressure should be felt. If the pressure is weak remove the adjusting screw and check that the spring is not broken. Renew the spring if required.

4 Remove the grease nipple and insert the plunger of a DTI through the grease nipple hole and the matching hole in the pressure pad. By moving the rack itself

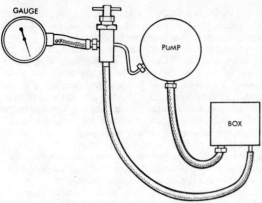

FIG 10:6 Testing the power assisted steering hydraulic system

up and down against the pressure of the spring the play can be measured. If required, adjust so that the play is at its minimum without the rack binding at any point throughout its travel. The maximum play must not exceed .010 inch (.254 mm). If no DTI is available, operations 1 and 2 will provide a reasonably accurate setting.

Wear on the ball joints:

This may be apparent as a knock when the steering is turned, due to wear on the inner ball joints. If the outer ball joints are worn they can be renewed after they have been disconnected from the steering arms on the suspension. The inner ball joints are renewed as follows:

1 Disconnect the tie rod ball joint from the steering arm (see **Chapter 9, Section 9:5**).
2 Remove the bellows retaining clips and pull the bellows back until the inner ball joints are accessible. Free the ears on the tabwashers and remove the ball joint and tie rod as a unit. Collect the spring from the end of the rack.
3 Measure the distance between the ball joint centres. Both the tie rods must be the same length, which should be 8.75 inch (22.2 mm).
4 Slacken the locknut and remove the outer ball joint. Renew it if required. **The inner ball joint must not be dismantled** and if it is faulty a new tie rod and ball joint assembly complete must be fitted.
5 Fit the outer ball joint to the tie rod assembly so that the dimension between centres is correct. Refit the parts in the reverse order of dismantling using a new tabwasher and smearing the inner ball joint housing liberally with grease. The front wheel alignment must be checked after reassembly.

Front wheel alignment:

This must be checked on a level surface, with the car fully fuelled, and using accurate garage equipment. The wheels are locked in the straight-ahead position by inserting a centralizing tool Jaguar Part No. 12297 into the adjuster pad through the grease nipple hole in the steering rack unit. The correct toe-in, as on all models, is $\frac{1}{16}$ to $\frac{1}{8}$ (1.6 to 3.2 mm). **Ensure that both tie rods are**

of equal length. If they vary greatly from the correct length the suspension should be examined for accident damage.

Hydraulic pressure:

Fit a pressure gauge into the return line from the steering rack. With the engine running at idle speed, turn the steering wheel to full lock and increase the turning effort until the pressure reaches a maximum. The pressure should not go higher than 950 to 1000 lb/sq in (66.8 to 70.3 kg/sq cm) even when the engine speed is increased. If the pressure is below 950 lb/sq in when the engine is idling but rises to the correct figure as the engine speed increases, then either there is major internal leakage in the steering unit or the relief valve in the pump is faulty.

If defective, fit the pressure gauge into the pressure line with an 'On/Off' cock fitted so that the cock shuts off the supply to the steering unit but not to the gauge, as shown in **FIG 10:6**. Start the engine and with the cock open check the hydraulic pressure at full lock. This should be 1000 lb/sq in (70.3 kg/sq cm). **Close the tap for a maximum of five seconds.** If the pressure reading is the same, then the leaks are in the steering rack unit and this should be overhauled. If the correct pressure is not reached then the fault lies in the pump. The pump cannot be serviced and an exchange pump must be fitted in its place.

Steering veers:

Before checking the power assisted system check that the veering is not caused by other faults as given in (b) Wander of **Section 10:10**.

When satisfied that the mechanical side of the steering is correct, connect a 0 to 100 lb/sq in (0 to 7 kg/sq cm) pressure gauge into the return pipe from the steering unit. Start the engine and leave it at idling speed. The gauge should read 40 lb/sq in (2.8 kg/sq cm). Turn the steering wheel by an equal small amount in either direction. The pressure should increase by an equal amount irrespective of which direction the steering is turned in. The valve and pinion assembly must be renewed if the pressure rise is not equal on both sides and there is a slight drop followed by the increase on one side. The assembly must also be renewed if the steering kicks to one side when the engine is started.

The valve and pinion assembly can be renewed without taking the steering unit out of the car, but note the following points:

1 The rack adjusting screw must be slackened right off and then reset correctly after the valve and pinion assembly has been fitted.
2 Note the position of the pinch bolt slot in the input shaft before removal and replace with the slot in the same position on reassembly. Allow for the spiral in the pinion when reassembling.

10:14 Servicing the steering rack unit

This is removed and replaced in exactly the same way as the normal unassisted rack unit (see **Section 10:3**) but with the addition of connecting and disconnecting the hoses. When disconnecting the hoses have a container ready as the oil will drain from the hoses.

When the steering rack has been refitted refill the reservoir. Start the engine and allow it to run at idle speed, adding fluid to the reservoir as it is drawn into the system. Turn the steering from lock to lock a few times to bleed the system. Finally top up to the correct level with the engine off. Ensure that the hoses are connected to their correct unions on reassembly.

Dismantling:

Before starting dismantling, plug the inlet and outlet connections and thoroughly clean the outside of the unit.

1 Remove the tie rods (see **Section 10:13**). The inner ball joints cannot be serviced and if they are worn they must be replaced using a new complete tie rod and ball joint.
2 Slacken the rack adjusting screw locknut and remove the adjusting screw, spring and plunger.
3 Mark the position of the pinion housing in relation to the rack housing. Remove the three nuts and withdraw the housing, noting the position of the pinch bolt slot. The valve and pinion housing assembly must be renewed if defective. Examination of the parts will be dealt with separately.

Valve and pinion assembly:

1 Drift out the valve and pinion assembly from the housing, using a soft-nosed drift. The top and back up seals can be renewed after removing the circlip.
2 Examine the Teflon rings. They should be free in their grooves and the outer surface should be unscratched and unmarked. Check that there is no relative movement at the trim pin between the valve sleeve and shaft, and that there is no free movement between the input and output shafts. Examine the housing bore for signs of wear. Examine the needle roller bearings for signs of wear. If any defects are found the complete assembly must be renewed.
3 The pipe union seats can be renewed if they are worn or damaged. Tap a suitable thread in the seat. Fit a nut onto a setscrew and screw these into the pipe seat, with a washer between the nut and housing. Screw down the nut to withdraw the seating. A new seating is fitted by carefully tapping it into position, using a soft-nosed drift.
4 Reassemble the parts in the reverse order of dismantling.

The rack assembly:

1 **Mark the end cap so that it will be replaced in the same relative position on the housing.** Unscrew the ring nut and remove the end cap.
2 Remove the union from the rack tube and push out the centre seal housing from the pinion housing end of the tube. Remove the outer circlip and withdraw the piston. Renew the piston and ring if either are worn or scored. Renew the O-ring on the shaft and replace the piston, securing it with the circlip. If the end float between the piston and circlips is greater than .010 inch (.254 mm) add extra shims to bring the end float within limits. **Check that the piston rotates freely between the circlips.**

3 Remove the old O-rings and seal from the centre seal housing and fit new ones in their place. Insert the housing back into the tube, with the lips of the seals pointing inwards. Align the holes in the seal housing with that in the tube and secure the housing in place with the union. Insert the rack back into the housing, **taking great care not to damage the oil seal by the teeth on the rack.**
4 Renew the oil seal and O-ring in the end cap. Examine the Clevite bush and if it is worn or damaged renew it. **It is essential that the Clevite bush is pressed in using a snug fitting stepped mandrel to prevent the new bush collapsing.** Refit the end cap so that the originally made marks align. Make sure that the end cap does not turn when tightening the ring nut.

Reassembly:

New seals and gaskets should be used throughout, and these are obtainable in a complete seal kit.

1 Fit the new gasket over the three studs on the rack housing, and refit the valve and pinion housing so that it is replaced in the original position. When engaging the pinion into the rack teeth make sure that the pinch bolt slot is also in its original position. Note that there is a spiral on the pinion and this must be allowed for so that the parts are correct when refitted, not before reassembly.
2 Refit the ball joints and tie rods as described in **Section 10:13**. Coat both the ballhousings with 2 oz (56.7 grammes) of grease and refit the bellows. Both tie rods should be 8.75 inches between ball joint centres.
3 Set the rack play adjusting plunger and screw as described in **Section 10:13**. Replace the grease nipple and inject 1 oz (28.35 grammes) of grease into the unit. **Do not over-lubricate otherwise the air transfer pipe may become blocked.**
4 The wheel alignment must be checked after the steering unit has been refitted to the car (see **Section 10:13**).

10:15 Fault diagnosis

This section is only applicable to Part III of this Chapter but it should be used in conjunction with the Fault Diagnosis for Parts I and II (see **Section 10:10**).

(a) Noisy operation

1 Air in the system
2 Loose belt (especially noticeable when parking or turning the wheels when stationary)
3 Defective pump
4 Hoses rubbing on body or frame
5 Rack rattle (most noticeable on rough surfaces)
6 Inner ball joint knock (occurs when changing direction on steering)

(b) High steering effort

1 Check 1, 2 and 3 in (a)
2 Low oil level
3 Internal leaks in steering unit
4 Blocked or damaged connecting hoses

(c) Steering effort too light

1 Defective pinion and valve assembly (broken torque shaft or worn torsion dowel pins)

(d) Steering veers

1 Defective pinion and valve assembly (can also cause a kick to the steering when the engine is started)

(e) Excessive fluid loss

1 Defective hoses
2 Hose connections not properly tightened
3 Gasket on reservoir cover damaged
4 Defective pump unit (seals on shaft failed)
5 Damaged seals or gaskets on steering unit
6 Defective or damaged pipe union seals on steering unit

CHAPTER 11

THE BRAKING SYSTEM

11:1 Description

Disc brakes are fitted to operate on all four road wheels. The front disc brakes are mounted directly by the wheel, the caliper being mounted on the suspension stub axle carrier and the disc fixed to rotate with the wheel hub. The rear disc brakes are mounted inboard on either side of the differential unit of the rear axle, and act on the rear wheels through the drive shafts.

All four disc brakes are hydraulically operated, pressure being generated in a master cylinder when the brake pedal is depressed. On all models the hydraulic system is so arranged that the front brakes are operated independently from the rear brakes and in spite of hydraulic failure in one half, this will still ensure that the other half of the system operates at its full efficiency.

The handbrake operates on the rear brake discs but uses pads and mechanism separate from the hydraulically operated brake. The linkage between the handbrake lever and mechanism on the rear brakes is mechanical and cable operated.

Wear is automatically taken up on all the hydraulically operated disc brakes and no adjustment points are provided. The brake pads are easily renewable, and can be inspected for wear without removal. It is essential that brake pad wear is checked regularly otherwise brake efficiency will be impaired if the pads wear to less than their minimum thickness. If they are allowed to wear excessively the brakes may become damaged.

A vacuum operated servo is fitted to augment the pedal pressure on all models covered by this manual. If the vacuum fails or the unit itself fails, it is so designed that the brakes are still operated by the brake pedal though a higher pressure will be required on the brake pedal to produce retardation.

Though the basic principles are the same on all models, the actual construction and design varies considerably. Some information is applicable to different models but this Chapter has been divided into three parts to cover the three variants. The Fault Diagnosis Section at the end of this Chapter covers all three parts, and so does the Routine Maintenance Section which follows.

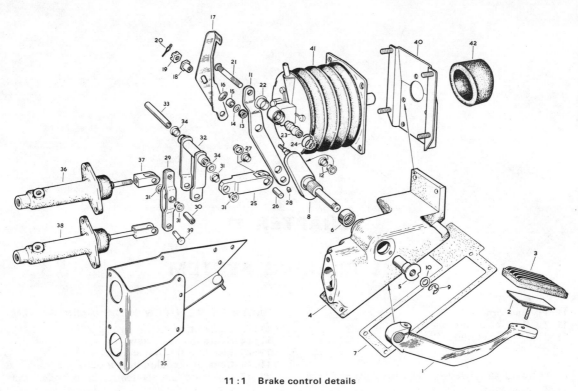

11 : 1   Brake control details

Key to Fig 11 : 1   1 Brake pedal   2 Steel pad   3 Rubber pad   4 Pedal housing   5 Bush   6 Bearing   7 Gasket
8 Pedal shaft and pin   9 Circlip   10 Washer   11 Power lever   12 Nylon bush   13 Rubber buffer   14 Plain washer
15 Spacing collar   16 Belleville washer   17 Operating lever   18 Eccentric barrel nut   19 Slotted nut   20 Splitpin (Return
spring on later models)   21 Serrated pin   22 Nylon bush   23 Eccentric bush   24 Spring   25 Fork end   26 Joint pin
27 Nylon bush   28 Grub screw   29 Balance link   30 Spacing tube   31 Nylon bush   32 Pivot bracket   33 Sleeve
34 Nylon bush   35 Mounting bracket   36 Rear brake master cylinder   37 Fork end   38 Front brake master cylinder
39 Clevis pin   40 Mounting bracket   41 Servo assembly   42 Rubber seal

11 : 2 Routine maintenance

1 At regular intervals check the fluid level in the two
brake reservoirs. The reservoirs are translucent and
the level can be checked without removing the top.
If the fluid is below the 'Fluid Level' mark on the
reservoir, wipe the top free from dirt and remove the
cap. Top up to the level mark with the correct grade
of fluid and replace the cap. The clutch reservoir is
easily identifiable from the three reservoirs as it is
the one not fitted with a level warning switch. A slow
steady fall in the fluid level is to be expected as the
brake pads wear, but any rapid or sudden fall must
be investigated immediately as it indicates a leak in
the system.

   **Use Castrol/Girling Crimson Clutch and
   Brake Fluid conforming to specifications
   SAE.J1703A or SAE.70.R3.** Other fluids may be
   used provided they also conform to the correct
   specification. **Fluids not conforming to this
   specification are dangerous to use as they can
   attack the seals and lead to complete brake
   failure.**

2 All the brake pads should be inspected at intervals not
exceeding 6000 miles, and renewed if they are worn
down to the minimum thickness specified.

3 3.8 litre models only. At 2500 mile intervals adjust
the handbrake pads on early models, and lubricate
the brake pedal bearing with engine oil.

11 : 3 Disconnecting a flexible hose

   Never try to release a flexible hose by turning the ends
with a spanner. The correct procedure is as follows:

   Unscrew the metal pipeline union nut from its connection with the hose. Hold the adjacent hexagon on the
hose with a spanner and use another spanner to release
the locknut which secures the hose to the bracket. The
hose can now be removed, without twisting the flexible
part, by using a spanner on the hexagon at the other end.

   Replace a flexible hose in the reverse order of removal,
ensuring that the flexible portion is not twisted or strained.

PART I THE 3.8 LITRE MODEL BRAKING SYSTEM

11 : 4 Description

   The mounting for the brake pedal, servo unit and
master cylinders is shown in **FIG 11 : 1**. The parts of the
servo unit are shown in **FIG 11 : 2**. When the brake pedal
is depressed the linkage moves the balance link to press
in the pushrods of both master cylinders 36 and 38 to
generate pressure in them. The movement also opens

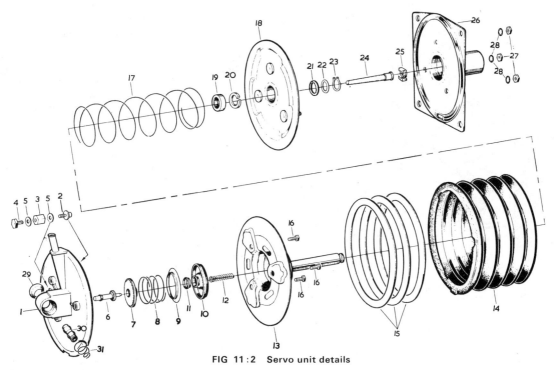

FIG 11:2 Servo unit details

Key to Fig 11:2   1 Valve housing   2 Nipple   3 Adaptor   4 Plug   5 Gasket   6 Air valve   7 Vacuum valve
8 Return spring   9 Balancing washer   10 Balancing diaphragm   11 Retainer   12 Control spring   13 Retainer sleeve
14 Bellows   15 Support ring   16 Bolt   17 Main return spring   18 Mounting hub   19 Seal   20 Guide sleeve
21 Rubber buffer   22 Stop washer   23 Circlip   24 Air filter   25 Baffle   26 Mounting plate   27 Nut   28 Lockwasher
29 Nylon bush   30 Eccentric bush   31 Spring

the vacuum valve and closes the air valve in the servo unit to allow vacuum from a reservoir to pass into the bellows of the servo unit. The vacuum contracts the bellows until a point of balance, dependent on the pressure required, is set up and the servo unit ceases to contract. The pressure from the servo unit is also applied to the brake cylinders through the linkage. The augmented hydraulic pressure from the master cylinders is then fed through the system of pipelines and flexible hoses to operate the pistons in the disc brake calipers.

11:5 Renewing friction pads

The friction pads must be renewed when the friction material has worn to less than $\frac{1}{4}$ inch (7 mm). The rear brake pads are accessible from underneath the car when it is on a ramp. The adjustment for the brakes is done automatically by a special bush sliding along a retractor pin as the lining wears. The lining is drawn back by a spring when the brake pressure is released to ensure that there is clearance between the lining and the disc.

Remove the nut, bolt and retaining plate, as shown in **FIG 11:3**. Use a hooked tool or a pair of long-nosed pliers to grip the protruding tag on the pad and withdraw it from the caliper. Similarly remove the other pad. The piston must now be pressed in so that the adjuster is reset and the bush travels back up the pin. Use tool Part No. 7840, as shown in **FIG 11:4**, to press the piston back in.

The convex side of the tool faces against the piston and the spigot on the tool locates in the retaining plate bolt hole. The level in the reservoir will rise during this operation and it is advisable to syphon half of it out of the reservoir to prevent it overflowing and damaging paintwork.

Clean out the recess for the pad and refit the pad in the reverse order of removal. Pump the brake pedal several times hard to adjust the brake and then top up the level in the reservoir to the correct level.

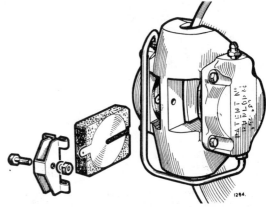

FIG 11:3 Friction pad removal

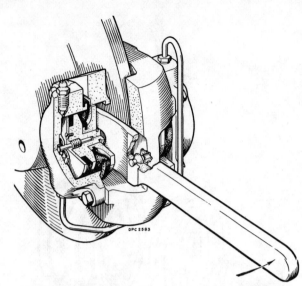

FIG 11:4 Resetting the pistons using special tool No. 7840. Note the sectional view of the early type of piston assembly

11:6 Disc brake description

The details of the front brakes are shown in **FIG 11:5**, and those of the rear brake in **FIG 11:6**.

The handbrake mechanism is removed from the rear caliper by freeing the tabwasher 27 and unscrewing the two pivot bolts 27. The details of the handbrake mechanism will be dealt with in **Section 11:12**.

Once the handbrake assembly has been removed the front and rear brake calipers are serviced in exactly the same manner. Earlier types of brakes are fitted with a spring washer to provide the clearance between the lining and disc, while later types of brakes use a modified adjuster mechanism which has a coil spring to provide the necessary clearance. The later type of brake may be identified by the letter C cast into the body by the inlet hole.

11:7 Removing a front brake

The removal of both the brake caliper and the brake disc has been covered in **Chapter 9, Section 9:3**.

The replacement has also been covered in this section but note the following points:

1 If the bridge pipe 12 has been removed, it must be refitted so that the hairpin bend is furthest away from

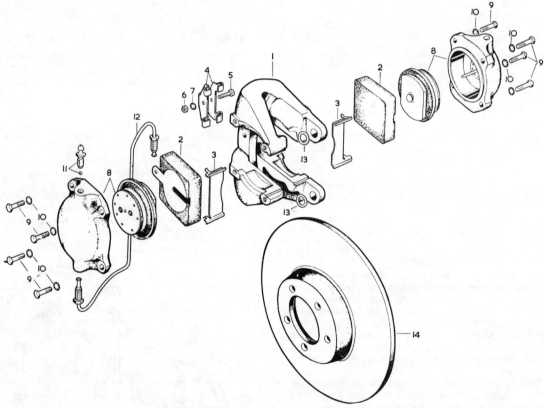

FIG 11:5 Front brake details

Key to Fig 11:5   1 Caliper body   2 Friction pad   3 Support plate   4 Retaining plate   5 Bolt   6 Nut
7 Lockwasher   8 Piston and cylinder   9 Bolt   10 Lockwasher   11 Bleed screw and ball   12 Bridge pipe
13 Shim   14 Disc

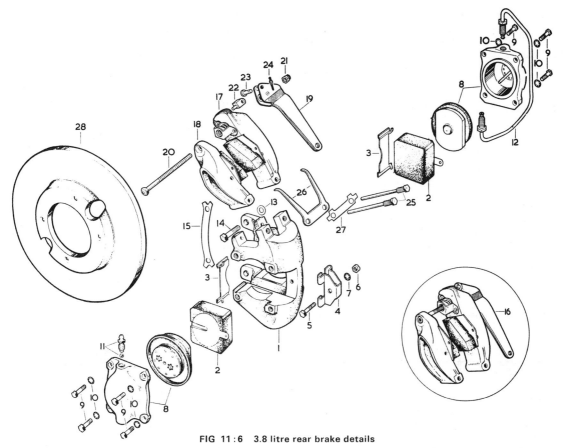

FIG 11:6   3.8 litre rear brake details

Key to Fig 11:6   1 Caliper body   2 Friction pad   3 Support plate   4 Retaining plate   5 Bolt   6 Nut
7 Lockwasher   8 Piston and cylinder   9 Bolt   10 Lockwasher   11 Bleed screw and ball   12 Bridge pipe   13 Shim
14 Setscrew   15 Tabwasher   16 Handbrake assembly   17 Inner pad carrier   18 Outer pad carrier   19 Operating lever
20 Bolt   21 Self-locking nut   22 Pivot seat   23 Clevis pin   24 Splitpin   25 Pivot bolt   26 Retractor plate
27 Tabwasher   28 Disc

the road wheel. The pipe is fitted with a rubber sleeve marked 'Inner Top'.

2 When the wheel hub and brake have been refitted with the correct end float refit the brake caliper, with the shims 13 originally fitted. Use feeler gauges to measure the gap between the caliper and the brake disc on both sides of the disc and at both top and bottom. If the dimensions vary by more than .010 inch (.25 mm) shims 13 must be fitted so as to centralize the caliper about the brake disc.

11:8 Removing a rear brake

The rear suspension assembly must be removed from the car for this operation (see **Chapter 8, Section 8:3**).

1 Invert the suspension and remove the damper and spring assemblies (see **Chapter 8, Section 8:5**).

2 Remove the four steel-type locknuts securing the halfshaft inner universal joint and brake disc to the driving flange on the differential unit. Withdraw the halfshaft from the bolts and collect the camber

shims, storing them safely for reassembly. Similarly disconnect the other halfshaft.

3 Free the handbrake assemblies from the calipers (see **Section 11:6**) and remove them through the rear aperture on the suspension crossmember.

4 Remove the friction pads (see **Section 11:5**). Disconnect the hydraulic pipes from the caliper inlets. Free the locking on the caliper securing bolts and remove the bolts through the access holes in the brake disc. Carefully note the number and position of the shims 13. Withdraw the calipers through the aperture in the front of the crossmember.

5 Tap back as far as possible the bolts that secure the halfshaft to the driving flange. Lift the halfshaft, hub carrier and lower wishbone as high as possible and remove the brake disc from the four bolts.

6 Refitting the brake caliper and disc is the reversal of the removal procedure. The shims 13 should be replaced in their original positions and then the centralizing of the caliper about the disc should be checked, and adjusted if necessary, in the same manner as the front brake caliper (see **Section 11:7**).

Disc run-out :

All the brake discs, including the front brakes, should be checked by mounting a DTI so that the plunger rests vertically on the face of the disc. If run-out exceeds the maximum allowed of .006 inch (.15 mm) the components should be checked for damage.

11 : 9 Servicing a brake caliper
Early type :

1 Remove the caliper from the car and remove the brake pads 2. Remove the bridge pipe 12 connecting the cylinders.
2 Remove the cylinder assemblies 8 from the body 1 by unscrewing the bolts 9. Thoroughly clean the outside of all the parts before dismantling any further.
3 Connect each cylinder in turn to the brake pipe on the car. Apply pressure to the brake pedal and carefully blow out the piston from the cylinder. Do the outer assembly first and then transfer the bleed screw and ball 11 to the inner assembly to block the outlet.
4 Remove the screws securing the backing plate to the piston and take off the plate and piston seal and withdraw the retractor bush. Use a sharp knife to cut away the dust cover. Lay the assembly into a bush or piece of tubing so that the outer edge of the assembly rests on the bush. Press on the spigot of the piston proper to separate the parts. To assist in identification of the parts a sectioned view of the piston assembly is shown in **FIG 11 : 4**.
5 Carefully fit into place a new dust seal and press the two halves of the piston assembly together. Wet a new piston seal with hydraulic fluid and place it into position on the piston. Insert the retractor bush and replace the backing plate. Peen the screws after the backing plate has been secured.
6 Make sure that the piston and cylinder bore are perfectly clean, with no signs of damage or scoring. Smear the cylinder bore with clean hydraulic fluid. Insert the piston assembly into the cylinder bore so that the retractor pin enters the bush. Taking great care, press the piston back into the cylinder bore. If care is not taken the piston sealing ring will either be displaced, cut or damaged, in which case a new sealing ring must be fitted.
7 Engage the outer lip of the dust seal in its groove. Put the two support plates 3 into position and refit the cylinder assemblies to the caliper body 1. Replace the bridge pipe 12 so that the hairpin bend is furthest away from the road wheel.
8 Replace the caliper on the car, refit the brake pads and bleed the brakes.

Later types :

The later type of caliper, identifiable by the letter C on the castings, differs from the earlier type in that the piston assembly is one piece and cannot be dismantled.

The caliper is serviced in exactly the same manner as the earlier type except for operations 4 and 5. In this case the seal and dust cover must be removed using a small blunt screwdriver. Wet both the seal and the inner lip of the dust cover with clean hydraulic fluid and use only the fingers to refit them to the piston, working them both around so that they seat squarely.

11 : 10 Bleeding the brakes

This operation must be carried out whenever a braking system has been dismantled, or the level in the reservoir has fallen so low that air has been drawn into a master cylinder. If air is left in the system the brake pedal will have a spongy feel.

The first fluid that is bled through the system must always be discarded. Later fluid should be discarded also but if it is absolutely clean it may be stored in a sealed container for future use. **Never return fluid that has just been bled back to the reservoir.** It should be allowed to stand in a sealed container for at least 24 hours to allow it to de-aerate.

Fluid will be continuously used throughout the bleeding operation and if the reservoir is not kept topped up the level will fall so low that it will allow air to enter the system once again. Before starting bleeding operations wipe the top of the reservoir, remove the cap and fill it right up with fresh fluid. It should be noted that the upper master cylinder is for the rear brakes and the reservoir connected to this is also for the rear brakes.

As the front and rear brakes are hydraulically independent only the system that has been dismantled needs to be bled.

1 Attach a length of small-bore plastic or rubber hose to the bleed nipple on the brake furthest from the master cylinder. Immerse the free end of the hose in a little clean brake fluid contained in a glass container.
2 Open the bleed nipple by about a half-turn, and have a second operator slowly pump the brake pedal through its full range of movement. Continue pumping until the fluid coming out of the hose is free of all air bubbles. Have the second operator hold the brake pedal down in the depressed position and tighten the bleed nipple. Similarly bleed the other nipple.
3 If difficulty is experienced in removing all the air, or the pedal still feels spongy after bleeding, first bleed the other half of the system. If the sponginess is still present change the method of bleeding. Tighten the bleed nipple every time the brake pedal is at the bottom of its stroke, allow the pedal to return and then apply slight pressure before re-opening the bleed nipple.
4 Top up the reservoirs to the correct level. Have the second operator apply heavy pressure to the brake pedal and check the system and all connections for leaks.

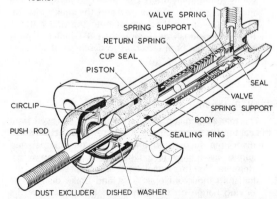

FIG 11 : 7 Sectioned view of 3.8 litre master cylinder

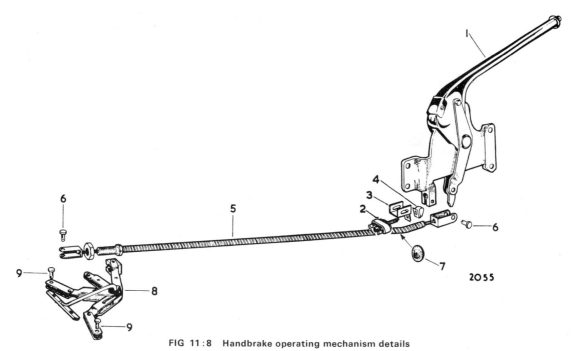

FIG 11:8 Handbrake operating mechanism details

Key to Fig 11:8   1 Handbrake lever assembly   2 Warning light switch   3 Mounting bracket   4 Spring striker
5 Handbrake cable   6 Clevis pin   7 Grommet   8 Compensator linkage   9 Clevis pin

11:11 The master cylinders

The mounting points for the master cylinders are shown in **FIG 11:1**. It should be noted that only the top cylinder 36 is fitted with an adjustable pushrod. A sectioned view of a master cylinder is shown in **FIG 11:7**.

When the brake pedal is depressed, the linkage presses the plunger assembly down the bore of the cylinder and the fluid is forced out of the side outlet to operate the brakes. The valve connecting the cylinder to the reservoir is closed immediately by the pressure of the valve spring. The master cylinders are of exactly the same type as the clutch master cylinder and are serviced in exactly the same manner. Refer to **Chapter 5, Section 5:3** for instructions on servicing.

Removal:

1 Syphon the fluid out of the reservoirs. Unscrew and withdraw all the pipe unions from the ends of the master cylinders, taking care to note the correct connections and labelling the pipes if necessary.
2 Remove the two bolts and nuts securing the top master cylinder 36 to the mounting bracket 35. Pull out the master cylinder and slacken the locknut securing the fork end 37. Unscrew the master cylinder pushrod from the fork end to free the top master cylinder.
3 Remove the nuts and bolts securing the bottom master cylinder 38 to the mounting bracket. Pull out the master cylinder until the clevis pin 39 is accessible and remove the clevis pin to free the master cylinder.

Replacement:

The master cylinders are replaced in the reverse order of removal. The free travel on the pushrods must be correctly set. Screw in the pushrod until the distance which the balance lever 29 moves when it is first pulled firmly towards the top master cylinder and then pushed away is $\frac{1}{16}$ inch (1.6 mm). Tighten the locknut on the top master cylinder to hold the pushrod in this position.

11:12 The handbrake

The handbrake cable assembly is shown in **FIG 11:8**. Early models are fitted with a handbrake mechanism which must be adjusted at regular intervals, to compensate for pad wear. Roll back the carpet and remove the cover from over the rear axle. Place a .004 inch (.10 mm) feeler gauge between a pad and the disc on each brake and turn the adjusting bolt, using the special key provided in the tool kit, until the pad just grips the feeler gauge. The method is shown in **FIG 11:9**. Remove the feeler gauge and replace the cover and carpet.

If the handbrake lever still has excessive travel after the brakes have been adjusted then adjust the cable. Screw in the adjuster on each brake until the pads are firmly in contact with the discs, making sure that the handbrake lever is fully off. Slacken the locknut on the handbrake cable, arrowed in **FIG 11:10**, and screw in the adjuster until all the slack is removed from the cable. Only remove slack but do not tension the cable. Reset the parking brake pads to the correct clearance of .040 inch.

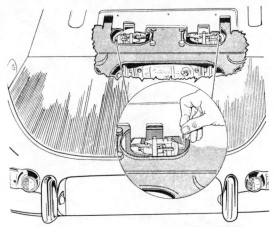

FIG 11:9 Early type handbrake adjustment

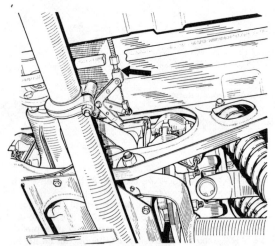

FIG 11:10 Handbrake cable adjustment

Renewing early type pads:

Free the compensator arm from the operating lever and, referring to **FIG 11:6**, remove the two pivot pins 25 to free the handbrake mechanism 16 and then lift them out from the rear of the suspension. Slacken the nuts on the outside of the carriers 17 and 18, and insert a hooked tool through the holes in the pads and withdraw the pads using this. Refit the new pads, tighten the nuts holding the pad securing bolts in place and refit the assembly back to the brake caliper. The adjusting bolt 20 will have to be slackened off to allow the new pads to pass over the brake disc. Adjust the pads as described earlier.

Later self-adjusting handbrakes:

The details of the later type are shown in **FIG 11:11**. The mechanism works normally in the same manner as the non-adjustable type. When the operating lever A is pulled away from the carrier B the action pulls together both carriers and clamps the friction pads F against the brake disc. The pawl C rides on the same tooth of the

ratchet nut D. When the wear on the pads becomes excessive the additional movement raises the pawl C onto the next tooth of the ratchet nut D and as the brakes are released the ratchet nut is turned by the pawl. The nut then screws itself along the adjusting bolt E and automatically resets the correct clearance.

The mechanism is removed and replaced from the rear calipers in exactly the same manner as the earlier type, and the friction pads are also renewed in a similar manner.

Before refitting the assembly when new pads have been fitted, remove the splitpin which locks the head of the adjusting bolt E and unscrew the bolt to open the clearance between the pads F. The gap between the pads should be set at $\frac{7}{16}$ inch (11.1 mm) so that when the caliper is refitted there will be a clearance of $\frac{1}{16}$ inch (1.6 mm) between the pads and the brake disc. Fit a new splitpin to lock the adjusting bolt and then refit the assembly to the brake caliper. Put on and release the handbrake lever several times until the ratchet nut stops 'clicking over' and the correct clearance is set.

Handbrake cable adjustment (later models):

Leave the handbrake lever in the fully off position. From underneath the car slacken the locknut at the rear of the cable and turn the adjuster until the operating levers on both handbrake assemblies just start to move. Simultaneously press both operating levers towards the calipers, opening the handbrakes to their widest, and check that there is no appreciable movement of the compensator mechanism. A small amount of movement is to be expected, but any larger amount shows that the handbrake cable is too tight and needs to be slackened off. **Do not attempt to remove all the slack from the cable.** When correctly adjusted, tighten the locknut securing the adjuster.

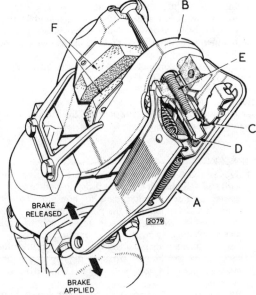

FIG 11:11 3.8 litre self-adjusting handbrake mechanism
Key to Fig 11:11   **A** Operating lever
B Friction pad carrier   **C** Pawl   **D** Ratchet nut
E Adjuster bolt   **F** Friction pads

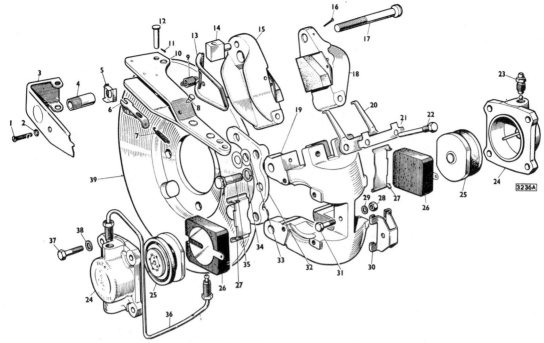

FIG 11:12   4.2 litre rear brake details

Key to Fig 11:12   1 Bolt   2 Shakeproof washer   3 Rear protection cover assembly   4 Adjusting nut
5 Friction spring   6 Pawl assembly   7 Tension spring   8 Anchor pin   9 Return spring   10 Operating lever   11 Splitpin
12 Hinge pin   13 Front protection cover assembly   14 Pivot seat   15 Inner pad carrier   16 Splitpin   17 Bolt
18 Outer pad carrier   19 Rear caliper   20 Retraction plate   21 Tabwasher   22 Bolt   23 Bleed screw and ball assembly
24 Brake cylinder   25 Piston   26 Friction pad   27 Support plate   28 Nut   29 Lockwasher   30 Retaining plate   31 Bolt
32 Locking plate   33 Shim   34 Spring washer   35 Setscrew   36 Bridge pipe   37 Bolt   38 Lockwasher   39 Disc

PART II THE 4.2 LITRE MODEL BRAKING SYSTEM

11:13 Description

The dual-line braking system has a master cylinder operated directly from the brake pedal. This is connected both hydraulically and pneumatically to a tandem slave cylinder which is in conjunction with a vacuum-operated servo. The tandem slave cylinder is connected to the wheel brakes. This system is described more fully in the next section.

The front brakes are of a similar type to the front brakes fitted to the later models of the 3.8 litre, and they are removed, serviced and replaced in exactly the same manner.

The rear brakes, the details of which are shown in **FIG 11:12**, are similar enough to the rear brakes fitted to the later 3.8 litre to be serviced in the same manner.

11:14 Hydraulic operation

A schematic diagram of the brake hydraulics is shown in **FIG 11:13**. The figure shows the layout for the later model. The earlier models differ only in that the pipeline J to the rear brakes is connected to the outlet B on the tandem master cylinder, and the pipeline K to the front brakes is connected to the outlet D, thus reversing their positions.

The brake pedal is connected to the pushrod on the master cylinder N. When the pedal is depressed the pushrod moves the plunger down the bore increasing the pressure in the chamber of the master cylinder, and this pressure is fed by the pipe to the primary chamber A in the tandem slave cylinder L. The pressure in the master cylinder N at the same time moves the secondary piston which closes the diaphragm G, isolating the chamber F from the chamber E in the vacuum cylinder M. Further movement of the secondary piston partially opens the spool I which allows atmospheric pressure to pass through the filter H and into the chamber F of the vacuum cylinder M. The diaphragm in the vacuum cylinder M is drawn by the vacuum towards the tandem slave cylinder L. The combined pressures, from the vacuum cylinder and the hydraulic pressure in the primary chamber A, combine to press the plunger of the tandem slave cylinder down the bore. Pressure builds up in the fluid in front of this and is fed out of the outlet B to operate the front brakes (rear brakes on earlier models). At the same time this pressure moves the plunger of the tandem slave cylinder down the bore and the pressure build-up in front of this is fed to the rear brakes (front brakes on earlier models) through the outlet D.

When the servo operates, the diaphragm G will have vacuum on one side and atmospheric pressure on the front side. This pressure differential will move the diaphragm back against the pressure of the secondary piston

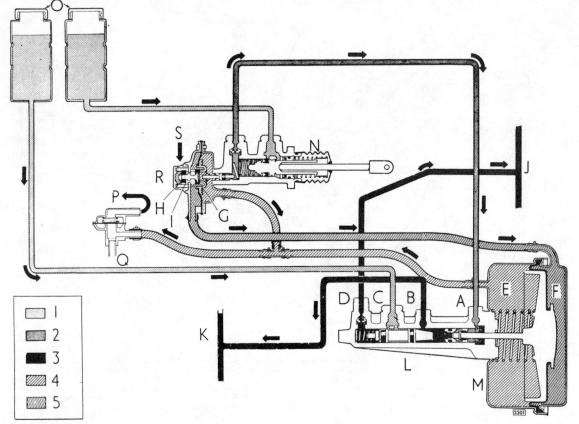

FIG 11:13 Dual-line servo braking system (Later cars). Earlier cars are the same but J connects to B and K connects to D

Key to Fig 11:13   1 Fluid at feed pressure   2 Fluid at master cylinder delivery pressure   3 Fluid at system delivery pressure
4 Vacuum   5 Air at atmospheric pressure   A Primary chamber, slave cylinder   B Outlet port   C Inlet port, secondary piston
D Outlet port   E Vacuum   F Air pressure   G Diaphragm   H Filter   I Air control   J To rear brakes   K To front brakes
L Tandem slave cylinder   M Vacuum cylinder   N Master cylinder   O Fluid reservoirs   P To manifold   Q To reservoir
R Reaction valve   S Atmospheric pressure

in the master cylinder N, and at the point of balance the spool I will shut to cut off further vacuum. If further pressure is then exerted on the brake pedal, the pressure in the chamber of the master cylinder will rise correspondingly and the increase in pressure will again move the spool I to open and increase the vacuum. Up to its maximum therefore, the servo will exert a pressure proportional to the brake pedal pressure.

When the brake pedal is released the pressure in the chamber of the master cylinder N is also released. The secondary piston then returns allowing the diaphragm to interconnect the chambers E and F so the vacuum cylinder M ceases to exert pressure, and with no hydraulic pressure either the plunger of the tandem slave cylinder L returns to release the brakes.

The system is so designed that individual component failure still allows the brake pedal to be effective. A plate is fitted into the master cylinder N so that, if the hydraulic part of the circuit between it and the tandem slave cylinder fails completely, the plunger will mechanically operate the secondary piston in the reaction valve R. The valve

will then function to operate the vacuum cylinder M and apply the brakes by this alone. Conversely a leak in the pipes of the pneumatic circuit, or a loss of vacuum, will lose the assistance of the vacuum chamber but the brakes will be applied by hydraulic pressure alone. If the brakes served by the outlet D leak, then the secondary plunger will move down until the return spring is coil bound and the pressure will then rise normally through the outlet B. If the B circuit leaks or fails the plunger will move down until it contacts the secondary plunger mechanically and the two together will then operate the other half of the circuit.

11:15 Bleeding the brakes

Make sure that both reservoirs are filled right up with clean fresh hydraulic fluid and see that they are kept constantly topped up. Discard all dirty fluid, and only re-use clean fluid after it has been left to stand in a sealed container for 24 hours.

The following instructions refer to bleeding later model cars. On earlier models the connections at the tandem

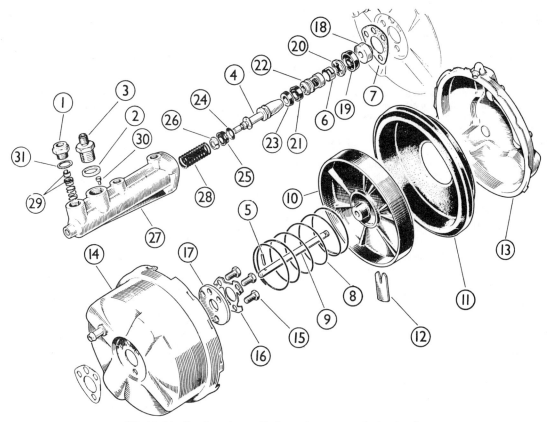

FIG 11:14 Tandem slave cylinder and vacuum cylinder details

Key to Fig 11:14   1 Outlet connection   2 Gasket   3 Inlet connection   4 Piston   5 Pin   6 Retaining clip
7 Gasket   8 Spring   9 Pushrod   10 Diaphragm support   11 Diaphragm   12 Key   13 Cover   14 Vacuum cylinder shell
15 Screw   16 Locking plate   17 Abutment plate   18 Bearing   19 Seal   20 Spacer   21 Cup   22 Piston   23 Cup
24 Piston washer   25 Seal   26 Retainer   27 Slave cylinder body   28 Spring   29 Trap valve   30 Stop pin   31 Gasket

slave cylinder are reversed (check using **FIG 11:13** and tracing the actual connections on the car). If it is an earlier model the front brakes should be bled first following the instructions given for the rear brakes, and the rear brakes then bled according to the instructions for the front brakes.

1 Attach a length of small-bore plastic or rubber tube to each of the bleed nipples on the rear brakes, and immerse the free ends in glass containers.

2 Open the bleed nipples on the rear brakes at least one full turn and allow the fluid to run through on its own. If the fluid is slow to start or run, assist it with a few very slow light strokes of the brake pedal. Release the pedal slowly as well as pressing it down slowly.

3 Allow the fluid to run through for a few minutes, or until it is fairly bubble free. Close both bleed nipples and remove one of the bleed tubes and containers.

4 Fit the bleed tube to the nipple on the front brake furthest from the master cylinder. Open the bleed nipple half a turn and have a second operator pump the brake pedal with steady full strokes. When air bubbles stop coming out of the tube and only clean fluid is ejected, have the brake pedal held down and

close the bleed nipple. Similarly bleed the other front brake.

5 Refit the bleed tube to the rear brake bleed nipple. Open both bleed nipples and allow the fluid to run through until it is clear of bubbles. Close the bleed nipples and remove the bleed tubes.

If the master cylinder has been removed, it is suggested that, once it has been replaced and the reservoirs filled, the banjo bolt on the inlet should be slackened until fluid seeps out. Retighten the banjo bolt immediately and use rags to absorb the seepage.

11:16 General servicing instructions

The individual components will be dealt with in separate sections, but certain factors apply to all of them.

Repair kits are available separately for each of the hydraulic cylinders and the reaction valve. These kits contain the complete set of new seals required to service the unit, and it is advisable to obtain the appropriate kit before starting dismantling operations.

After the parts have been dismantled remove the old seals and discard them. A blunt small screwdriver can be used for this, but take great care not to damage the part from which the seal is being removed.

Wash all the parts in clean methylated spirits and use only non-fluffy cloth to dry them with. **Cleanliness is essential.** Lay the clean parts on clean paper or cloth to ensure that they stay dirt free. Dip all the internal parts into clean hydraulic fluid as they are being assembled and fit them wet. Use only the fingers to replace new seals, and work them around to make sure that the seals are squarely and properly fitted. Examine the bores of cylinders and the working faces of pistons. Scores, wear, pitting or corrosion will necessitate the fitting of a new assembly

Check all hoses and pipelines for leaks. Small hydraulic leaks are most easily found if hard pressure is applied to the brake pedal whilst the pipelines are being examined.

11:17 Servicing the tandem slave cylinder and vacuum cylinder

Removal:

1 Remove the floor recess plate from inside on the left-hand side of the car and take off the three nuts securing the vacuum cylinder to the bulkhead. Syphon the fluid out of the reservoirs and disconnect the four brake pipe unions and two vacuum hoses from the assembly. Label the pipes and hoses to ensure that they will be reconnected correctly.
2 Disconnect and remove the battery. Take out the carrier bracket for the battery tray and unscrew the bolt which holds the tandem slave cylinder to its mounting bracket.
3 The assembly can now be lifted out.

The assembly is refitted in the reverse order of removal, but the system will have to be bled.

Dismantling the vacuum cylinder:

The details of the parts are shown in **FIG 11:14**.

1 Mount the cylinder shell 14 in a pair of shaped blocks held in a vice. Fit the cover removing tool (Churchill No. J.31) to the three studs on the cover 13 and turn the cover in an anticlockwise direction till the lugs are free and the cover can be removed.
2 Ease the diaphragm 11 off the support 10. Remove the assembly from its mountings in the vice. Holding the shell 14 by hand, press in the diaphragm support 10 and shake the key 12 loose. The support 10 and spring 8 can then be removed.
3 Free the tabs on the locking plate 16 and undo the three screws 15 to free the tandem slave cylinder from the shell 14. Collect the locking plate 16, abutment plate 17 and gasket 7.

Dismantling the tandem slave cylinder:

1 Gently pull on the pushrod 9 to withdraw the piston assembly with the bearing 18 and seal 19. Slide the bearing and seal off the pushrod. Slide back the clip 6 and push out the pin 5 to free the piston 22 from the pushrod. Discard the piston 22 and cup 21 as new parts are supplied in the kit.
2 Remove the adaptor 3 and copper gasket 2. Extract the stop pin 30. Removing the stop pin will be made easier if the secondary piston is gently pressed down the bore of the cylinder.

3 Carefully shake out the secondary piston assembly and the return spring 28. Remove the spring retainer 26 (a new item is supplied in the kit) from the piston 4 and then remove the seal 25 and washer 24.
4 If required, remove the adaptor 1 to free the trap valve assembly 29.

Reassembling the tandem slave cylinder:

1 Fit new seals 23 and 24 to the secondary piston 4 after the washer 24 has been fitted, convex side towards the piston. The seals must be fitted so that their lips face away from each other.
2 Press the spring retainer 26 onto the piston and fit onto it the return spring 28. Insert the assembly very carefully into the bore of the cylinder, using hydraulic fluid as a lubricant, and taking extra care not to bend back or damage the lips of the seal 25. Once in, press the assembly down the bore, using a pencil or similar object, until the drilled flange on the piston 4 is past the position of the stop pin 30. Hold the secondary piston assembly in place. Refit the stop pin 30 and hold it in place by screwing in adaptor 3 with a new copper gasket 2. The secondary plunger assembly will now be held in place.
3 Fit the pushrod 9 to the piston 22 and use a small screwdriver to compress the coil spring in the piston so that the pin 5 can be fitted to lock the parts together. The pin 5 must not pass through the coils of the spring, and the spring must be acting fully between the heel of the piston and the pin 5. Refit the retaining clip 6 and make sure it is fully seated and not standing proud from the piston. Refit the seal 21 so that its lips will face into the bore of the cylinder. Carefully, so as not to damage the seal 21, insert the piston assembly back into the bore of the cylinder. Slide down the pushrod and into the bore the spacer 20, seal 19 and bearing 18. Leave the bearing protruding slightly from the bore.

Reassembling the vacuum cylinder:

1 Refit the tandem slave cylinder to the shell 14 in the reverse order of removal. Tighten the three screws 15 to a torque of 150 to 170 lb in (1.7 to 1.9 kg m) before locking them with the tabs on the washers 16.
2 Replace the return spring 8 and diaphragm support 10, securing them in place with the key 12 which fits into a slot in the diaphragm support.
3 Liberally smear the outside edges of the diaphragm 11 with clean hydraulic fluid and stretch it into position over the diaphragm support 10. The bead on the inside of the diaphragm must fit snugly into the groove of the support and the diaphragm must fit so that it is smooth and wave free.
4 Refit the end cover 13 so that the pipe for the air hose is aligned with the row of unions on the tandem slave cylinder.

11:18 Servicing the master cylinder and reaction valve

The details of the parts are shown in **FIG 11:15**.

Removal:

Syphon the fluid out of the reservoirs. Disconnect the two hydraulic pipes from the master cylinder and the

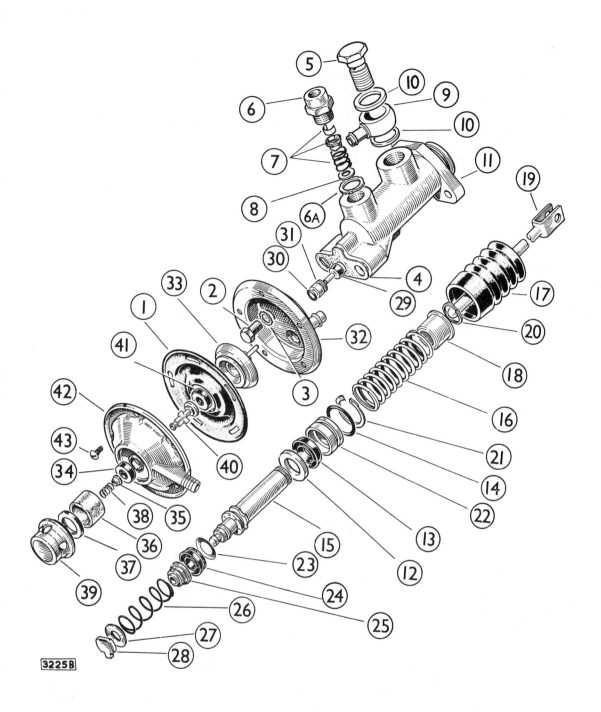

FIG 11:15   Master cylinder and reaction valve details

Key to Fig 11:15   1 Diaphragm   2 Screw   3 Shakeproof washer   4 Gasket   5 Bolt   6 Outlet adaptor
6A Copper gasket   7 Trap valve body   8 Washer   9 Banjo   10 Copper gasket   11 Body   12 Bearing   13 Secondary cup
14 Seal   15 Piston   16 Return spring   17 Rubber boot   18 Spring retainer   19 Pushrod   20 Spirolox circlip   21 Circlip
22 Bearing   23 Piston washer   24 Main cup   25 Retainer   26 Spring   27 Retainer   28 Lever   29 Seal   30 Seal
31 Piston   32 Valve housing   33 Diaphragm support   34 Valve rubber   35 Valve cap   36 Filter   37 Sorbo washer
38 Spring   39 Filter cover   40 Valve stem   41 Valve rubber   42 Valve cover   43 Screw

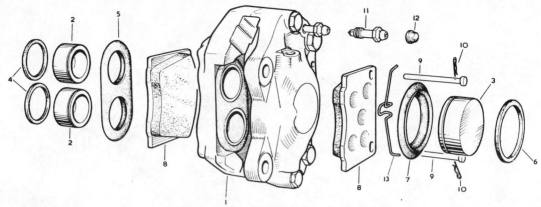

FIG 11 : 16   4.2 litre (Series 2) front brake details

Key to Fig 11 : 16   1 Caliper body   2 Outer piston   3 Inner piston   4 Seal   5 Dust seal   6 Seal   7 Dust seal
8 Friction pad   9 Retaining pin   10 Clip   11 Brake bleed nipple   12 Dust cap   13 Anti-chatter clip

hoses from the reaction valve. Withdraw the clevis pin securing the master cylinder pushrod to the brake pedal. Undo the securing bolts and on lefthand drive cars remove the assembly from the car. On righthand drive cars take off the top of the air cleaner and separate the reaction valve from the master cylinder so as to give sufficient room to remove the master cylinder.

Refit the parts in the reverse order of removal and bleed the brakes afterwards.

Dismantling:

1 Pull back the rubber boot 17 from the body 11. Hold the pushrod and press the spring retainer 18 into the bore of the cylinder to compress the return spring 16. Unwind the now exposed Spirolox circlip 20 to free the pushrod 19, spring retainer 18 and return spring 16.

2 Unscrew the union 6 and carefully remove the parts of the trap valve 7. Press the piston 15 down the bore of the cylinder and remove the circlip 21, taking great care not to damage the bore of the cylinder. Special circlip pliers part No. 7066 should be used to remove the circlip. Shake or tap out the internal parts of the cylinder. A little gentle air pressure at the outlet connection will assist in removing the parts.

3 Slide off the bearing 22, secondary seal 13 and bearing 12 from the piston 15. Hold the piston 15 head downwards against a bench and use a slim open-ended spanner behind the spring retainer 25 to press it off the piston. Discard the old retainer, which has probably been damaged in removal, as a new retainer is supplied in the kit. Slip off the seal 24 and washer 23.

4 Carefully pull off the filter cover 39 and remove the sorbo washer 37, filter 36 and spring 38. Undo the five screws 43 securing the cover 42 and remove the cover. Remove the valve rubber 34 by prising off the snap-on clip which secures it.

5 Withdraw the valve stem 40 and valve rubber 41, separating them after removal. Separate the diaphragm 1 from the support 33. Undo the two bolts 2 and remove the housing 32 from the body 11.

6 Insert a small blunt screwdriver through the outlet port and press out the piston 31 until it can be gripped and withdrawn, **using only the fingers.**

Reassembling:

1 Hold the body up at an angle of 25 deg. and slide the lever 28, tab foremost, down the bore so that the lever drops into position with the tab in the recess provided. Drop the pressed steel spring retainer 27 down the bore, followed by the return spring 26. Check that the lever 28 is still in position and adjust it if required.

2 Fit the washer 23, convex side first, to the piston 15 and then fit a new seal 24 and retainer 25. The lips of the seal 24 must face into the bore of the cylinder on reassembly. Very carefully, taking great care not to damage the lips of the seal, fit the piston assembly back into the bore of the cylinder. Fit in the bearing 12, seal 13 and bearing 22 complete with O-ring, taking great care of the lips of the seal. Secure the parts in place using the special circlip pliers to fit the circlip 21.

3 Refit the spring 16, retainer 18 and Spirolox circlip 20 in the reverse order of dismantling.

4 Fit a new seal 29 and O-ring 30 to the piston 31 and slide the assembly carefully back into its place. Refit the housing 32 using a new gasket 4 and tightening the bolts 2 to a torque of 160 to 180 lb in (1.8 to 2.0 kg m).

5 Fit the diaphragm 1 back onto the support 33 carefully stretching it into place. Pass the pin of the diaphragm support 33 through the housing 32 so that it engages in the recess in the piston 31. Fit the valve rubber 41 so that its recess fits over the end of the valve stem 40 and pass the valve stem through the hole in the valve cover. Refit the valve rubber 34 onto the other end of the valve stem and secure it in place with the clip.

6 Refit the cover and diaphragm assembly using the five screws 43 and ensuring that both pipe connections align below the assembly.

7 Hold the assembly vertically upright with the reaction valve at the top. Lay the spring 38, filter 36 and sorbo

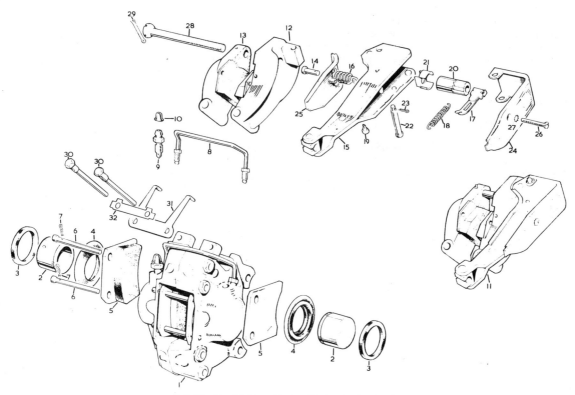

FIG 11:17   4.2 litre (Series 2) rear brake details

Key to Fig 11:17   1 Righthand rear caliper assembly   2 Piston   3 Seal   4 Dust seal   5 Friction pad   6 Pin
7 Clip   8 Bridge pipe   9 Bleed screw   10 Dust cap   11 Handbrake mechanism assembly   12 Pad carrier assembly
(Righthand outer)   13 Pad carrier assembly (Righthand inner)   14 Anchor pin   15 Operating lever   16 Return spring
17 Pawl assembly   18 Tension spring   19 Anchor pin   20 Adjusting nut   21 Friction spring   22 Hinge pin   23 Splitpin
24 Protection cover   25 Protection cover   26 Belt   27 Washer   28 Bolt   29 Splitpin   30 Bolt   31 Retraction plate
32 Tabwasher

washer 37 back into place and secure them by firmly
pressing on the filter cover 39.
8 Refit the trap valve assembly 7, new copper gasket 6A
and union 6 in the reverse order of removal.

PART III THE 4.2 LITRE (SERIES 2) MODEL BRAKING SYSTEM

11:19 Description

The Series 2 4.2 litre model uses exactly the same type
of dual-line braking system as the earlier 4.2 litre models
shown in **FIG 11:13**. The system is serviced and bled as
instructed in Part II of this Chapter.

On all the earlier models Dunlop type disc brakes were
used. On the models covered by this part of the Chapter
Girling disc brakes are used instead. These are similar
enough to the Dunlop type of brakes for all instructions
regarding removal and replacement, as well as instructions
on the handbrake, to be still applicable. The details of the
front brake are shown in **FIG 11:16** and the details of the
rear brake are shown in **FIG 11:17**.

Renewing the friction pads:

**These must not be allowed to wear less than ⅛
inch (3.2 mm).** On the front brakes the pads can be
withdrawn after removing the clips 10, withdrawing the
retaining pins 9 and removing the anti-chatter clip 13.
The rear brake pads are similarly removed after removing
the clips 7 and withdrawing the pins 6, noting that no
anti-chatter clips are fitted to the rear brakes. Lever the
pistons back into the bores, **taking care that no fluid
overflows from the reservoirs** and fit the new pads in
the reverse order of removing the old ones.

11:20 Servicing the calipers

Remove the calipers from the car and withdraw the
friction pads. If the pistons cannot be pulled out carefully
on their own, use hydraulic pressure to blow them out.
Remove the old seals from the cylinder bores and the
dust seals from the pistons. Thoroughly clean all the
parts using methylated spirits. Check that the bores and
the pistons are not scored. **The two halves of the
caliper must not be separated.** Refit the seals to their
recesses in the bores, and the dust covers to the pistons.
Use new seals if there has been any sign of leakage or

damage. Very carefully press the pistons back into their bores, using clean hydraulic fluid as lubricant. Take extra special care not to roll the seals out of their recesses or otherwise damage them when refitting the pistons.

11:21 Fault diagnosis

(a) Spongy pedal

1 Leak in the hydraulic system
2 Worn master (or tandem slave) cylinder(s)
3 Leaking seals on brake calipers
4 Air in the system

(b) Excessive pedal movement

1 Check 1 and 4 in (a)
2 Excessive pad wear
3 Very low fluid level in reservoir or reservoirs

(c) Brakes grab or pull to one side

1 Scored, cracked or distorted disc
2 Disc not running true
3 Wet or oily pads
4 Front or rear suspension anchorages loose or perished
5 Worn steering connections
6 Mixed pads of different grades
7 Uneven tyre pressures

CHAPTER 12

THE ELECTRICAL EQUIPMENT

12:1 Description

The 3.8 litre models use a 12 volt system in which the 'positive' terminal of the battery is earthed to the chassis. The supply for the battery is produced by a belt-driven generator. A 12 volt system is still used on the 4.2 litre models but the 'negative' terminal of the battery is connected to earth, and an alternator supplies the charging current.

Always observe the correct polarity of the system when making or breaking connections, particularly when an alternator is fitted in place of the generator. Any circuit containing transistors (such as alternators, radios, automatic parking lamp etc), is polarity sensitive and may be damaged if incorrectly connected. Such circuits should be disconnected if the battery is to be boost-charged or any arc welding operations are to be carried out on the car.

If an alternator is fitted, never disconnect or reconnect any parts of the charging circuit while the engine is running.

Test the continuity of a circuit using either a 0–15 voltmeter or a low-wattage test bulb. Connect the tester between a good earth point on the car and a suitable tapping point in the circuit to be tested. With the circuit correct and switched on, the voltmeter should give the same reading as across the battery terminals, and the bulb should glow as brightly as when connected directly across the battery terminals. When making performance checks, or adjusting components, first class instruments are essential. Cheap and unreliable instruments will not measure to the accuracy required, and inaccurate settings may introduce further faults.

Wiring Diagrams to enable those with electrical experience to trace and correct wiring faults are given in Technical Data. Detailed instructions for servicing the electrical equipment are provided in this Chapter. Equipment which is seriously defective, electrically or mechanically, should be replaced by either new or reconditioned units which can be obtained on an exchange basis.

12:2 The battery

This is of the 12 volt lead/acid type. The battery has to meet heavy demands of current, especially in winter, and unless it is correctly and carefully maintained it may fail and cause difficult starting or none at all.

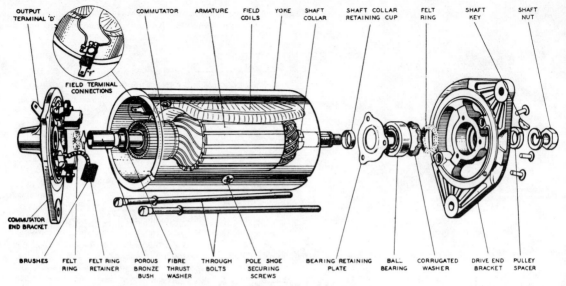

FIG 12:1 C.42 Generator details

Top labels: OUTPUT TERMINAL 'D' — COMMUTATOR — ARMATURE — FIELD COILS — YOKE — SHAFT COLLAR — SHAFT COLLAR RETAINING CUP — FELT RING — SHAFT KEY — SHAFT NUT

FIELD TERMINAL CONNECTIONS

COMMUTATOR END BRACKET

Bottom labels: BRUSHES — FELT RING — FELT RING RETAINER — POROUS BRONZE BUSH — FIBRE THRUST WASHER — THROUGH BOLTS — POLE SHOE SECURING SCREWS — BEARING RETAINING PLATE — BALL BEARING — CORRUGATED WASHER — DRIVE END BRACKET — PULLEY SPACER

Regularly carry out the following operations:

1 Clean and dry the top of the battery and its surroundings. Dampness can cause leakage between the battery terminals or to any metal part in contact with the battery. Clean off corrosion from the metal parts of the battery mountings using dilute ammonia. Wash them with clean water and paint when dry with anti-sulphuric paint.

2 If the terminal posts or connectors are corroded, disconnect the battery and remove the corrosion compounds with dilute ammonia. Smear the posts and connectors with petroleum jelly before refitting the connectors. Make sure the terminal screws are tight. High electrical resistance at the battery connections is often responsible for lack of sufficient current to operate the starter motor effectively.

3 At regular intervals top up the electrolyte level, using distilled water only. The correct level is just above the separator guards. On the later type of battery with an Aqualok device, remove the cover and fill the trough until the tubes, one in each cell, are filled with distilled water, then replace the cover. The level is then automatically correct.

Never use a naked light when inspecting the battery. Hydrogen given off by the battery forms a potentially explosive mixture with oxygen in the air.

Testing:

Use a hydrometer to draw up sufficient electrolyte from each cell in turn to float the float in the instrument. The specific gravity of the electrolyte indicates the state of charge of the battery. Each cell should have approximately the same reading, and if one cell differs radically from the rest it is suspect. Electrolyte which looks dirty or contains small particles is a further indication of a poor cell. Electrolyte containing acid should never be added to the battery except to replace spillage or leakage. Make up electrolyte to the correct specific gravity by adding acid

to water. **Never add water to acid** as the heat produced will cause the acid to sputter out dangerously. The specific gravity of the electrolyte gives the following indications:

Climates below 32°C (90°F):

1.270 to 1.290	Cell fully charged
1.190 to 1.210	Cell half charged
1.110 to 1.130	Cell discharged

Use electrolyte of 1.270 specific gravity to replace spillage.

Climates above 32°C (90°F):

1.210 to 1.230	Cell fully charged
1.130 to 1.150	Cell half charged
1.050 to 1.070	Cell discharged

Use electrolyte of 1.210 specific gravity to replace spillage. These figures are based on a standard electrolyte temperature of 16°C (60°F). Convert the actual reading to standard by adding .002 for each 3°C (5°F) increase of actual electrolyte temperature and subtracting .002 each decrease in actual temperature.

Those batteries where the inter-cell connectors are accessible may also be tested using a heavy-discharge tester. Never use this test on a semi-discharged battery. A good cell will maintain a reading of 1.2 to 1.5 volts, depending on the state of the charge, for at least 6 seconds. A rapid fall in voltage indicates a faulty cell.

If the car is not in use, or the battery has been removed for storage, the battery should be given a freshening charge every month otherwise the plates will sulphate, running the battery.

12:3 The generator

Type C.45 PVS.6 generators are fitted to the earlier models of the 3.8 litre and type C.42 to the later models. The main difference between the two models is that the earlier type is fitted with windows in the yoke for servicing the brushgear. A cover band covers these apertures to prevent the ingress of dirt. Ballbearings are fitted to both

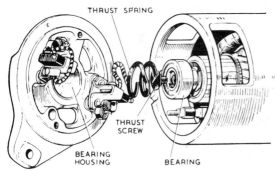

FIG 12:2 Commutator end bracket removed from C.45 PVS.6 generator

the armature ends on the earlier generator, but the later one uses a pressed-in bush for the commutator end bearing.

FIG 12:1 shows the details of the type C.42 generator, and **FIG 12:2** the commutator end bracket removed on the earlier C.45 PVS.6 generator.

Routine maintenance :

1 Every 5000 miles inject a few drops of engine oil through the hole in the centre of the commutator end bracket to lubricate the bush on the later type of generators. The ballbearings are packed with grease on assembly and do not require lubrication.

2 The brush gear should be inspected every 24,000 miles.

Testing when the generator is not charging :

1 Check that the driving belt is at the correct tension and is not damaged or slipping. On earlier models the tension is adjusted by pivoting the generator about its lower mountings while on later models a jockey pulley and spring are fitted to ensure correct tension.

2 Check that the connections on the generator and control box are correct. Disconnect the cables from the D and F terminals on the generator and short these two terminals together with a piece of wire. Connect a first-class moving coil 0−20 volt voltmeter between one terminal of the generator and a good earth point on the car. Start the engine and gradually increase the speed up to 1000 rev/min. The generator output should rise steadily without fluctuation, but do not let it reach 20 volts and do not race the engine in an attempt to increase a low reading.

3 If no reading is obtained repeat the test with the radio suppression capacitor removed from between the terminals. If a correct reading is now obtained then the capacitor is faulty and must be renewed. If the maximum reading is about 1 volt the field coils may be faulty. A maximum of 4 to 5 volts indicates a faulty armature and no reading indicates faulty brush gear.

4 If the generator appears satisfactory restore the original connection leaving the link in place. Remove the lead connected to the D terminal on the control box and repeat the test with the voltmeter connected between this cable and a good earth. Reconnect the D lead and repeat the test on the lead connected to the F terminal on the control box. In both cases the voltmeter should

give the same readings as when connected directly to the generator. No reading on either lead indicates a broken or defective cable.

Removal :

Slacken all the mounting and pivot bolts securing the generator and remove the driving belt from the generator pulley. Disconnect both electrical cables from the terminals on the generator and take out the generator after withdrawing the securing bolts.

The generator is replaced in the reverse order of removal and the driving belt set to the correct tension.

Dismantling :

Unscrew the shaft nut and remove the spring washer. Carefully draw off the driving pulley. Remove the two long through-bolts and ease off the commutator end bracket. The armature and driving end bracket assembly can then be withdrawn from the yoke. Do not remove the armature from the driving end bracket unless the driving end bearing is to be replaced.

Reassembly is the reversal of the dismantling procedure. Lift up the brushes in the brush boxes and hold them in position with the springs against the sides of the brushes. The commutator end bracket can then be replaced without damaging the brushes on the commutator end.

Servicing the brushgear :

Examine this with the engine running. Excessive sparking indicates a faulty commutator. On the earlier models the brushgear can be examined by removing the metal cover band. On the later models the brushgear can be seen with the engine running by using a mirror and

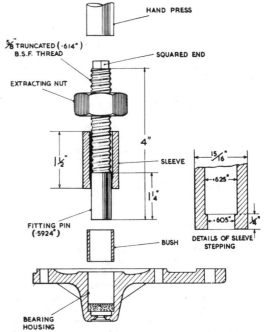

FIG 12:3 Method of fitting porous bronze bush to generator

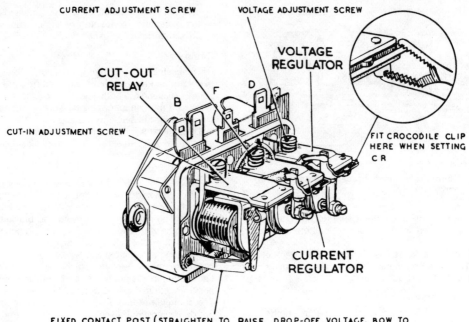

CURRENT ADJUSTMENT SCREW　　VOLTAGE ADJUSTMENT SCREW

CUT-OUT
RELAY

VOLTAGE
REGULATOR

B　F　D

CUT-IN ADJUSTMENT SCREW

FIT CROCODILE CLIP
HERE WHEN SETTING
C R

CURRENT
REGULATOR

FIXED CONTACT POST (STRAIGHTEN TO RAISE DROP-OFF VOLTAGE, BOW TO
REDUCE DROP-OFF VOLTAGE)

FIG 12:4　RB.310 control box details

looking in through the cooling air outlets in the commutator end bracket. Further examination requires dismantling of the generator.

If this has been done, refit the commutator end bracket to the commutator, without the yoke in place. Hold back the springs and move each brush in turn by gently pulling on the flexible connector. The brush should move freely. If the movement is sluggish remove each brush in turn and polish the sides on a smooth file. Clean the brush holder with petrol-moistened rag. Refit the brushes and springs. Use a spring balance to check the tension of the springs. On the model C.42 the brush tension should be 33 ozs with new parts reducing to a minimum serviceable of 16 ozs with worn brushes. Renew the springs if weak and the brushes if they are shorter than $\frac{1}{4}$ inch (6.4 mm). The springs and brushes on the earlier C.45 PVS.6 model are checked in a similar manner but the spring tension should lie between 20 to 28 ozs, depending on the wear on the brush. Brushes must be renewed if shorter than $\frac{11}{32}$ inch (8.7 mm).

The commutator:

In good condition this should be smooth and free from pitting or burned segments. Clean the commutator with a petrol-moistened cloth and if necessary polish with glasspaper. If the commutator is scored it may be skimmed in a lathe, using high-speed and a sharp tool. Ideally the insulator should be undercut and then a light polishing cut taken using a diamond tipped tool. Grind a hacksaw blade exactly to the thickness of the insulation and use this to undercut it squarely. If a diamond tipped tool is not available lightly polish the commutator using glasspaper, **never emerycloth**.

The armature:

Apart from servicing the commutator, little can be done to the armature. Never try to straighten or machine the armature core to cure a bent shaft. Specialist equipment is required for checking the armature coils and the only test readily available is to substitute a known satisfactory armature for a suspect one.

Field coils:

Leave the coils in the yoke and measure their resistance between the yoke and the F terminal. Use either an ohmmeter or an ammeter connected in series with a 12 volt supply. The resistance on the C.42 field coils should be 4.5 ohms and if the current method is used the ammeter should read 2.7 amps. On the C.45 PSV.6 the equivalent readings should be 6.0 ohms or 2 amps. Very high resistance and no current indicates an open circuit. Low resistance and high current indicate that the insulation of the field coils has broken down. Renewing field coils is an operation best left to a service station as the coil securing screws must be slackened and tightened on a special wheel screwdriver.

Bearings:

If there is excessive sideways movement on the armature shaft or if the bearings are noisy, they should be renewed. Take out the key from the armature shaft and use a press to separate the bracket from the armature. Drill out the rivets to free the retaining plate and remove the parts. Refit in the reverse order of dismantling, making sure that the new bearing is packed with grease. Use new rivets to secure the parts in place.

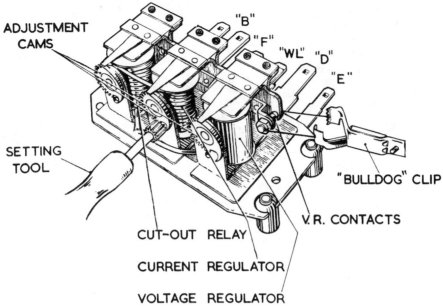

FIG 12:5 RB.340 control box details

Labels on figure: ADJUSTMENT CAMS, "B", "F", "WL", "D", "E", SETTING TOOL, "BULLDOG" CLIP, V.R. CONTACTS, CUT-OUT RELAY, CURRENT REGULATOR, VOLTAGE REGULATOR

Remove the commutator end bearing using an extractor after the thrust screw has been removed. Press the new bearing fully back onto the shoulders of the shaft.

On later models fitted with a phosphor/bronze porous bush screw a $\frac{5}{8}$ inch tap squarely into the old bush and withdraw the bush using the tap. The new bush must be soaked in engine oil for 24 hours at room temperature, or the period can be reduced by soaking in oil at a temperature of 100°C and allowing it all to cool before fitting the bush. Use a press and mandrel, as shown in **FIG 12:3**, to fit the new bush. Screw down the nut to withdraw the mandrel without pulling out the bush again. The bush must not be bored or reamed after fitting and using the correct highly-polished mandrel ensures that the bush is of the correct fit and finish.

12:4 The generator control box

This controls the output of the generator in relation to the demands of the system and the state of charge of the battery. An RB.310 regulator box is fitted with the earlier C.45 PVS.6 generator and an RB.340 regulator box with the later C.42 generator. They are similar in construction and the servicing and adjusting instructions apply equally to both. The only difference is in their performance characteristics. Before making adjustments to the control box carry out the following tests:

1 Check that the driving belt is not slipping.
2 Check that the generator is supplying current correctly.
3 Check the wiring between the generator, control box and battery for continuity and to ensure all connections are secure.
4 Check the earth connections on the control box and battery.
5 Check that the battery is capable of holding a charge.
6 Make certain that the low state of the battery is not just due to low-mileage journeys in which the

generator has not time to recharge the battery from the demands made by the starter and lights.

When these points have been checked the control box may be adjusted. After long service the points in the control box may be dirty, causing irregular operation. Clean them as follows:

Regulator contacts:

Use a fine carborundum stone, silicone carbide paper or fine emerycloth and clean away dust and dirt with methylated spirits.

Cut-out contacts:

Use only fine glasspaper, **never emerycloth, silicone carbide or carborundum.** Again clean with methylated spirits.

The parts of the RB.310 control box are shown in **FIG 12:4** and those of the RB.340 control box in **FIG 12:5**. A special tool is required to adjust the RB.340 model, as shown in **FIG 12:5**.

Voltage regulator adjustment:

This may be checked without even removing the cover, but adjustments will necessitate the cover removal. **The importance of using good quality moving coil instruments cannot be over-emphasized.**

1 Disconnect the leads from the B terminal. Check that battery voltage is available at the battery supply cable and then connect the ignition lead and battery lead together with a jumper lead.
2 Connect a 0–20 voltmeter between the D terminal and a good earth point on the car. Start the engine and take readings within 30 seconds. **Adjustments must also be made within 30 seconds of starting the engine otherwise the coils will heat up and produce spurious results.** Run the engine at 2000

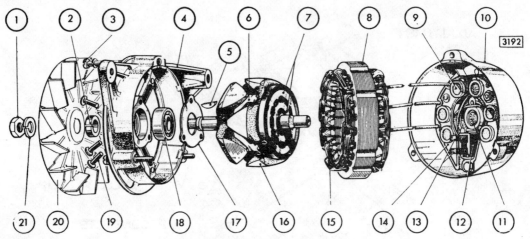

FIG 12:6 Lucas 11.AC alternator details

Key to Fig 12:6   1 Shaft nut   2 Bearing collar   3 Through fixing bolts   4 Drive end bracket   5 Key
6 Rotor (field) winding   7 Slip rings 8 Stator laminations 9 Silicon diodes 10 Slip ring end bracket 11 Needle roller bearing
12 Brush box moulding   13 Brushes   14 Diode heat sink   15 Stator windings   16 Rotor   17 Bearing retaining plate
18 Ballbearing   19 Bearing retaining plate rivets   20 Fan   21 Spring washer

rev/min and check that the voltage reading is within the following limits.

Ambient temperature	Open circuit voltage setting	
	RB.310	RB.340
10°C (50°F)	15.1 to 15.7	15.0 to 15.6
20°C (68°F)	14.9 to 15.5	14.8 to 15.4
30°C (86°F)	14.7 to 15.3	14.6 to 15.2
40°C (104°F)	14.5 to 15.1	14.4 to 15.0

3 If the reading is outside the limits stop the engine and remove the control box cover. Turn the voltage regulator adjuster clockwise to raise the setting and anticlockwise to lower the setting. Only small adjustments will be necessary. Stop the engine every time an adjustment is made and restart it to check.

4 When the adjustment is satisfactory replace the cover and connect the leads to the B terminal after removing the jumper lead.

Current regulator adjustment:

If the battery is still not charging satisfactorily after adjusting the voltage regulator set, adjust the current regulator as follows:

1 Disconnect the leads from the B terminal and connect them together as before. Remove the cover and isolate the voltage regulator by clipping its points together with a clip as shown in the figures.

2 Connect a high-quality 0–40 moving coil ammeter between the leads and the B terminal. Run the engine at about 2700 rev/min. On the RB.310 the ammeter should read between 24 and 26 amps while on the RB.340 the reading should be 30 ± 1½ amps.

3 If the reading is outside the limits turn the centre adjuster clockwise to raise the setting or anticlockwise to lower it. Restart the engine and check that the setting is correct. Once satisfied remove the clip, reconnect the leads and replace the cover.

Cut-out adjustment:

Checks and adjustments on this must be completed within 30 seconds to avoid spurious results from coils heating.

Cut-in voltage:

1 Partially withdraw the lead from the D terminal and connect a 0–20 voltmeter between the partially exposed D terminal and a good earth point on the car.

2 Start the engine and slowly increase speed, noting the voltage reading continuously. The needle should rise steadily, reach a peak and then drop slightly as the points operate. The peak reading for the RB.310 should be 12.7 to 13.3 volts and for the RB.340, 12.6 to 13.4 volts.

3 If the voltage reading is incorrect turn the adjuster by small increments, clockwise to raise the setting and anticlockwise to lower, stopping the engine when making each adjustment until the correct reading is given.

4 If the point at which the points operate is difficult to determine, switch on the headlamps to reduce the battery voltage.

Drop-off voltage:

1 Disconnect the leads from the B terminals, connect them together with a jumper lead, and connect a voltmeter between the leads and the B terminal.

2 Start the engine and run it up above the cut-in speed. Slowly decrease engine speed. Watch the voltmeter needle. It will fall, then suddenly drop to zero indicating that the points have opened. Note the minimum reading just before the points open. On the RB.310 this should be 9.5 to 11.0 volts and on the RB.340 9.25 to 11.25 volts.

3 Carefully bend or straighten the fixed contact support to adjust the drop-off voltage. Closing the gap will raise the voltage and opening the gap will lower the voltage.

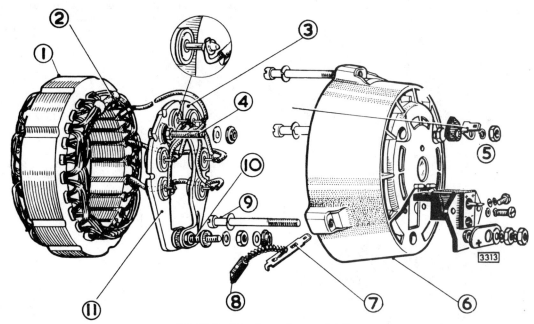

FIG 12:7   Slip ring end cover details

Key to Fig 12:7   1 Stator   2 Star point   3 Negative heat sink anode base diodes (black)   4 Warning light terminal 'AL'
5 Field terminal (2)   6 Slip ring end cover   7 Terminal blade retaining tongue   8 Rotor slip ring brush (2)   9 'Through' bolts (3)
10 Output terminal (+)   11 Positive heat sink and cathode base diode (red)

12:5 The alternator

FIG 12:6 shows the details of the alternator, and **FIG 12:7** shows the details of the slip ring end cover. On later models the design of the brush gear was changed to the type shown in **FIG 12:8**.

Testing when the alternator is not charging:

1 Before carrying out any tests on the alternator, check that the driving belt is not slipping, and that all connections are secure with undamaged cables.

2 Disconnect the battery. Disconnect the brown output cable from the alternator and connect an accurate 0–60 ammeter between the cable and the terminal on the alternator. Disconnect all three cables from the contacts on the 4.TR alternator control. Join the brown/green and black cables, which were connected to the alternator control, by a short jumper lead so as to connect full battery voltage through the field coils.

3 Reconnect the battery and start the engine. Gradually increase engine speed to 2000 rev/min and, without allowing the alternator to heat up, note the reading on the ammeter. The correct reading is approximately 40 amps. A low reading indicates a faulty alternator, provided that the circuit wiring is correct.

4 If the output is nil, disconnect the two cables from the field terminals on the alternator and check that there is battery voltage between them. If there is no voltage, check through associated wiring and check the isolating relay.

5 If the output is low, connect an ohmmeter between the two field terminals on the alternator, with the cables

disconnected. The rotor field coil should have a resistance of approximately 3.8 ohms. A high resistance indicates an open circuit so check the slip ring and the field coil. A low reading indicates a short-circuit. An ammeter and 12 volt supply may be used instead of an ohmmeter in which case the current reading should be 3.2 amps.

Dismantling the alternator:

Disconnect the cables from the terminals on the alternator and either note the colours or label the cables to ensure correct reconnections on reassembly. Free the driving belt and remove the securing bolts.

1 Refer to **FIG 12:6**. Remove the nut 1 and spring washer 21. Withdraw the pulley and cooling fan 20. Indelibly mark the drive end bracket 4, stator laminations 8 and slip ring end bracket 10 so that they will be reassembled in the correct angular relationship. Break the staking on the nuts and undo the three through-bolts 3. If the threads are damaged new nuts and bolts should be fitted on reassembly.

2 Withdraw the drive end bracket 4 complete with the rotor assembly 16. These need not be separated unless the bearing 18 needs to be changed. If this is required, first remove the key 5 and bearing collar 2. Use a press to remove the rotor from the end bracket. Drill out the rivets 19 to free the retaining plate 17 and remove the old bearing. Press in a new bearing, making sure that it is packed with grease, and use new rivets 19 to secure the parts in place.

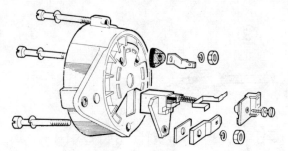

FIG 12:8 Brush removal, later model alternators

The minimum length of a brush is $\frac{5}{32}$ inch and it must be replaced if shorter than this. If possible check that the spring exerts a pressure of 4 to 5 ozs when compressed to a length of $\frac{25}{32}$ inch.

Later brush gear:

This type is shown in **FIG 12:7** and the brush is held in place by a cover secured by a screw. If at least .2 inch (5 mm) of brush protrudes from the brush box when in the free position then the brush is fit for further service. Press each brush flush with the face of the brush box and check that the spring pressure is 8 to 16 oz. If the brush sticks, clean the parts with a fuel-moistened rag and lightly polish the sides of the brush on a smooth file. Renew the assembly if it is outside the limits given.

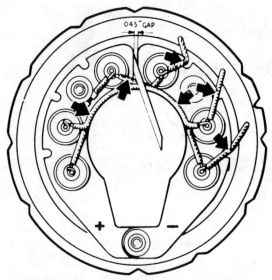

FIG 12:9 Correct connections to the diodes. Note the correct gap between the free ends of the diode heat sinks

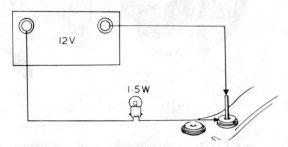

FIG 12:10 Circuit for testing diodes

3 Remove the nuts, bolt or screw securing the brush gear and field terminals in place and withdraw the stator assembly and diode heat sink assemblies from the slip ring end bracket 10. If the needle bearing 11 is defective a new end bracket complete with new bearing must be fitted.

Reassembly is the reversal of the dismantling operation. The three through-bolts 3 should be tightened to a torque of 45 to 50 lb in (.518 to .576 kg m) and the nuts restaked after assembly. The diode heat sink assemblies must be refitted with a gap of .045 inch (1.28 mm) between their free ends, as shown in **FIG 12:9**. Do not overtighten the brush gear securing screws.

Early brush gear:

The brushes are removed by closing up the securing tongue and withdrawing the brush, spring and terminal, and replaced by pushing the assembly home until the tongue clicks into place. Make sure that the tongue makes an angle of 30 deg. with the assembly to ensure security.

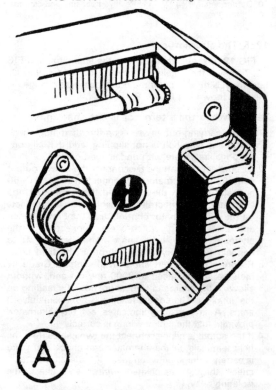

FIG 12:11 Potentiometer adjuster on 4TR alternator control

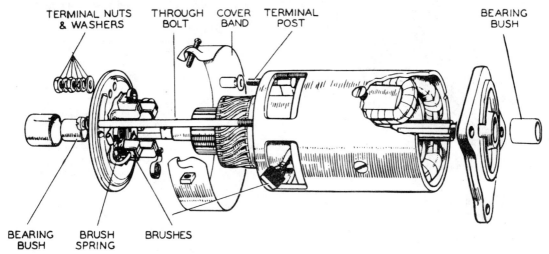

TERMINAL NUTS & WASHERS   THROUGH BOLT   COVER BAND   TERMINAL POST   BEARING BUSH

BEARING BUSH   BRUSH SPRING   BRUSHES

FIG 12:12   Details of starter motor fitted to 3.8 litre models

The rotor:

Check that the slip rings 7 are smooth and clean. As they take little current and are in continuous contact only light marks should show and these can be cleaned off with fine glasspaper. **Never machine the slip rings as the high-speed performance of the unit will be upset.**

Check that the resistance of the field coils, measured between the slip rings, is approximately 3.8 ohms. A 110 volt AC lamp should be used between each slip ring and the stator 16 to ensure that the insulation has not broken down. Replace the rotor if it is defective.

The stator:

Carefully note the exact positions of the three stator wires on the diode heat sink, shown in **FIG 12:9**, and unsolder them quickly. When soldering or unsoldering wires to the diodes grip the diode pin carefully with a pair of pliers which will act as a heat sink to prevent excessive heat reaching the diode.

Check any pair of stator wires using a 36 watt test bulb and 12 volt supply. The bulb should light. Leave one wire still connected to the test bulb circuit and connect in the third wire. The bulb should again light. Use a 110 AC volt test bulb and check that this does not light between each wire in turn and the metal outside on the stator assembly. Renew the stator if it is defective.

The diodes:

Connect up a circuit as shown in **FIG 12:10**, and test each diode in turn. Test each diode twice, reversing the polarity of the circuit. The bulb should light for one polarity but stay out for the other. If the bulb either lights in both directions or does not light at all the diode is defective and that heat sink assembly must be replaced. Solder the connections, using pliers as a heat sink, so that the connections are as shown in **FIG 12:9**. Use 44/55 tin/lead solder and ensure the wires are neatly arranged to prevent them chafing. Use MMM.EC.1022 adhesive tape to hold the wires in place.

12:6 The alternator control unit

A 4 TR model unit is fitted to control the output of the alternator in relation to the demands made by the battery, and electrical system and to compensate for outside temperature variations.

Before checking or adjusting the control unit make sure that the battery is fully charged and that the alternator has been tested and found satisfactory.

Partially ease off the brown/purple cable from the unit + terminal and the black cable from the — terminal of the unit. Connect an accurate voltmeter between the partially exposed + and — terminals. Switch on ancillaries, such as sidelights, to give a discharge rate of 2 amps. Start the engine and allow it to run at 1500 rev/min for at least eight minutes to allow the system to stabilize. The voltmeter should give a reading of 13.9 to 14.3 volts at an ambient temperature of 68 to 78°F (20 to 26°C).

If the voltage remains at battery terminal voltage or increases uncontrollably then the unit is defective and a new unit must be fitted. If the voltage is outside the limits but is stable above the battery terminal voltage then a simple adjustment is necessary. Stop the engine and remove the control unit from the bulkhead, without disconnecting the wires. Scrape away the sealant from the potentiometer adjuster, shown in **FIG 12:11**. Start the engine and run it at 1500 rev/min and turn the potentiometer clockwise to increase the setting and anti-clockwise to decrease the setting. Take care to turn the adjuster by small movements only as even these have a large effect on the voltage.

Warning light control:

On later models a model 3.AW unit is fitted to operate the alternator warning light. The unit is very similar to the flasher unit for the indicators but may be identified from it by the distinctive green label. If the unit is faulty a new one must be fitted as units are sealed and cannot be rectified. Before changing the unit, check to make sure that the warning bulb has not blown. Before fitting the new unit check that the voltage between the alternator AL terminal and earth is 7 to 7.75 volts at an engine speed

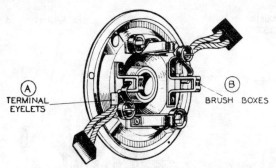

FIG 12:13   Commutator end bracket brush connections

of 1500 rev/min. If this is exceeded, first check all connections, then check the alternator diodes. If a new warning light unit is fitted when the voltage exceeds the limits given the unit will rapidly fail.

12:7 The 3.8 litre starter motor

The details of this are shown in **FIG 12:12**. A view of the commutator end bracket and the brush connections is shown in **FIG 12:13** and **FIG 12:14** gives the details of the starter drive.

Starter does not operate:

Check that the battery is charged. Make sure that the battery connections are clean and tight as high resistance here is often a cause of starter motor failure. Provided the battery is satisfactory, switch on the lights and operate the starter. If the lights go dim then current is reaching the starter and it is being prevented from rotating. The probability is that the starter pinion is jammed in the flywheel teeth. Either rock the car backwards and forwards in gear or remove the cover and turn the starter motor shaft by the squared end, now exposed on the front end of the armature shaft. If this fails the starter will have to be removed for further examination.

If the lights do not go dim, trace through the wiring until the fault is found. If the starter solenoid is defective it will have to be renewed. If the starter motor does not operate although current is reaching it, it will have to be removed for further examination.

Starter motor renewal:

Disconnect the battery. Remove the brake vacuum servo from the bulkhead, labelling the two hoses for correct reassembly. Disconnect the cable from the starter motor terminal. Remove the two nuts from the starter motor securing bolts. Support the starter motor and remove the two bolts. Withdraw the starter motor through the chassis frame.

Replace the starter motor in the reverse order of removal.

Starter motor servicing:

The starter motor is of very similar construction to the generator fitted to the 3.8 litre cars. Dismantling is the same except for the drive end bracket which can only be removed after the starter drive has been removed. Four brushes are fitted instead of the two on the generator.

The brushes must be renewed if less than $\frac{5}{16}$ inch long. The flexible connectors are soldered into place, so take care to prevent the solder from creeping up the flexible connector when fitting new brushes. The new brushes are preformed and require no bedding in.

The commutator and armature are cleaned and serviced in exactly the same manner as the generator armature, but **the insulation on the starter commutator must not be undercut.**

Test the field coils for continuity using a test lamp and 12 volt supply between the starter motor terminal and the field coil brush connections. The insulation should be tested using a 110 AC volt test lamp between the field coil connections and the yoke. If the field coils are defective either renew the starter motor or have new field coils fitted at a garage.

Renew the brush springs if their tension is less than 30 to 40 oz.

The starter motor drive:

Refer to **FIG 12:14**. Remove the cover over the squared end of the armature shaft. Withdraw the splitpin A and holding the squared end of the shaft with a spanner undo the nut B. The parts can then be drawn off the armature shaft. Wash all the parts in clean fuel and examine them for wear. If the pinion and screwed sleeve assembly E are worn they must be renewed as a set. Check the spring C to ensure that there are no cracks in it.

Reassemble the parts in the reverse order of dismantling, but do not lubricate them as any oil or grease will cause dirt to stick to the parts and cause jamming.

12:8 The 4.2 litre starter motor

A sectioned view of this is shown in **FIG 12:15**. When the solenoid is actuated two coils draw it in. The initial movement engages the pinion on the roller clutch assembly 6 with the teeth on the flywheel. Further movement then makes the contacts in the solenoid and power is directed to the starter motor. At this point one of the coils in the solenoid is shortened out, leaving the solenoid held in by the weaker coil. If the teeth on the pinion abut then the springs compress, allowing the solenoids to make the contacts. The teeth engage with the first rotation of the starter motor. A roller clutch is fitted so that when the engine starts the starter motor is not driven at high-speed by the engine. Centrifugally operated brake shoes are fitted in the commutator end bracket to slow the starter motor armature immediately after disengagement and ensure that the starter motor will not be operated again with the pinion spinning.

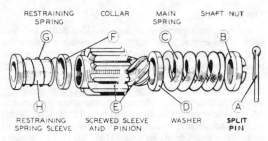

FIG 12:14   Starter drive details

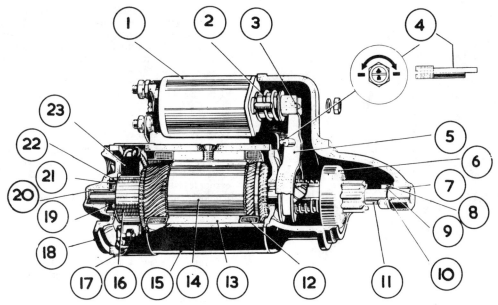

FIG 12:15 Details of starter motor fitted to 4.2 litre models

Key to Fig 12:15   1 Actuating solenoid   2 Return spring   3 Clevis pin   4 Eccentric pivot pin   5 Engaging lever
6 Roller clutch   7 Porous bronze bush   8 Thrust collar   9 Jump ring   10 Thrust washer   11 Armature shaft extension
12 Field coils   13 Pole shoe   14 Armature   15 Yoke   16 Commutator   17 Band cover   18 Commutator end bracket
19 Thrust washer   20 Porous bronze bush   21 Brake shoes and cross-peg   22 Brake ring   23 Brushes

Both the roller clutch and the solenoid assemblies are sealed units and must be renewed if defective. The roller clutch should never be washed in solvent otherwise the internal grease will be washed out.

Starter motor removal:

1 Disconnect the battery. Remove the transmitter unit from on top of the oil filter. Disconnect the leads and cables to the starter motor solenoid.
2 Remove the distributor clamp plate retaining screw ∨ and withdraw the distributor. Do not slacken the clamp pinch bolt or the ignition timing will be lost.
3 Free the tabwashers and remove the two setscrews securing the starter motor in place. The two setscrews can be reached either from underneath the car or after removing the access cover from the righthand side of the transmission cover.
4 Gently bend the carburetter drain pipes and remove the starter motor through the chassis frame.

Dismantling:

1 Disconnect the cables and link from the starter solenoid. Remove the two nuts securing the solenoid to the drive end bracket and withdraw the solenoid. Carefully remove the clevis pin 3 to disconnect the solenoid from the operating lever 5.
2 Remove the cover band 17 and lift the four brushes free off the commutator, holding them up by allowing the springs to rest on the side of the brushes. Remove the through-bolts so that the commutator end bracket 18 and yoke 15 can now be drawn off the armature.
3 Remove the rubber seal from the drive end bracket. Slacken the locknut on the adjusting pin 4, unscrew the

pin, and withdraw it. Separate the drive end bracket from the armature. Tap back the thrust collar 8 towards the armature, using a suitable piece of pipe after removing the thrust washer 10. Prise out the jump ring 9 and withdraw the parts of the drive assembly from the armature shaft.

Brush gear and commutator:

These are serviced in the same manner as the brush gear and commutator on the generator fitted to the 3.8 litre models (see **Section 12:3**). The brushes must be renewed if they are shorter than $\frac{5}{16}$ inch (7.94 mm) and the springs if they have a tension less than 52 oz (1.47 kg) when in place with a new brush. Commutator damage may be skimmed off on a lathe but the diameter must not be reduced to less than $1\frac{17}{32}$ inch (38.89 mm) **Do not undercut the insulation.**

If any commutator segments have lifted suspect that the starter motor has overspeeded and check the roller clutch assembly. This should rotate freely in one direction and take up drive instantaneously in the other direction. If there is any defect the clutch assembly must be renewed.

Field coils:

Check these for continuity using a 12 volt test lamp and check the insulation using a 110 AC volt test lamp. If defective they should be renewed by a garage.

Bearings:

These are phosphor/bronze porous bushes and must be renewed if worn. Extract the old bushes by screwing in a $\frac{9}{16}$ inch tap and using this to withdraw the bush. After

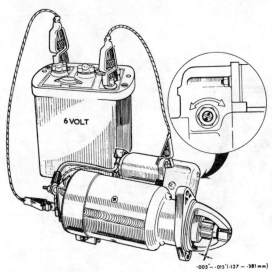

FIG 12:16 Setting pinion movement

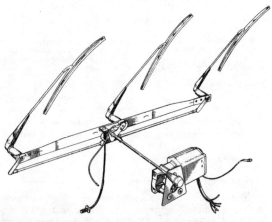

FIG 12:17 DL3 wiper motor and linkage fitted to 3.8 litre models

soaking the new bushes in oil for 24 hours press them into place, using a highly polished stepped mandrel .0005 inch (.013 mm) larger in diameter than the armature shaft, again in a similar manner to the bush on the later type of generator fitted to the 3.8 litre models.

Reassembly:

This is the reversal of the dismantling procedure. Torque loads are given in Technical Data. Seat the brake shoes squarely and then turn them so that the ends of the cross-pegs in the armature shaft engage correctly with the slots in the shoes. After the starter motor has been reassembled reset the pinion clearance as follows:
1 Ensure that the arrow on the eccentric pin is in the 180 deg. segment between the arrows on the body. Connect a 6 volt battery as shown in FIG 12:16. Do not use a 12 volt battery otherwise the armature will turn.

2 When the connections are completed the pinion will be thrown into the engaged position. Measure the gap between the pinion and thrust collar with feeler gauges and turn the eccentric pin, ensuring that the arrow still points to the correct segment, until the gap is correct at .005 to .015 inch.
3 Disconnect the battery and secure the eccentric pin in position by tightening the locknut.

12:9 Windscreen wiper motor

All models of E type are fitted with two-speed self-parking windscreen wiper motors. The motors are the same on the 3.8 litre models as on the 4.2 litre models except for later lefthand drive models. The 4.2 litre Series 2 model is fitted with a different motor again.

3.8 litre model motor removal:

The motor and linkage is shown in FIG 12:17 and the parking adjuster nut is shown in FIG 12:18.
1 Disconnect the battery. Disconnect the ball joint from the throttle control at the pivot bracket and remove the bracket.
2 Release the snap connector from its clip on the bulkhead and disconnect the cables.
3 Lower the centre instrument panel, by removing the two top securing screws and tilting it outwards. Disconnect the ball joint of the link from the wiper motor at the centre wheel spindle assembly.
4 Remove the four setscrews securing the motor and withdraw the motor complete with the link rod.

Refitting the motor is the reverse of the removal operations. Make sure that the throttle control rod is central in its bearing, the bracket has slotted securing holes so the adjustment can be made correctly. Make sure that the lengths of the three link rods are not altered, otherwise the wipers will be out of synchronization. If the parking position of the blades needs to be altered turn the nut, shown in FIG 12:18, a couple of clicks at a time until the position is correct.

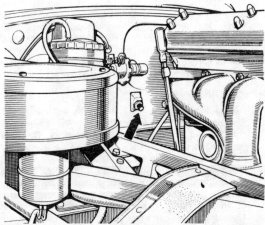

FIG 12:18 The windscreen wiper parking adjuster screw on 3.8 litre models

Lefthand drive 4.2 litre motor removal :

This is removed and replaced in exactly the same manner as the motor fitted to the 3.8 litre models. The motor (Lucas DL3A) is shown in **FIG 12:19**. The parking position of the blades is altered by slackening the three screws arrowed and turning the switch carrier plate until the motor stops in the required position.

4.2 litre motor removal :

The motor is again removed in a similar manner except on 4.2 litre (Series 2) 2 + 2 models. On these the top facia panel must be removed as the motor link is connected to a ball joint on the lefthand wheelbox. The park position is set by altering the positions of the wiper arms on the wheelbox spindles. The details of the motor fitted (Lucas 15W) are shown in **FIG 12:20**.

Testing the motor :

If the motor fails to operate, first check the appropriate fuse. If the fuse is unblown check through the wiring and check that the supply is reaching the wiper motor.

If the wiper motor operates sluggishly, check that excess friction in the linkage or of the blades on the glass is not the cause before carrying out other tests.

Disconnect the wiper motor from the linkage and check the free running current. On the DL3 model (fitted to 3.8 litre models) connect the 'Green' cable to the negative battery terminal. Connect the 'Blue' and the 'White' cables together. To check the slow speed connect both the 'Brown' and 'Red' cables to the battery positive terminal. To check the fast speed connect both the 'Yellow' and 'Red' cables to the battery positive terminal. The motor should operate at a speed of 44 to 48 cycles/min and at a current of 2.5 to 3.2 amps at slow speed, and 58 to 68 cycles/min at a current of 1.7 to 2.4 amps at high speed. If the motor exceeds these limits it should be renewed.

The circuit diagram for the 15W model (fitted to 4.2 litre models) is shown in **FIG 12:21**. Connect the negative terminal of the battery to terminal No. 1 and for high-speed connect terminal No. 3 to the positive terminal.

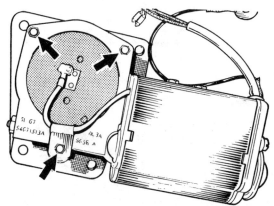

FIG 12:19 Adjusting the parking position of windscreen wiper blades on lefthand drive 4.2 litre models. The arrows indicate the three screws to be slackened before the switch carrier plate can be turned

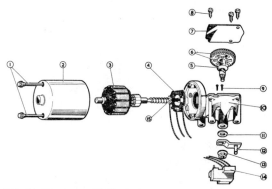

FIG 12:20 Lucas 15.W windscreen wiper motor details, fitted to 4.2 litre Series 2 models

Key to Fig 12:20
1 Yoke fixing bolts
2 Yoke assembly comprising two permanent-magnet poles and retaining clips and armature bearing bush   3 Armature
4 Brushgear, comprising insulating plate and brushboxes, brushes, springs and fixing bolts   5 'Dished' washer
6 Shaft and gear   7 Gearbox cover   8 Cover fixing screws
9 Limit switch fixing screws   10 Gearbox
11 Flat washer   12 Rotary link   13 Link fixing nut
14 Limit switch assembly   15 Nylon thrust cap

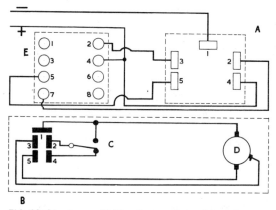

FIG 12:21 Lucas 15.W wiper motor wiring diagram

Key to Fig 12:21   **A** Moulded terminal connector on cable harness   **B** Terminal connector on wiper motor
C Limit switch   **D** Armature   **E** 152.SA switch
Switch internal connections
Off   *Normal speed*   *High speed*
(5-7)   (4-5)   (2-4)

Connect the positive terminal of the battery to terminal No. 5 for normal speed. The motor should take a current of 1.5 amps at normal speed and 2.0 amps at high-speed. If the motor exceeds these currents it should be dismantled and the brush gear and commutator checked. The housing contains a permanent magnet so it is essential that it is replaced in the same relative position on reassembly. When the housing is removed the armature will be drawn out by the magnet so take care not to damage the brushes either on dismantling or reassembly. The complete brush gear assembly must be renewed if the main brushes are worn to less than $\frac{3}{16}$ inch (4.8 mm) or if the high-speed brush is worn so that the narrow portion is worn away and the brush is bearing on its full width. The

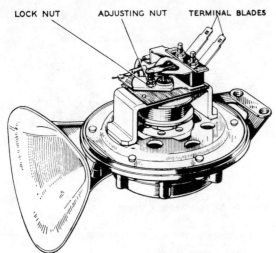

FIG 12:22 The adjusting screw on 3.8 litre models

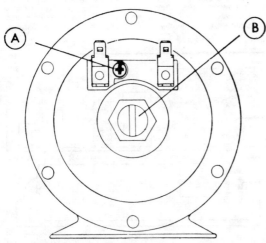

FIG 12:23 The adjusting screw on the Lucas 9H horn is screw A. The screw and locknut B must not be turned

brush gear assembly must also be renewed if the spring pressure is less than 5 to 7 oz (140 to 200 gr) when the outer end of the brush is level with the end of the slot in the brush box.

12:10 The fuses

All the fuses are accessible after lowering the centre instrument panel by removing the two top securing screws and hinging it forwards. A fuse indicator panel will also be exposed.

Electric clock:

The back of this is exposed when the centre instrument panel is hinged forwards. On all 4.2 litre models the clock is run from a mercury cell battery which will run the clock accurately for 18 months, after which the battery should be renewed.

12:11 The horns

The 3.8 litre models are fitted with horns as shown in **FIG 12:22**, and the Lucas 9H fitted to the 4.2 litre models is shown in **FIG 12:23**.

The 3.8 litre model is adjusted after the cover has been removed until it is taking a current of 13 to 15 amps. **The centre slotted screw and locknut must not be disturbed on the 9H model.** Instead turn the adjusting screw until the horn operates on a current of 6.5 to 7 amps. If either of the horns is adjusted when removed from the car then their mounting brackets must be securely gripped in a vice.

12:12 The headlamps

Earlier models had the headlamps recesses faired in with a moulded glass fairing, but this is omitted on later models to conform with USA safety regulations. The glass moulding is held in place by six setscrews. The headlamps and lenses vary to suit the local current lighting regulations so ensure that only the correct parts are refitted if a headlamp unit fails.

Two screws, those for the 4.2 litre model being shown in **FIG 12:24**, set the adjustment of the headlights. The beam setting is best left to a competent garage where they will have the correct equipment to ensure that the headlamps are accurately aligned in accordance with local regulations. These screws should not be touched when removing or replacing the headlamp. Three cross-headed screws secure the rim and headlamp into position.

12:13 The voltage stabilized instruments

The fuel gauge and water temperature gauge take their supply from a voltage stabilizing unit. The unit operates using a bi-metallic strip, whose action produces the equivalent of a continuous steady voltage at the terminals, though at any point in time the actual voltage at the terminals will either be battery voltage or nil. For this reason special test equipment is required to test the system. If a fault develops, the wiring should be checked for continuity, loose connections or defective insulation.

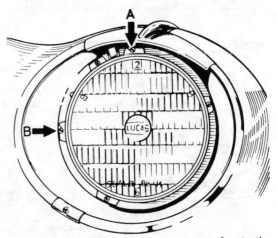

FIG 12:24 Headlamp adjustment screws. A sets the vertical alignment and B sets the horizontal. This figure shows the position on 4.2 litre models, on 3.8 litre models the screw A is at the bottom

If no fault is found in the wiring the components should be checked individually, by substituting known satisfactory items. The actual instruments themselves function by the heating of a bi-metallic strip moving the pointer.

The oil pressure gauge uses a similar voltage stabilized circuit, but in this case the voltage stabilizer is incorporated in the transmitter.

12:14 Fault diagnosis

(a) Battery discharged

1 Terminals loose or dirty
2 Shortcircuit in the system
3 Alternator/generator not charging
4 Control unit functioning incorrectly
5 Battery internally defective
6 Loose alternator/generator driving belt

(b) Battery will not hold charge

1 Low electrolyte level
2 Battery plates sulphated
3 Electrolyte leakage from cracked casing or top sealing compound
4 Plate separators ineffective

(c) Alternator output low or nil

1 Loose alternator driving belt
2 No battery supply to field coils
3 Defective wiring
4 Control unit failed
5 Diodes failed in rectifier pack
6 Brushes excessively worn or slip rings dirty

(d) Generator output low or nil

1 Loose generator driving belt
2 Defective wiring
3 Control box either failed or incorrectly adjusted
4 Defective brush gear
5 Defective field or armature coils
6 Mechanical defects in generator

(e) Starter motor lacks power or will not operate

1 Battery discharged, loose connections
2 Starter pinion assembly damaged or jammed in mesh
3 Starter switch defective
4 Starter solenoid defective
5 Brush gear faulty
6 Commutator worn or dirty
7 Armature or field coils defective
8 Engine abnormally stiff

(f) Starter motor runs but does not turn engine

1 Pinion engaging mechanism failed
2 Broken teeth on pinion or flywheel gears
3 Failed roller clutch assembly (4.2 litre models only)

(g) Starter motor rough or noisy

1 Mounting bolts loose
2 Damaged pinion or flywheel teeth
3 Weak or broken return spring

(h) Lamps inoperative or erratic

1 Battery low
2 Bulbs burned out
3 Defective wiring
4 Blown fuse (check for cause)
5 Faulty earth points
6 Lighting switch faulty

(i) Wiper motor sluggish, taking high current

1 Commutator dirty or shortcircuited
2 Excessive friction of wiper blades on glass
3 Faulty armature

(j) Fuel or temperature gauges do not register

1 No battery supply to voltage stabilizer
2 Defective voltage stabilizer
3 Cable between tank unit or temperature transmitter broken
4 Defective gauge
5 Poor earth on transmitter or tank unit

(k) Fuel or temperature gauges intermittent

1 Defective wiring
2 Defective voltage stabilizer
3 Defective transmitting units
4 Defective gauges

CHAPTER 13

THE BODYWORK

13:1 Bodywork finish

Large scale repairs to body panels are best left to expert panel beaters. Even small dents can be tricky as too much hammering will stretch the metal and make things worse instead of better. Filling minor dents and scratches is probably the best method of restoring the surface. The touching-up of paintwork is well within the powers of most owners, particularly as self-spraying cans of the correct colours are now readily available. Paint changes colour with age so it is better to spray a whole panel rather than touch-up a small area.

Cellulose paint must never be sprayed over a synthetic finish, as the synthetic paint will lift off in blisters. If there is any doubt try a spot of paint in an area where it will not show.

Before spraying it is essential to remove all traces of wax polish with white spirits. More drastic treatment is required if silicone-based polishes have been used. Lightly scuff the area to be sprayed and mask off surrounding areas with newspaper and masking tape to prevent spray dust settling on them. Use a primer surfacer or paste stopper according to the amount of filling required. Keep paste as level and smooth as possible as this will save time and effort in rubbing down later. When the surface is dry and hard rub it down using 400 grade 'wet and dry'

paper, with plenty of water as a lubricant, until it is smooth and flush with the surrounding areas. If required, use further coats of stopper and filler to achieve a perfect result. Spend plenty of time in obtaining the best surface possible as this will control the final effect. Small blemishes which are hardly noticeable on the matt surface will stand out glaringly on the polished finish.

Apply the retouching spray evenly. If the area is only part of a panel 'feather' the spray at the edges. It is better to apply two light coats, rubbing down between each, than one thick one which may run.

When the paint is dry and hard, use a cutting compound to polish the surface lightly and remove any spray dust. A final careful polish with a proprietary metal polish will produce an excellent finish. Let the paint dry for at least a couple of days before applying wax polish.

13:2 Seat belts

Instructions for fitting the seat belts are supplied with the appropriate Jaguar seat belt kits. It is strongly advised that the correct Jaguar seat belts are fitted, as not all types of belt will be suitable. If the owner has any doubts as to his ability to install seat belts correctly he should leave the work to an authorized dealer as incorrectly fitted seat belts can be of more danger than none at all.

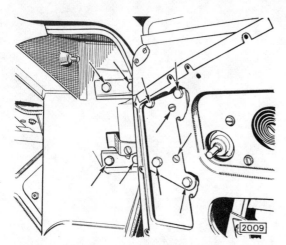

FIG 13:1 Screws and bolts securing the door hinges

13:3 The doors

The doors on all the models covered by this manual are of very similar design. On the Series 2 4.2 litre models the door locks were changed to the anti-burst type.

Removing door trim:

On the earlier models the interior door handles are secured by pins. Fit a screwdriver between the handle and spring-loaded trim cap and press the cap back against the door trim. The pin will now be exposed and can be tapped out with a suitable punch to free the handle. Later model handles are recessed and secured by a central accessible screw.

Insert a thin screwdriver under the door top chrome strip at the hinge end, and lever the strip away from its spring clip. Remove the chrome strip by similarly levering it away from the four remaining spring clips. Remove the spring clips by unscrewing the screw securing each one.

Insert a thin-bladed screwdriver between the trim panel and the door and by levering out, free the twenty-one clips holding the panel to the door. A clear plastic sheet is stuck to the door and this will have to be peeled off before the door parts are accessible.

The trim is replaced in the reverse order of dismantling, but use a glue which can be peeled off to hold the plastic sheet in place.

Door removal:

The bolts and screws securing the door to the hinge and the hinge to the car are shown in FIG 13:1. They can only be reached after the trim has been removed. Free the door from the hinge, marking the position of the hinge so that the door will fit correctly on refitting. Some degree of adjustment is provided to ensure that the door fits smoothly with the body.

Door glass removal:

Remove the door trim and loosely refit the window winder handle. Wind the window down until the window regulator roller is accessible through the bottom large aperture in the door, as shown in FIG 13:2, and unscrew the regulator stop pin from the front of the channel.

Unscrew the six screws securing the closing strip to the top of the door and remove the closing strip. Wind the window up until the regulator channel is above the door. Ease the regulator slide from the channel and lift the glass out of the door.

Door window frame:

This can be removed from the door after the window glass has been taken out. Remove the three screws securing the frame to the top of the door, carefully noting the position of any shims fitted between the frame and the door. Remove the nuts, bolts and washers securing the frame to the two brackets on the door lower panel and withdraw the frame.

Window regulator:

This can be removed after the door glass and window frame have been taken away. Undo all the screws and bolts arrowed in FIG 13:2 and lower the mechanism so that it can be withdrawn through the large lower aperture.

All the parts are replaced in the reverse order of removal. Lubricate the regulator and sliding metal parts with grease.

13:4 The door locks

The details of the earlier door lock are shown in FIG 13:3 and the antiburst lock fitted to later 4.2 litre models is shown in FIG 13:4. The only differences in servicing procedure between the two types of locks is that the splitpin P and rod U are not required when refitting the anti-burst type lock mechanism.

At monthly intervals a few drops of oil should be injected into the oil hole V on the locks and into the private key slots.

When refitting the parts of the locks lubricate moving parts with protective grease, such as Astrolan. The private lock cylinders should never be lubricated with grease.

Removing the parts:

1 Remove the door trim panel and plastic sheet.
2 Disconnect the arm from the remote control unit at the door lock by removing the clip and washers H. The

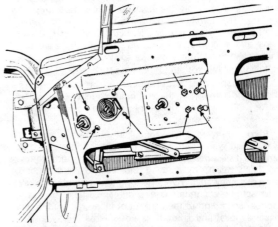

FIG 13:2 Nuts and screws securing the window regulator mechanism

152

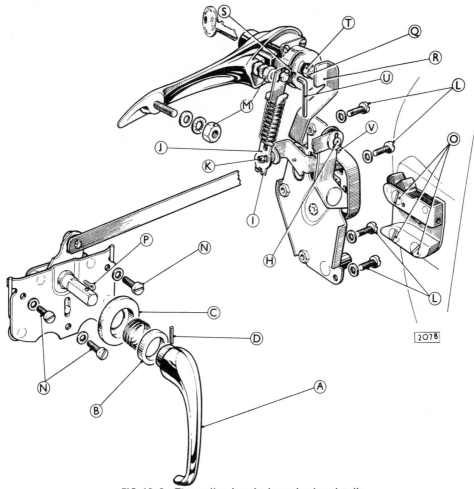

FIG 13:3 The earlier door lock mechanism details

Key to Figs 13:3 and 13:4   **A** Interior handle   **H** Lever pin, wave washer and clip   **I** Spring clip   **J** Adjustable link
K Dowel   **L** Latch fixing screw   **M** Exterior handle fixings   **N** Remote control fixing screw   **O** Striker fixing screws
P Adjusting pin   **Q** Striker   **R** Striker lever   **T** Locknut   **U** Bent adjusting pin   **V** Lubrication point

remote control unit can be removed through the
aperture in the inner door panel after removing the
three screws N.

3 Disconnect the clip I from the dowel K to free the
adjustable arm J from the door lock. The door lock
can then be removed after taking out the four securing
screws L from the rear of the door. The lock may have
to be pressed both inwards and downwards to pass
it around the window channel.

4 The outside door handle may be removed by taking
off the nuts and washers M.

Replacing parts:

The door lock itself is replaced in the reverse order of
removal. Refit the remote control unit in the reverse order
of removal. On the earlier type of lock the remote control
unit must be refitted in the locked position, using a splitpin
P to hold it in this position. Loosely secure the remote control unit in place with the screws N and then slide it along

towards the lock until the operating lever is in contact
with the lock casing. Tighten the screws N and remove
the pin P, checking that the remote control unit operates
satisfactorily. On the later anti-burst lock sufficient
adjustment is provided on the slotted holes to set the
remote control unit, but if a new unit is fitted to the earlier
type of lock the four elongated holes may have to be
further enlarged to give the correct adjustment.

The outside door handles are marked LH or RH to
ensure that they are fitted to the correct side. Hold the door
handle firmly in position and check visually through the
aperture in the door that the gap between the plunger Q
and lever R is $\frac{1}{32}$ inch. The gap must be checked through
the door aperture as pressing in the button will not give
a sufficiently accurate measurement. If the gap is incorrect, set the operating lever S to the unlocked position
and press in the door lock button. Slacken the locknut T
and screw the plunger Q in the direction required. Tighten

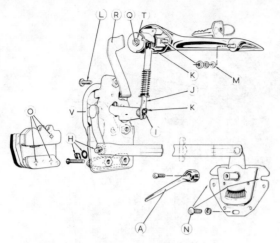

FIG 13:4   Anti-burst door lock details

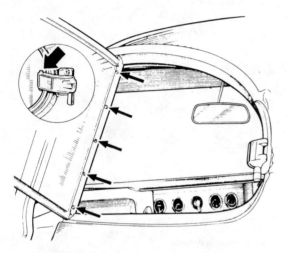

FIG 13:5   Removing no-draught ventilator

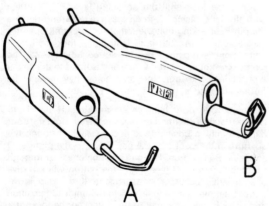

FIG 13:6   Special tools for refitting windscreen glass

the locknut T before releasing the button. Recheck the gap and readjust if required.

Set the remote control unit to the locked position and hold it there with the pin P. Turn the operating lever S to the locked position and hold it there with a piece of bent $\frac{1}{8}$ inch rod U. Refit the adjustable link J to the operating lever S if they have been separated. Manoeuvre the link J and pin U through the slot in the door so that they both hang vertically downwards when the handle is secured in place with the nuts and washers M. Secure the link J to the dowel K. Remove both pins P and U, loosely refit the interior door handle and check that the mechanism operates satisfactorily.

Door striker :

The three screws O securing the striker plate to the body should not normally be slackened. If a new striker plate is fitted, or the door requires adjustment, leave the screws sufficiently slack to allow the striker plate to be moved by firm hand pressure. Adjust the correct position by a process of trial and error, pushing the door carefully shut and never slamming it. When the plate is positioned so that the door neither rises or falls when shutting, and the plate is in line with the shutting of the door, fully tighten the securing screws.

No-draught ventilator :

This is only fitted to fixed head coupés. It can be taken off, as shown in **FIG 13:5**, by removing the two screws securing the catch to the body of the car, opening the NDV wide, and undoing the five screws securing it to the post.

13:5 The windscreen

If a windscreen glass has broken make sure that all glass particles are removed, **especially from the windscreen demister ducts.** Disconnect the hoses to the ducts to make sure no particles remain as otherwise they may be blown into the passenger's or driver's face by the action of the heater.

The windscreen rubber is sealed to both the glass and the frame, so removal is bound to damage the rubber. Always fit a new windscreen rubber when fitting new glass or replacing the old windscreen. The special tools required for replacing a screen are shown in **FIG 13:6**.

FIG 13:7 Using special tool A to refit windscreen rubber over glass

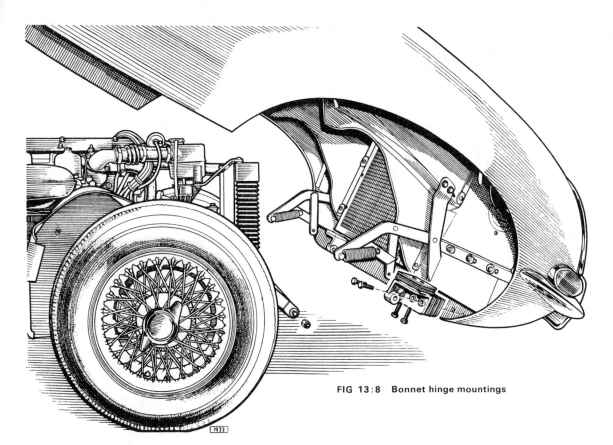

FIG 13:8   Bonnet hinge mountings

Open cars:

1 Remove the screen pillar cappings from the top of the pillars by undoing the two screws securing each capping. The flat-headed screw must always be on the inside face of the pillar otherwise it will prevent the hood from seating properly.

2 Free the screen pillar trim welts from their clips on the flanges of the pillars. Drill out the two 'pop' rivets securing each chrome finisher to the screen pillars and prise away the chrome finisher from the screen rubber.

3 Extract one end of the screen rubber insert and then pull free the complete length after removing the chrome strip. Run a thin blunt tool around the outside of the windscreen to break the seal between the rubber and the windscreen aperture. Start at a top corner and hit the glass with the flat of the hand to force it out. Work downwards and then around the glass to free it. Break the seal between the top frame sealer and glass, using a thin blunt tool, and gently remove the top frame.

4 If the windscreen glass has broken spontaneously and not by impact with anything, check the flange of the windscreen aperture for bumps or distortions. Dress out distortions and file away the bumps. Clean away any old sealant.

5 Fit a new windscreen rubber to the aperture so that the flat side of the rubber is towards the rear. Refit the new glass to the rubber, using tool A (shown in **FIG 13:6**) as shown in **FIG 13:7**. Start at the bottom of the screen and work in both directions from the same spot. **Do not start in two separate places.** Use a pressure gun fitted with a copper nozzle to seal between the windscreen rubber and metal body flange and then between the rubber and glass. Thread one end of the screen rubber insert through the loop in the special tool B, shown in **FIG 13:6**, and use the tool to refit the insert, rounded wide edge outside. Wipe away excess sealant using rag and **white spirits only.**

6 Fit the chrome strip over the screen rubber and bend it to shape if required. Remove it and coat the inside with Bostik 1251. When the Bostik is tacky refit the chrome strip using special tool A to lift the screen rubber over it and into place.

7 Refit the windscreen top frame, using a new sealing strip. Lubricate the sealing strip and glass with soft-soap solution if the frame is difficult to refit.

8 Coat the inner surface of the screen pillar finisher with Bostik 1251 at the points where it will contact the screen rubber. When the Bostik is tacky, refit the finisher using special tool A to lip the rubber over the finisher. Secure the finisher in place with two pop rivets in each of the original holes in the finishers. Refit the screen pillar cappings, ensuring that the flat-headed screws are on the inside faces. Refit the trim welts.

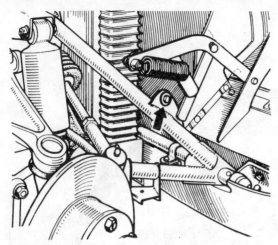

FIG 13:9 Bonnet balance spring mechanism pivots

Fixed head coupé:

Apart from the differences in the trim the windscreen glass is removed and replaced in exactly the same manner as that on the open cars.

Rear glass:

The rear glass on the detachable hard top is made of a clear tough plastic which will not break under normal circumstances, but may be renewed if the old light becomes excessively scratched. The rear light on the coupés is of glass. Both are removed and replaced in a similar manner to the windscreen glass on the open models..

13:6 The bonnet

Early 3.8 litre bonnet locks:

These are a coach-type lock opened by a separate T-shaped handle. With these locks released the rear of the bonnet is still secured by a safety lock. The safety lock is opened by inserting the fingers under the rear edge of the bonnet and pressing the catch.

Adjustment to the locks is made by the addition or removal of packing pieces under the lockplates attached to the body. The quantity of packing should be adjusted under each lockplate until the bonnet is held securely shut.

All later bonnet locks:

The locks are operated by two small levers located on the door hinge posts. Each lever is held in by a bayonet-type fitting to ensure against accidental operation. A safety lock is still fitted under the rear edge of the bonnet.

Adjustment is provided by means of rubber buffers attached to adjustable spigot pins. Slacken the locknuts on the pins and turn them until the bonnet lock pawls hold the bonnet firmly in the locked position. Tighten the locknuts after adjustment.

Bonnet removal:

1 Disconnect the multi-cable connector at the lefthand side front of the bonnet. The pins are graded in size so that the socket can only be refitted in one position.

2 Refer to **FIG 13:8**. Remove the locknuts and washers securing the hinges to the front subframe mounting pin. Referring to **FIG 13:9** remove the nuts, bolts and washers securing the balance spring assemblies to the subframe.

3 Mark around both hinges to facilitate refitting. Referring to **FIG 13:8**, remove the four setscrews and washers securing the lefthand hinge to the bonnet and remove the hinge, carefully noting the quantity and position of the packing shims. Support the bonnet while removing the lefthand hinge and, still supporting the bonnet, slide it towards the righthand side to free it from the righthand pivot pin and lift it free from the car.

4 On 4.2 litre models the number plate tie rod fork must also be detached from the chassis front cross tube by removing the splitpin and withdrawing the clevis pin, before the bonnet can be slid sideways for removal.

The bonnet is replaced in the reverse order of removal. A limited degree of adjustment is provided in the bolt holes to ensure that the bonnet aligns smoothly with the body.

Radiator grille:

With the introduction of Series 3 in 1971 a slatted grille was added to the radiator air intake. This is easily removed by taking out the screws and nylon nuts securing it to the mounting brackets.

If it is required also to remove the grille surround, the front bumper must first be removed by unscrewing the two securing bolts on each side. Two screws secure the upper portion to the bonnet, and after they have been removed the strip can be prised out of its retaining clips. The lower portion is similarly held by screws.

13:7 The facia parts

Before doing any work, either requiring removal of the facia or on connections behind the facia, disconnect the battery.

There are differences between righthand drive and lefthand drive models as well as minor differences between models, but if the following instructions are used as a guide and care is taken over connections they will be adequate for all models.

FIG 13:10 Attachment points on side facia panel (righthand drive version shown)

Instrument side facia panel:

The location of the attachment points is shown in **FIG 13:10**.

1 Unscrew the two chrome bezels securing the speedo-meter trip and clock control cables. Remove the securing screws and take off the under scuttle casings by drawing them out of their clips.

2 Withdraw warning lamps, panel lights and their holders from the back of the panel. Label them if required to ensure correct replacement. Some may not be accessible at this stage, but bear in mind that all must be removed before the panel is taken out.

3 Disconnect the speedometer drive cable from the back of the instrument. Disconnect the tachometer electrical cables at the connector, never at the instrument itself.

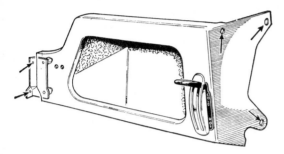

FIG 13:11 Attachment points on glove box (righthand version shown)

4 Release the upper steering column clamp and allow the steering column to rest on the driver's seat. Disconnect the direction indicator wires at the connector behind the facia panel. Unscrew the chrome bezel securing the dipswitch and push the switch out at the back of the panel.

5 Undo the two screws securing the centre instrument panel in position and lower it down horizontally. Remove the three setscrews and washers securing the panel to the instrument panel support bracket. On righthand drive models also remove the nut, bolt and washer securing the mixture control bracket to the panel support. Remove the two nuts and washers securing the facia panel to body by the door hinge post.

6 Pull out the panel and detach the remainder of the connections.

Glove box:

1 Remove the under scuttle casing. Lower the centre instrument panel down to its horizontal position.

2 Remove the grab handle. Two of the setscrews are on the inner face of the glove box. On early models of the 3.8 litre lift the draught rubber and pull away the trim to expose the third screw.

3 Disconnect the map light and withdraw the choke warning light if fitted. Disconnect the cables to the control levers (heater or choke depending on whether the model is lefthand or righthand drive).

4 The attachment points are shown in **FIG 13:11**. Remove the nuts, bolts and washers securing the glove box, and after checking that all connections are detached remove the glove box.

Top facia panel:

The attachment points for the 3.8 litre model are shown in **FIG 13:12**. The remainder of the models are similar but will have more demister ducts, and 2+2 4.2 Series 2 models have the top panel connected to a separate demister panel.

1 Remove the under scuttle casings. Remove the central console panel. If a radio is fitted disconnect the aerial lead and power cables leaving the radio in the console.

2 Lower the centre instrument panel. Undo and remove the nuts and bolts holding the top panel.

3 Disconnect the electric cables attached to the map light. Disconnect the flexible hoses for the demister ducts and lift the top panel away.

All the parts are refitted in the reverse order of removal.

13:8 The heater

The same type of heater is fitted to all the models covered by this manual. The details of the heater fitted to the 3.8 litre models are shown in **FIG 13:13**. Though the heater is the same the controls have been altered. **FIG 13:14** shows the controls on the 3.8 litre models and **FIG 13:15** shows the controls on the 4.2 litre Series 2 models. Though appearing different the controls are used in the same way but there is the addition of the heater outlet controls D on later models. On earlier models two doors just under the scuttle control the distribution of the air between the screen and car. On the later models rotation of the knobs D controls the distribution. Fully rotating the righthand knob clockwise and the lefthand knob anticlockwise directs all the supply to the screen and none to the car. Rotating the knobs in the opposite directions progressively increases the amount of air to the car until, when they are fully in the opposite directions, all the air is sent to the car and little to the screen.

The air control lever A regulates the amount of air passed through the heater so that the flow can be set to the desired rate. The temperature control lever B operates a valve which controls the amount of hot water passing through the heater. The valve can be set progressively from no hot water flow to full flow, and thus within limits can vary the temperature of the air coming out of the heater.

An electrically operated fan is fitted to boost the air flow when the car is stationary or travelling slowly. At higher speeds the fan is unnecessary as the motion of the car will provide an adequate air flow.

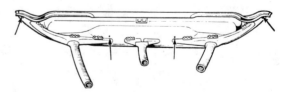

FIG 13:12 Attachment points on 3.8 litre model top facia panel

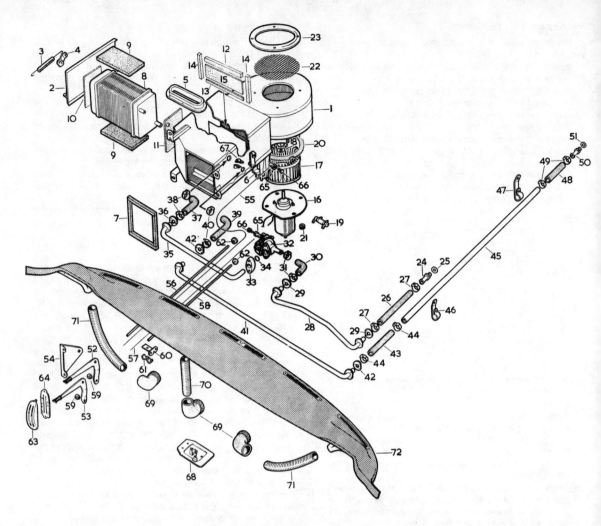

FIG 13:13   3.8 litre model heater details

Key to Fig 13:13   1 Heater case   2 Side panel   3 Spring   4 Flap lever   5 Air release duct   6 Mounting bracket
7 Seal between heater case and dash   8 Water radiator for heater   9 Felt seal   10 Seal   11 Seal   12 Seal on air control flap
13 Seal on heater case   14 Seal on air control flap   15 Air release duct seal   16 Fan motor   17 Fan   18 Spire nut
19 Electrical resistance   20 Sealing ring   21 Grommet   22 Wire mesh   23 Wire mesh securing ring
24 Manifold heater pipe adaptor   25 Copper washer   26 Water hose   27 Hose clip   28 Water feed pipe
29 Feed pipe flange   30 Water hose elbow   31 Hose clip   32 Water control tap   33 Control tap mounting block
34 Sealing ring   35 Feed pipe from water control tap   36 Feed pipe securing flange   37 Water hose elbow   38 Hose clip
39 Water hose elbow   40 Hose clip   41 Water return pipe   42 Securing flange   43 Water hose   44 Hose clip
45 Water return pipe   46 Return pipe mounting clip   47 Return pipe mounting clip   48 Water hose   49 Hose clips
50 Water pump adaptor   51 Copper washer   52 Air flap control lever   53 Water control tap lever   54 Control lever
support bracket   55 Air flap control cable   56 Conduit for air flap control cable   57 Water tap control cable
58 Conduit for water tap control cable   59 Control cable retaining clip   60 Cable abutment clamp bracket   61 Abutment clamp
62 Grommet   63 Control lever escutcheon   64 Plate   65 Inner control cable trunnions   66 Setscrew   67 Abutment clamp
68 Heater doors   69 Rubber elbow   70 Demister hose   71 Demister hose   72 Screen rail

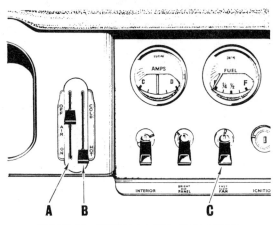

FIG 13:14   3.8 litre model heater controls

Key to Figs 13:14 and 13:15
B Heater temperature controls
D Heater outlet controls

A Heater air controls
C Heater fan switch

Maintenance:

The heater requires no separate maintenance, but when flushing the cooling system disconnect the hoses 43 and 26 and flush through the heater radiator and system in the reverse direction of normal flow until the water comes out clean. At long intervals it may become necessary to use an air-line to blow out any accumulations of dirt and dust in the heater.

Removal:

1 Drain the cooling system and disconnect the battery.
2 Disconnect and remove the two rubber elbow pipes 37 and 39.
3 Slacken the pinch bolt 66 and the pinch bolt securing the clamp 67 so that the inner cable 55 and its conduit 56 can be freed from the body of the heater.
4 Remove the four sets of bolts, plain and serrated washers securing the heater body to the scuttle. Remove the two screws securing the heater bracket to the subframe and lift out the heater.

The heater is replaced in the reverse order of removal. After replacement set the heater controls correctly.

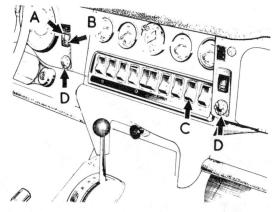

FIG 13:15   4.2 litre Series 2 model heater controls

If the heater fails to produce hot air after the system has been drained and refilled, even though the engine is hot, suspect an air lock. Slacken each hose clip in turn, while running the engine, in the same order as the direction of the water flow. Retighten the hose clip as soon as water seeps from the connection. Use rags and a bowl to prevent drips from staining the carpets or trim.

Cable adjustment:

Slacken the pinch bolts securing the outer cable 56 and the inner cable 55 to the heater. Set the facia control in the car to the 'On' position and press the flap lever on the heater to the fully forward position, as shown in **FIG 13:16**. Tighten the pinch bolts to hold the inner and outer cables in place.

Slacken the pinch bolts securing the inner cable 57 and the outer conduit 58 to the water control tag 32. Set the temperature control lever to 'Hot' and press the lever on the water valve fully forward, as shown at B in **FIG 13:16**. Tighten both pinch bolts to hold the inner and outer cables in position. If the water valve is defective it must be renewed as these are sealed items and cannot be repaired.

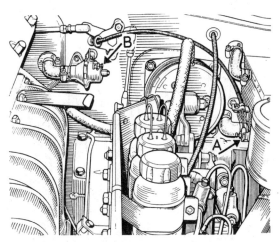

FIG 13:16   Setting the heater operating cables

13:9 The air-conditioning system

This can be fitted as an optional extra to 4.2 litre models. **Under no circumstances should the owner disconnect any of the high-pressure flexible hoses or connections in the system.** The system is pressurized with refrigerant and any work on the car requiring disconnection of the system must be taken to a garage specializing in air-conditioning systems.

Routine maintenance:

1 Ensure that the condenser, whose mounting points are shown in **FIG 13:17**, is kept clear of dirt and insects. Use a hosepipe and flush through in the

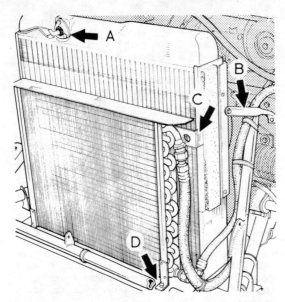

FIG 13:17 Air-conditioner condenser mountings

Key to Fig 13:17

B Radiator mounting strap   **A** Fan thermostat switch
D Condenser lower mounting   **C** Condenser upper mounting

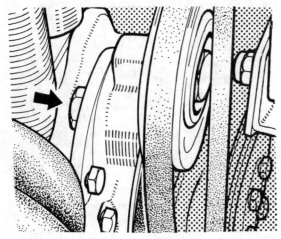

FIG 13:18 Air-conditioner compressor drive belt adjusting point

opposite direction to the airflow to remove any accumulations of dirt.

2 Periodically check that the driving belt tension is correct. The belt adjustment point is shown in **FIG 13:18**.

3 Select the air-conditioning system on and run the engine at a fast idle speed. Watch the fluid as it passes through the sight glass E, shown in **FIG 13:19**. The fluid should be clear with no trace of frothing. Repeat the test at 1800 rev/min and, provided that the fluid is still clear, gradually increase the engine speed. If at any time frothing appears it shows that the refrigerant

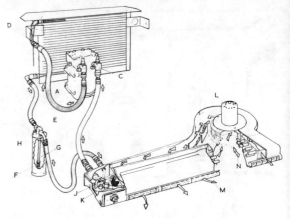

FIG 13:19 Air-conditioner schematic circuit

Key to Fig 13:19   **A** Compressor   **B** Discharge valve
C Suction valve   **D** Condenser   **E** Sight glass
F Cotton bobbin   **G** Dessicant   **H** Receiver drier assembly
J Expansion valve   **K** Capillary tube   **L** Blower assembly
M Air flow outlet   **N** Air flow inlet

level is low. **A low refrigerant level must only be topped up by qualified personnel.** It also indicates a possible leak in the system which again should only be checked by qualified personnel.

4 At 12 month intervals the oil level in the compressor should be checked and topped up as necessary. As this requires a special procedure it is recommended that the car be taken to a qualified garage and the opportunity taken for the system to be given a complete check over.

Description and operation:

The components of the system are shown in **FIG 13:19**. The mounting of the condenser D has already been shown in **FIG 13:17**. The evaporator unit is mounted under the facia and the mounting points for the compressor A and receiver/drier H are shown in **FIG 13:20**.

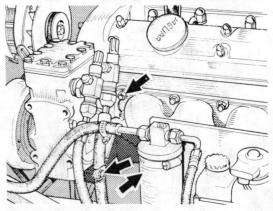

FIG 13:20 Air-conditioner compressor mounting points and receiver/drier unit

The compressor is belt driven from the engine through a magnetic clutch assembly. The magnetic clutch only operates when a current passes through it. The current is controlled by a thermostatic switch so that the system does not operate when the interior of the car drops to the temperature selected. When running, the compressor draws the vapour from the evaporator unit, leaving a low pressure in the unit. The compressor compresses the vapour and after passing through the condenser, where the heat is removed, all the refrigerant passes as liquid through the sight glass E and receiver/drier assembly H. The refrigerant is both filtered and dried of any moisture by the cotton bobbin F and dessicant G. The liquid refrigerant then passes through the controlled expansion valve J where the pressure drop causes it to expand into a very cold vapour. This vapour then picks up heat from the air blown by the blower assembly L over the coils of the evaporator unit before being once more drawn back through the compressor.

The air is also drawn in over some of the coils in the evaporator unit, causing the temperature of the vapour at that point to be proportional to the temperature in the car. This temperature is fed by a thermal bulb and capilliary tube K to operate the expansion valve J so that only vapour and not liquid passes into the evaporator unit.

The air drawn through the evaporator unit is cooled and the moisture in it immediately condenses on the coils. Drains are provided under the evaporator unit to lead this condensed water away. If the weather outside is temperate and humid this water, instead of running away, can freeze on the coils and impair the effective running of the system. Under such conditions a warmer internal car temperature should be selected.

Two concentric rotary switches are fitted to the evaporator unit. The outer switch controls the speed of the blower motor as well as supplying power to the system when the ignition is on and the system is selected. The inner switch is for the temperature and progressively lowers the temperature at which the thermostat switch

opens as it is rotated in the 'Cooler' direction. When the system senses that the temperature in the car is lower than the temperature set by the control switch the points on the thermostat switch open and the power supply to the magnetic clutch is cut off so that it stops driving the compressor. As the temperature rises the switch points close and power is again restored to the magnetic clutch.

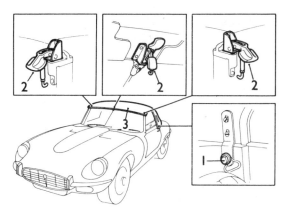

FIG 13:21   Removing the hard top, Series 3. For key see text

13:10 Detachable hard top

This optional fitting to the open models of Series 3 cars is quickly removed as follows:

Refer to **FIG 13:21**. Remove the bolts securing the locating brackets to the body trim (Inset 1), then release the toggles securing the front edge of the hard top to the windscreen rail (Inset 2). Lift off the hard top and secure the sides of the tonneau cover to the Velcro strip. Replace the securing bolts.

Refitting is the reverse of the above procedure.

APPENDIX

TECHNICAL DATA

Engine Fuel system Ignition system Cooling system
Clutch Gearbox Automatic transmission Rear axle
Rear suspension Front suspension Steering
Power steering Brakes Electrical system
Wheels and tyres Special tools Torque wrench settings

STANDARD MEASURE AND METRIC EQUIVALENTS

FRACTIONAL AND METRIC EQUIVALENTS

HINTS ON MAINTENANCE AND OVERHAUL

GLOSSARY OF TERMS

INDEX

Inches	Decimals	Milli-metres	Inches to Millimetres — Inches	mm	Millimetres to Inches — mm	Inches
1/64	.015625	.3969	.001	.0254	.01	.00039
1/32	.03125	.7937	.002	.0508	.02	.00079
3/64	.046875	1.1906	.003	.0762	.03	.00118
1/16	.0625	1.5875	.004	.1016	.04	.00157
5/64	.078125	1.9844	.005	.1270	.05	.00197
3/32	.09375	2.3812	.006	.1524	.06	.00236
7/64	.109375	2.7781	.007	.1778	.07	.00276
1/8	.125	3.1750	.008	.2032	.08	.00315
9/64	.140625	3.5719	.009	.2286	.09	.00354
5/32	.15625	3.9687	.01	.254	.1	.00394
11/64	.171875	4.3656	.02	.508	.2	.00787
3/16	.1875	4.7625	.03	.762	.3	.01181
13/64	.203125	5·1594	.04	1.016	.4	.01575
7/32	.21875	5.5562	.05	1.270	.5	.01969
15/64	.234375	5.9531	.06	1.524	.6	.02362
1/4	.25	6.3500	.07	1.778	.7	.02756
17/64	.265625	6.7469	.08	2.032	.8	.03150
9/32	.28125	7.1437	.09	2.286	.9	.03543
19/64	.296875	7.5406	.1	2.54	1	.03937
5/16	.3125	7.9375	.2	5.08	2	.07874
21/64	.328125	8.3344	.3	7.62	3	.11811
11/32	.34375	8.7312	.4	10.16	4	.15748
23/64	.359375	9.1281	.5	12.70	5	.19685
3/8	.375	9.5250	.6	15.24	6	.23622
25/64	.390625	9.9219	.7	17.78	7	.27559
13/32	.40625	10.3187	.8	20.32	8	.31496
27/64	.421875	10.7156	.9	22.86	9	.35433
7/16	.4375	11.1125	1	25.4	10	.39370
29/64	.453125	11.5094	2	50.8	11	.43307
15/32	.46875	11.9062	3	76.2	12	.47244
31/64	.484375	12.3031	4	101.6	13	.51181
1/2	.5	12.7000	5	127.0	14	.55118
33/64	.515625	13.0969	6	152.4	15	.59055
17/32	.53125	13.4937	7	177.8	16	.62992
35/64	.546875	13.8906	8	203.2	17	.66929
9/16	.5625	14.2875	9	228.6	18	.70866
37/64	.578125	14.6844	10	254.0	19	.74803
19/32	.59375	15.0812	11	279.4	20	.78740
39/64	.609375	15.4781	12	304.8	21	.82677
5/8	.625	15.8750	13	330.2	22	.86614
41/64	.640625	16.2719	14	355.6	23	.90551
21/32	.65625	16.6687	15	381.0	24	.94488
43/64	.671875	17.0656	16	406.4	25	.98425
11/16	.6875	17.4625	17	431.8	26	1.02362
45/64	.703125	17.8594	18	457.2	27	1.06299
23/32	.71875	18.2562	19	482.6	28	1.10236
47/64	.734375	18.6531	20	508.0	29	1.14173
3/4	.75	19.0500	21	533.4	30	1.18110
49/64	.765625	19.4469	22	558.8	31	1.22047
25/32	.78125	19.8437	23	584.2	32	1.25984
51/64	.796875	20.2406	24	609.6	33	1.29921
13/16	.8125	20.6375	25	635.0	34	1.33858
53/64	.828125	21.0344	26	660.4	35	1.37795
27/32	.84375	21.4312	27	685.8	36	1.41732
55/64	.859375	21.8281	28	711.2	37	1.4567
7/8	.875	22.2250	29	736.6	38	1.4961
57/64	.890625	22.6219	30	762.0	39	1.5354
29/32	.90625	23.0187	31	787.4	40	1.5748
59/64	.921875	23.4156	32	812.8	41	1.6142
15/16	.9375	23.8125	33	838.2	42	1.6535
61/64	.953125	24.2094	34	863.6	43	1.6929
31/32	.96875	24.6062	35	889.0	44	1.7323
63/64	.984375	25.0031	36	914.4	45	1.7717

UNITS	Pints to Litres	Gallons to Litres	Litres to Pints	Litres to Gallons	Miles to Kilometres	Kilometres to Miles	Lbs. per sq. In. to Kg. per sq. Cm.	Kg. per sq. Cm. to Lbs. per sq. In.
1	.57	4.55	1.76	.22	1.61	.62	.07	14.22
2	1.14	9.09	3.52	.44	3.22	1.24	.14	28.50
3	1.70	13.64	5.28	.66	4.83	1.86	.21	42.67
4	2.27	18.18	7.04	.88	6.44	2.49	.28	56.89
5	2.84	22.73	8.80	1.10	8.05	3.11	.35	71.12
6	3.41	27.28	10.56	1.32	9.66	3.73	.42	85.34
7	3.98	31.82	12.32	1.54	11.27	4.35	.49	99.56
8	4.55	36.37	14.08	1.76	12.88	4.97	.56	113.79
9		40.91	15.84	1.98	14.48	5.59	.63	128.00
10		45.46	17.60	2.20	16.09	6.21	.70	142.23
20				4.40	32.19	12.43	1.41	284.47
30				6.60	48.28	18.64	2.11	426.70
40				8.80	64.37	24.85		
50					80.47	31.07		
60					96.56	37.28		
70					112.65	43.50		
80					128.75	49.71		
90					144.84	55.92		
100					160.93	62.14		

UNITS	Lb ft to kgm	Kgm to lb ft	UNITS	Lb ft to kgm	Kgm to lb ft
1	.138	7.233	7	.967	50.631
2	.276	14.466	8	1.106	57.864
3	.414	21.699	9	1.244	65.097
4	.553	28.932	10	1.382	72.330
5	.691	36.165	20	2.765	144.660
6	.829	43.398	30	4.147	216.990

TECHNICAL DATA

Unless otherwise stated the dimensions are in inches and the figures in the brackets are given in millimetres.

ENGINE

Type	6 cylinder in-line, twin camshaft OHV, watercooled, 'Brivadium' dry liners
Compression ratio	9:1 or 8:1 depending on pistons fitted

Bore (nominal)

4.2 litre	3.625 (92.07)
3.8 litre	3.4252 (87)
Firing order	1–5–3–6–2–4 (counting rear cylinder as No. 1)

Engine speeds

Maximum permissible	5500 rev/min
Normal maximum	5000 rev/min
Running-in maximum	2500 rev/min for first 1000 miles (1600 km)
	3000 rev/min for next 1000 miles

Compression test pressures

9:1 compression	180 lb/sq in (12.65 kg/sq cm)
8:1 compression	155 lb/sq in (10.90 kg/sq cm)
Cylinder head	Aluminium alloy, 'S' type with straight ports, 'Gold top'

Camshafts

Type	$\frac{3}{8}$ inch lift, cast iron with chilled faces
End float	.0045 to .008 (.11 to .20)
Bearings	Four sets per shaft, steel-backed white-metal. No undersize bearings
Journal diameter	$1.00 {}^{-.0005}_{-.001}$ $(25.4 {}^{-.013}_{-.05})$

Crankshaft

Type	Manganese/molybdenum steel, seven main bearings
Maximum wear or taper on journals or crankpins	.003 (.08) — regrind to cure
Minimum diameter for regrind	—.040 (—1.02)
Bearings (Big-end and main)	Steel-backed lead/bronze shells
Undersize bearings	—.010, —.020, —.030, —.040 (—.25, —.51, —.76, —1.02)
Crankpin diameter	$2.086 {}^{+.0006}_{-.000}$ $(52.98 {}^{+.015}_{-.00})$

Journal diameter

Front, centre, rear	2.750 to 2.7505 (69.85 to 69.86)
Intermediate	2.7495 to 2.750 (69.84 to 69.85)
End float	.004 to .006 (.10 to .15 mm) set by thrust washers

Thrust washer thickness

Standard	.092 ± .001 (2.33 ± .025)
Oversize	.096 ± .001 (2.43 ± .025)

Connecting rod

Type	Steel stampings with longitudinal drilling for oil to pass from big-end to small-end
Length	$7\frac{3}{4}$ (19.68) centre-to-centre
Small-end	Renewable steel-backed phosphor/bronze bush

Pistons

Maximum bore wear	.006 (.15) —rebore to cure
Oversize pistons available	+.010, +.020, +.030 (+.25, +.51, +.76)

Type

3.8 litre	Brico semi-split skirt, light alloy
4.2 litre	Similar to 3.8 litre on earlier models Hepworth and Grandage solid skirt (later)

Piston grades

3.8 litre

Grade	To suit cylinder bore size
F	3.4248 to 3.4251 (86.990 to 86.997)
G	3.4252 to 3.4255 (87.000 to 87.007)
H	3.4256 to 3.4259 (87.010 to 87.017)
J	3.4260 to 3.4263 (87.020 to 87.027)
K	3.4264 to 3.4267 (87.030 to 87.037)

4.2 litre

Grade	To suit cylinder bore size
F	3.6250 to 3.6253 (92.075 to 92.0826)
G	3.6254 to 3.6257 (92.0852 to 92.0928)
H	3.6258 to 3.6261 (92.0953 to 92.1029)
J	3.6262 to 3.6265 (92.1055 to 92.1131)
K	3.6266 to 3.6269 (92.1156 to 92.1123)

Skirt clearance	Measured at bottom of skirt 90 deg. to gudgeon pin axis)
Brico pistons	.0011 to .0017 (.028 to .043)
Hepworth and Grandage pistons	.0007 to .0013 (.018 to .03)

Piston rings

Number	3, 2 compression, 1 oil control
Side clearance in groove	.001 to .003 (.02 to .07)
Gap fitted	
All top compression rings	.015 to .020 (.38 to .51)
Second compression ring (3.8)	.015 to .020 (.38 to .51)
Second compression ring (4.2)	.010 to .015 (.254 to .38)
Oil control ring (3.8)	.011 to .016 (.28 to .41)
Oil control ring (4.2)	.015 to .033 (.38 to .82)
Maxiflex ring (4.2)	.015 to .045 (.38 to 1.143)

Valves

Material	
Inlet	Silicon/chrome steel
Exhaust	Austenitic steel
Seat angle	45 deg.
Head diameter	
Inlet	$1\frac{3}{4} \pm .002$ (44.45 $\pm$ .05)
Exhaust	$1\frac{5}{8} \pm .002$ (41.27 $\pm$ .05)
Stem diameter (both)	$\frac{5}{16} \begin{smallmatrix}-.0025\\-.0035\end{smallmatrix}$ $(7.95 \begin{smallmatrix}-.06\\-.09\end{smallmatrix})$
Valve clearance (set by shims)	
Touring	
Inlet	.004 (.10)
Exhaust	.006 (.15)
Racing	
Inlet	.006 (.15)
Exhaust	.010 (.25)

Valve springs
Free length
  Inner ... ... $1\frac{21}{32}$ (42.07)
  Outer ... ... $1\frac{15}{16}$ (49.2)
Fitted length and load
  Inner ... ... $1\frac{7}{32}$ (30.96) at 30.33 lbs (13.76 kg)
  Outer ... ... $1\frac{5}{16}$ (33.34) at 48.375 lbs (21.94 kg)
Number of free coils
  Inner ... ... 6 (12 SWG wire)
  Outer ... ... 5 (10 SWG wire)

Valve guides
Length
  Inlet ... ... $1\frac{13}{16}$ (46.04)
  Exhaust ... ... $1\frac{15}{16}$ (49.21)
Material ... ... Cast iron
Inside diameter
  Inlet ... ... $\frac{5}{16}\ {}^{-.0005}_{-.0015}\ (7.94\ {}^{-.013}_{-.038})$
  Exhaust ... ... $\frac{5}{16} \pm .0005$ (7.94 ± .013)
Interference fit in head ... ... .0005 to .0022 (.013 to .055)
Outside diameter
  No identification groove (standard) ... .501 to .502 (12.70 to 12.725)
  One groove (1st oversize) ... ... .503 to .504 (12.776 to 12.801)
  Two groove (2nd oversize) ... ... .506 to .507 (12.852 to 12.877)
  Three groove (3rd oversize) ... ... .511 to .512 (12.979 to 13.005)
Ream cylinder head
  2nd oversize ... ... $.505 \pm {}^{.0005}_{.0002}\ (12.83 \pm {}^{.012}_{.005})$
  3rd oversize ... ... $.510 \pm {}^{.0005}_{.0002}\ (12.95 \pm {}^{.012}_{.005})$
Protrusion above spring seat spot face ... $\frac{5}{16}$ (.8)

Valve seat inserts
Material ... ... Centrifugally cast, cast iron
Interference fit ... ... .003 (.08) produced by precision grinding, new seat fitted to cylinder head with head heated to 300°F (150°C)

Maximum distance between valve stem and back of cam ... ... .320 (8.13)

Valve tappet
Material ... ... Chilled cast iron
Outside diameter ... ... 1.3738 to 1.3742 (34.89 to 34.90)

Tappet guide
Material ... ... Austenitic iron
Internal reamed diameter ... ... $1.375\ {}^{+.0007}_{-.000}\ (34.925\ {}^{+.018}_{-.000})$ after fitment
Interference fit in head ... ... .003 (.07) produced by precision grinding, new guide fitted with cylinder head heated to 300°F (150°C)

Valve timing
Inlet valve opens ... ... 15 deg. BTDC
Inlet valve closes ... ... 57 deg. ABDC
Exhaust valve opens ... ... 57 deg. BBDC
Exhaust valve closes ... ... 15 deg. ATDC

3.8 litre cylinder liners
Bore size for fitting liners	3.561 to 3.562 (90.45 to 90.47)
Interference fit...	.001 to .005 (.025 to .125)
Overall length	6 $\frac{3}{32}$ (17.7 cm)

4.2 litre cylinder liners
Bore size for fitting liners	3.761 to 3.762 (94.03 to 94.04)
Interference fit...	.003 to .005 (.08 to .125)
Overall length	6.959 to 6.979 (17.39 to 17.45 cm)

Timing chains and sprockets
Type	Duplex $\frac{3}{8}$ pitch (9.5)
Top chain pitches	100
Bottom chain pitches	82
Crankshaft sprocket	21 teeth
Outer intermediate sprocket	28 teeth
Inner intermediate sprocket	20 teeth
Camshaft sprocket	30 teeth
Idler sprocket	21 teeth

Oil pressure (hot) ... ...   40 lb/sq in at 3000 rev/min

Oil capacity (refill) ... ...   15 Imperial pints (18 US pints, 8.5 litres)

FUEL SYSTEM

Fuel pump
3.8 litre	Lucas 2FP centrifugal pump
4.2 litre	Diaphragm operated pump

Fuel pressure (3.8 litre)
Early models	2 lb/sq in (.14 kg/sq cm)
Later models	3 to 3½ lb/sq in (.2 to .25 kg/sq cm) when carburetters fitted with 'Delrin' needles

Carburetters
Standard	Triple SU HD8 (2 inch 5.08 mm)
Exhaust emission	Twin Stromberg 175 CD2SE

Carburetter needle size
SU	UM
Stromberg	B1E, supplied in appropriate Red Emission Pack

Jet size
SU	.125 (3.17)
Stromberg	Not to be changed without renewing sub-assembly or carburetter

Emission control service kits
12,000 mile	Yellow Emission Pack Part No. 11549
24,000 mile	Red Emission Pack Part No. 11550
	Part No. 11791 for cars fitted with water-jacketed secondary throttle housing

Idling speed
3.8 litre, 4.2 litre automatic transmission ...	500 rev/min
4.2 litre manual transmission	700 rev/min
Emission control automatic transmission ...	650 rev/min
Emission control manual transmission	750 rev/min

Fuel tank capacity ... ...   Approximately 14 Imperial gallons (16¾ US gallons, 63.64 litres)

IGNITION SYSTEM

Distributor type
3.8 litre ... ... Lucas DMBZ.6A
4.2 litre ... ... Lucas 22D6

Ignition timing
8:1 compression ratio ... ... 9 deg. BTDC (static)
9:1 compression ratio ... ... 10 deg. BTDC (static)
Emission controlled ... ... 5 deg. approx (static) BTDC
10 deg. BTDC at 1000 rev/min

Emission control dynamic settings

Rev/min						Without exhaust hot spot	With exhaust hot spot
1200 ...	...	...	...	...	...	13 to 17 deg.	8 to 12 deg.
1600 ...	...	...	...	...	...	22 to 26 deg.	17 to 21 deg.
2900 ...	...	...	...	...	...	29 to 33 deg.	24 to 28 deg.
4400 ...	...	...	...	...	...	37 to 41 deg.	32 to 36 deg.

Distributor rotation ... ... Anticlockwise
Firing order 1–5–3–6–2–4
Points gap ... ... .014 to .016 (.36 to .41)
Sparking plugs
Type ... ... Champion UN.12Y (touring) Champion N.3 (racing)
Gap ... ... .025 (.64)

COOLING SYSTEM

Thermostat						Starts opening	Fully open
C.12867/2 ...	...	...	...	...	...	165°F (73.9°C)	187°F (86.1°C)
C.20766/2 ...	...	...	...	...	...	159°F (70.5°C)	168°F (75.5°C)
Thermostatic switch						Cuts in	Cuts out
3.8 litre ...	...	...	...	...	...	80°C	72°C
4.2 litre ...	...	...	...	...	...	86°C	74°C

Filler cap releases pressure
Early 3.8 litre ... ... 4 lb/sq in (.28 kg/sq cm)
FHC Righthand drive Chassis 861091 ... ...
   Lefthand Chassis 888241 ... ... Pressure raised to 9 lb/sq in
Open Righthand drive Chassis 850657 ...
Lefthand drive Chassis 879044 ... ... (.63 kg/sq cm) from these 3.8 litres on
4.2 litre ... ... 7 lb/sq in (.49 kg/sq cm)
4.2 litre with air-conditioning ... ... 13 lb/sq in
Capacity (including heater) ... ... 32 Imperial pints (38½ US pints, 18.18 litre)

CLUTCH

Early 3.8 litre
Make, model ... ... Borg and Beck 10 A6.G
Thrust springs
   Number 12
   Colour ... ... Violet
   Free length 2.68 (68)
Driven plate
   Type ... ... Borglite (Arcuate for racing)
   Facings ... ... Wound yarn (Cemented wound yarn for racing)

Driven plate damper springs
   Number 6
   Colour ... ... Brown/Cream (Buff for racing)

Later 3.8 litre and earlier 4.2 litre
Make, model ... ...   Laycock, 10 inch, diaphragm spring
Later 4.2 litre
(Commencing Chassis No. 7E.13501 E type and
7E.53582 2 + 2 model)
Make, model ... ...   Borg and Beck BB9/412G
Operation ... ...   Hydraulic
Fluid ... ...   Castrol/Girling Crimson Clutch and Brake Fluid

Earlier 3.8 litre ... ...   Specification SAE.J1703A
All other models ... ...   Specification SAE.70.R3

GEARBOX

3.8 litre
Type ... ...   Four forward speeds, one reverse speed synchromesh on top three speeds

Suffix ... ...   JS
Prefix ... ...   EB
Ratios

Rear axle	—	3.31:1	2.93:1	3.07:1	3.54:1
First and reverse ...	3.377:1	11.177:1	9.894:1	10.367:1	11.954:1
Second	1.86:1	6.156:1	5.449:1	5.710:1	6.584:1
Third	1.283:1	4.246:1	3.759:1	3.938:1	4.541:1
Top	1:1	3.31:1	2.93:1	3.07:1	3.54:1

Oil SAE.30
Layshaft end float on countershaft ... ...   .002 to .004 (.05 to .10)
Second and third gear end float on mainshaft...   .002 to .004 (.05 to .10)

4.2 litre
Type ... ...   Four forward speeds, one reverse, synchromesh on all four forward speeds

Prefix
All earlier models ... ...   EJ
Later 2 seaters ... ...   KE
Later 2 + 2 ... ...   KJS
Ratios

	First	Second	Third	Top	Reverse
EJ	2.68:1	1.74:1	1.27:1	1:1	3.08:1
KE and KJS	2.933:1	1.905:1	1.389:1	1:1	3.378:1

Oil ... ...   Hypoid type
First gear end float on mainshaft ... ...   .005 to .007 (.13 to .18)
Second gear end float on mainshaft ... ...   .005 to .008 (.13 to .20)
Third gear end float on mainshaft ... ...   .005 to .008 (.13 to .20)
Countershaft gear end float ... ...   .004 to .006 (.10 to .15)
Capacity ... ...   2½ Imperial pints (3 US pints, 1.72 litres)

AUTOMATIC TRANSMISSION

Make and model ... ...   Borg Warner Model 8
Ratios
Maximum ratio of torque converter 2:1
First gear reduction 2.40:1
Second gear reduction 1.46:1
Third gear 1.00:1
Reverse gear reduction 2.00:1

Pressure tests

Selector position	Control pressure* Idle rev/min	Control pressure* Stall rev/min
D2	50 to 60	150 to 185
D1	50 to 60	150 to 185
L	50 to 60	150 to 185
R	50 to 60	190 to 210
N	55 to 60	—

*in lb/sq in at normal operating temperature

Normal stall speed ... ... 1600 to 1700 rev/min

Shift speeds

2.88:1 rear axle ratio, 185 x 15 SP 41 HR tyres at correct pressures

Selector position	Throttle position	Upshifts			Downshifts	
		1 to 2	2 to 3	3 to 2	3 to 1	2 to 1
				Mile/hr		
	Minimum	7 to 9	12 to 15	8 to 14	—	4 to 8
D1	Full	38 to 44	66 to 71	23 to 37	—	—
	Kick-down	52 to 56	81 to 89	73 to 81	20 to 24	20 to 24
	Minimum	—	12 to 15	8 to 14	—	—
D2	Full	—	66 to 71	23 to 37	—	—
	Kick-down	—	81 to 89	73 to 81	—	—
L	Zero	—	—	60	—	12 to 20
				Kilometre/hr		
	Minimum	11 to 14	19 to 24	13 to 23	—	6 to 13
D1	Full	61 to 71	106 to 114	37 to 60	—	—
	Kick-down	83 to 90	130 to 143	118 to 130	32 to 39	32 to 39
	Minimum	—	19 to 24	13 to 23	—	—
D2	Full	—	106 to 114	37 to 60	—	—
	Kick-down	—	130 to 143	118 to 130	—	—
L	Zero	—	—	96	—	19 to 32

3.31:1 rear axle ratio, 185 x 15 SP 41 HR tyres at correct pressures

Selector position	Throttle position	Upshifts			Downshifts	
		1 to 2	2 to 3	3 to 2	3 to 1	2 to 1
				Mile/hr		
	Minimum	6 to 8	11 to 13	7 to 13	—	3 to 7
D1	Full	33 to 40	58 to 62	19 to 23	—	—
	Kick-down	45 to 49	70 to 78	63 to 71	17 to 21	17 to 21
	Minimum	—	11 to 13	7 to 13	—	—
D2	Full	—	58 to 62	19 to 33	—	—
	Kick-down	—	70 to 78	63 to 71	—	—
L	Zero	—	—	60	—	10 to 18
				Kilometre/hr		
	Minimum	9 to 13	18 to 21	11 to 21	—	5 to 11
D1	Full	53 to 64	93 to 100	31 to 53	—	—
	Kick-down	73 to 80	113 to 126	101 to 114	28 to 34	28 to 34
	Minimum	—	18 to 21	11 to 21	—	—
D2	Full	—	93 to 100	31 to 53	—	—
	Kick-down	—	113 to 126	101 to 114	—	—
L	Zero	—	—	96	—	16 to 29

Note: Shift points are approximate and not absolute values. Reasonable deviations from the above values are permissible.

| Oil | ... | ... | ... | ... | ... | Automatic transmission fluid Type A or Type A Suffix A |

Capacity
Total (including cooler) ... ... 16 Imperial pints (19 US pints, 9 litres)
Normal operating temperature ... ... 150 to 185°F (65.5 to 85°C)

REAR AXLE

Type ... ... Salisbury 4.HU fitted with Thornton 'Powr-Lok' differential unit

Ratios
3.8 litre 3.07:1
3.31:1
3.54:1

4.2 litre
USA, Canada ... ... 3.54:1 (Manual transmission only)
All other countires ... ... 3.07:1 (Manual transmission only)
USA, Canada ... ... 3.31:1 (Automatic transmission)
All other countries ... ... 2.88:1 (Automatic transmission)
Oil ... ... Hypoid type
Capacity ... ... $2\frac{3}{4}$ Imperial pints ($3\frac{1}{4}$ US pints, 1.6 litres)

REAR SUSPENSION

Type ... ... Independent rear suspension, using two coil springs and two dampers per wheel
Dampers ... ... Telescopic, non-adjustable, sealed
Track (standard) ... ... $50\frac{1}{4}$
Track, Series 3 53
Rear wheel camber ... ... $\frac{3}{4} \pm \frac{1}{4}$ deg. (wheels held in mid-laden position)

Road springs
Earlier cars
Free length ... ... 10.1 (256.5) approximately
Number of coils ... ... $9\frac{3}{8}$
Later cars
Free length ... ... 10.5 (266.7) approximately
Number of coils 10
Identification colour ... ... Red

FRONT SUSPENSION

Type ... ... Independently sprung using torsion bars and unequal length wishbones
Dampers ... ... Telescopic, non-adjustable, sealed
Castor angle ... ... $2 \pm \frac{1}{2}$ deg. positive
Camber angle ... ... $\frac{1}{4} \pm \frac{1}{2}$ deg. positive
Swivel pin inclination ... ... 4 deg.
Car standing height ... ... See Chapter 9, Section 9:9
3.8 litre ... ... Dimension A is $8\frac{3}{4} \pm \frac{1}{4}$ (22.2 ± .64 cm)
4.2 litre
2 seaters ... ... Dimension B is $3\frac{1}{2} \pm \frac{1}{4}$ (88.9 ± 6.35)
2 + 2 ... ... Dimension C is $3\frac{3}{4} \pm \frac{1}{4}$ (95.25 ± 6.35)
4.2 Series 2 ... ... Dimension B should be 9 (22.86) minimum to give 24 in dimension to headlight centre
Series 3 ... ... 6.25 ± .25

Dimensions for hole centres on torsion bar setting links

3.8 litre	$17\frac{13}{16}$ in (45.24 cm)
4.2 litre	
Early 2 seater	$17\frac{13}{16}$ (45.24 cm)
Early 2 + 2	$18\frac{1}{4}$ (46.36 cm)
*FHC (1E.35382 on) Lefthand drive ...	
*Open (1E.17532 on) Lefthand drive ...	$17\frac{3}{4}$ (45.1 cm)
*2 + 2 (1E.50875 on) Righthand drive	
(1E.77407 on) Lefthand drive ...	18 (45.7 cm)
4.2 litre with air-conditioning	
*2 seater	$17\frac{3}{4}$ (45.1 cm)
*2 + 2	$18\frac{1}{4}$ (48.87 cm)

*Larger diameter torsion bars—.780 to .784 (19.81 to 19.9)—are fitted to those cars', Chassis Numbers given in brackets.

4.2 litre Series 2	
2 seater Lefthand drive	$17\frac{25}{32}$ (45.16 cm)
2 seater Righthand drive	$17\frac{31}{32}$ (45.6 cm)
2 + 2 (all)	$18\frac{1}{8}$ (46.06 cm)
4.2 litre Series 2 with air-conditioning	
2 seater	$17\frac{31}{32}$ (45.6 cm)
2 + 2	$18\frac{5}{16}$ (46.5 cm)

STEERING

Type	Rack and pinion
Number of turns lock-to-lock	$2\frac{1}{2}$
Turning circle	37 feet (11.27 metres)
Front wheel alignment	$\frac{1}{16}$ to $\frac{1}{8}$ (1.6 to 3.2) — on all models

POWER STEERING

Make	Adwest Engineering Co. Ltd.
Oil pump	
Type	Hobourn-Eaton
Pressure	1000 lb/sq in (70.3 kg/sq cm)
Flow	2.2 Imperial gallons (21 US pints, 10 litres) per minute
Oil	Automatic transmission fluid type A

BRAKES

3.8 litre

Type	Dunlop disc brakes, two master cylinders
Diameter	
Front	11 (27.9 cm)
Rear...	10 (25.4 cm)
Lining material	
Early models	Mintex M.40 or M.33
Later models	Mintex M.59
Handbrake	Mintex M.34
Servo	
Type	Dunlop bellows operated unit
Maximum vacuum	20 inches (50.8 cm) of mercury

4.2 litre

Type	Dunlop disc brakes, with dual-line servo braking system
Diameter	
Front	11 (27.9 cm)
Rear...	10 (25.4 cm)

Lining material
   Main ... ... Mintex M.59
   Handbrake ... ... Mintex M.34
Servo unit ... ... Lockheed dual-line
Master cylinder bore ... ... $\frac{7}{8}$ (22.23)

4.2 litre Series 2
   Type ... ... Girling disc brakes, otherwise all details including lining material are the same as on earlier 4.2 litre models

Brake fluid (all models) ... ... Castrol/Girling Crimson Clutch and Brake Fluid to specification SAE.70 R3

ELECTRICAL SYSTEM

Type
   3.8 litre ... ... 12 volt Positive earth
   4.2 litre ... ... 12 volt Negative earth
Battery
   Type ... ... Lucas FRV11/7A   Lucas CA11/7
   Number of plates/cell 11   11
   Capacity at 10 hour rate ... ... 55 amp/hr   53 amp/hr
   Capacity at 20 hour rate ... ... 60 amp/hr   60 amp/hr
Generator (3.8 litre)
   Type
      Early ... ... Lucas C.45 PVS.6
      Later ... ... Later C.42
   Minimum brush length
      C.45 ... ... $\frac{11}{32}$
      C.42 ... ... $\frac{1}{4}$
   Brush spring tension
      C.45 ... ... 20 to 28 ozs
      C.42 ... ... 16 to 33 ozs
   Maximum output
      C.45 ... ... 25 amps at 2050 rev/min (max) at 13.5 volts
      C.42 ... ... 30 amps at 2200 rev/min (max) at 13.5 volts
   Field resistance
      C.45 ... ... 6.0 ohms
      C.42 ... ... 4.5 ohms
Generator speed to engine speed 3:2
Control box
   C.45 ... ... Lucas RB.310
   C.42 ... ... Lucas RB.340
Alternator (4.2 litre)
   Type ... ... Lucas 11.AC
   Polarity ... ... Negative earth only
   Control box ... ... Lucas 4TR
   Warning light ... ... Lucas 3AW
   Nominal maximum output (hot) ... ... 43 amps
   Stator resistance per phase ... ... .107 ± 5% at 68°F (20 °C)
   Rotor winding resistance ... ... 3.8 ± 5% at 68°F (20°C)
Alternator speed to engine speed 2:1

Starter motor

	3.8 litre	4.2 litre
Type	M.45.G	M.45.G pre-engage
Lock torque	22.0 lb ft with 430 to 450 amps at 7.8 to 7.4 volts	22.6 lb ft with 465 amps at 7.6 volts
Torque at 1000 rev/min	8.3 lb ft with 200 to 220 amps at 10.2 to 9.8 volts	9.6 lb ft with with 240 amps at 9.7 volts
Light running current	45 amps at 5800 to 6800 rev/min	70 amps at 5800 6500 rev/min

WHEELS AND TYRES

3.8 litre wheels

Make	Dunlop
Rim section	5K
Rim diameter	15 (381)
Number of spokes	72
Racing	Part No. C.18 (only on rear of car, never front)

3.8 litre tyres ... ...

Dunlop RS5 (fitted as standard equipment)

Dunlop SP.41 (not for speeds above 125 mile/hr)

Dunlop SP.41 HR 185 x 15

Dunlop R.5 6.00 x 15 (not recommended for road use)

3.8 litre tyre pressures

	Front	Rear
RS.5		
Up to 130 mile/hr (210 kil/hr)	23 lb/sq in (1.62 kg/sq cm)	25 lb/sq in (1.76 kg/sq cm)
Up to maximum	30 lb/sq in (2.11 kg/sq cm)	35 lb/sq in (2.46 kg/sq cm)
SP41	*Front*	*Rear*
Up to 125 mile/hr (200 kil/hr)	32 lb/sq in (2.25 kg/sq cm)	32 lb/sq in (2.25 kg/sq cm)
Up to maximum*	40 lb/sq in (2.81 kg/sq cm)	40 lb/sq in (2.81 kg/sq cm)
R.5		
Racing	45 lb/sq in (3.2 kg/sq cm)	45 lb/sq in (3.2 kg/sq cm)
Racing maximum	50 lb/sq in (3.5 kg/sq cm)	50 lb sq in (3.5 kg/sq cm)
Road use**	30 lb/sq in (2.1 kg/sq cm)	30 lb/sq in (2.1 kg/sq cm)

*Not ordinary SP.41 as these are limited to 125 mile/hr
**Not recommended as these tyres have side walls that are easily damaged.

4.2 litre Series 2 wheels

Standard equipment	Pressed spoke* Wire spoke (spray painted)
Special equipment	Wire spoke (chromium plated**)

*Secured in place by five studs and wheel nuts
**These wheels are protected by a clear lacquer, and if the lacquer is damaged they must be re-done using ICI 'Necol' before use

Rim section	
Pressed spoke	6.JK
Wire spoke	5.K

4.2 litre Series 2 tyres

Standard	...	...	...	...	...	Dunlop SP Sport 185.VR.15
Winter use	...	...	...	...	...	Dunlop Weathermaster SP.44, 185 x 15

Dunlop Weathermaster SP.44, 185 x 15
fitted to rear wheels only and limited
to 100 mile/hr (160 kilo/hr)

4.2 litre Series 2 tyre pressures:

SP Sport				*Front*	*Rear*
Up to 125 mile/hr (200 kil/hr)	...	...	32 lb/sq in (2.25 kg/sq cm)	32 lb/sq in (2.25 kg/sq cm)
Up to maximum	...	...	...	40 lb/sq in (2.81 kg/sq cm)	40 lb/sq in (2.81 kg/sq cm)
SP Weathermaster*	...	...	...	—	32 lb/sq in (2.25 kg/sq cm)

*Ordinary tubes cannot be used in these tyres. The special inner tubes are identified by 'Weathermaster only'.

Tyre changing

Because of the high performance of the E type, diagonal changing of tyres is not recommended. Fit new tyres (never remoulds) to the rear wheels. Fit the rear wheels with new tyres to the front of the car, and the front wheels with their part-worn tyres to the rear of the car, thus scrapping the original rear tyres when worn to the limit.

SPECIAL TOOLS

All special tools, including those needed for automatic transmissions, are available from:

V. L. Churchill & Co. Ltd.
London Road,
Daventry,
Northants.
England.
P.O. Box No. 3.

USA Service Department:

The Technical Service Department
600 Willow Tree Road,
Leonia,
New Jersey 07605

Canadian Service Department:

The Technical Service Department,
British Motor Holdings (Canada) Ltd.,
4445 Fairview Street,
P.O. Box No. 5033,
Burlington,
Ontario.

TORQUE WRENCH SETTINGS

	lb ft	Kg m
Engine		
Cylinder head nuts		
Copper gasket	54	7.5
Steel gasket	58	8.0
Main bearing bolts	83	11.5
Big-end bolts	37	5.1
Camshaft bearings	15	2.0
Flywheel-to-crankshaft	67	9.2
Sparking plugs	27	3.73
Automatic transmission		
Oil pan bolts	10 to 13	1.38 to 1.80
Oil drain plug	25 to 30	3.46 to 4.15
Rear band locknut	35 to 40	4.70 to 5.53
Front band locknut	20 to 25	2.76 to 3.46
Front band adjustment with correct spacer ...	10 lb in	.12
Rear band adjustment then back off 1½ turns ...	10	1.382
Governor inspection cover	50 to 60 lb in	.58 to .69
Governor body cover	20 to 30 lb in	.24 to .35
Governor body to transmission	50 to 60 lb in	.58 to .69
Rear axle		
Drive gear bolts	70 to 80	9.7 to 11.1
Differential cap bolts	60 to 65	8.3 to 9.0
Pinion nut	120 to 130	16.6 to 18.0
'Powr-Lok' bolts	40 to 45	5.5 to 6.2
Rear suspension		
Radius arm securing bolt	46	6.36
Wishbone fulcrum nuts	55	7.60
Wheel hub to halfshaft	140	19.3
4.2 litre starter motor		
Nuts on solenoid terminals	20 lb/in	.23
Solenoid fixing bolts	4.5	.62
Through-bolts	8.0	.83
Alternator through-bolts	45 to 50 lb in	.115

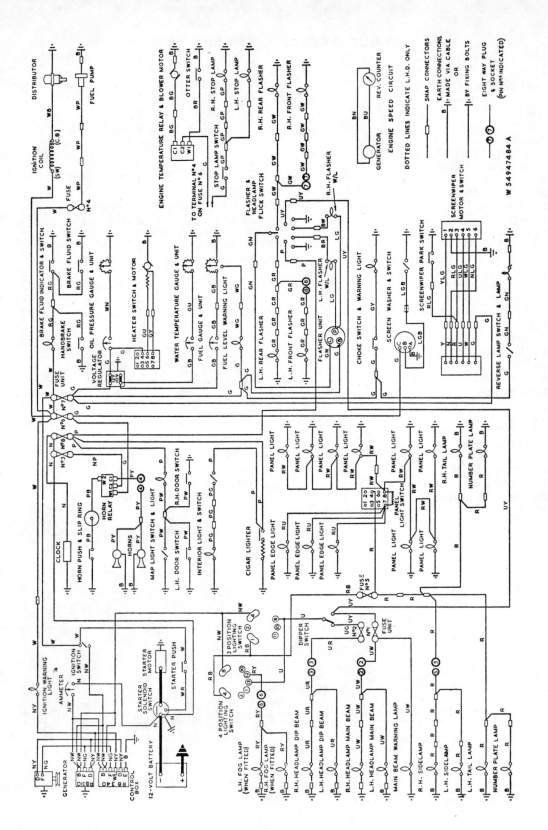

FIG 14:1 3.8 litre wiring diagram

Key to Figs 14:1, 14:2, 14:3 and 14:4   **Cable colour code**   **B** Black   **U** Blue   **N** Brown   **R** Red   **P** Purple   **G** Green   **S** Slate   **W** White   **Y** Yellow
D Dark   **L** Light   **M** Medium   When a cable has two colour code letters, the first denotes the main colour and the second denotes the tracer colour

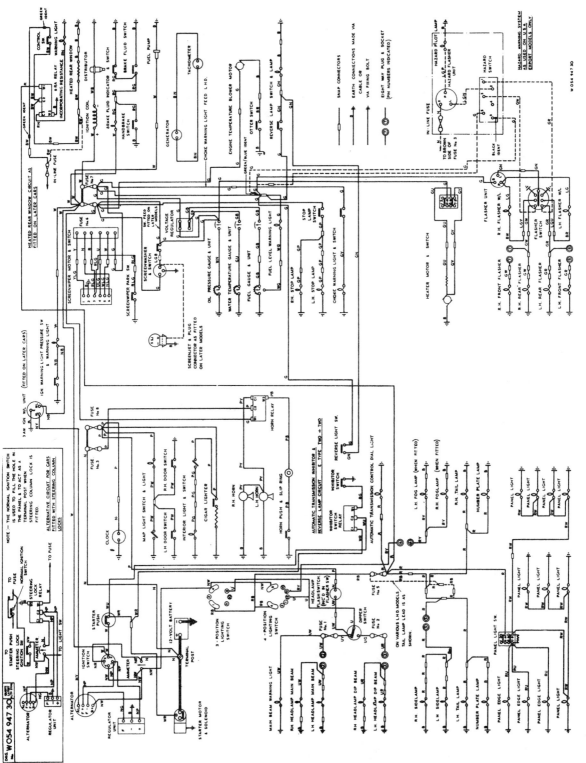

FIG 14:2   Early 4.2 litre wiring diagram

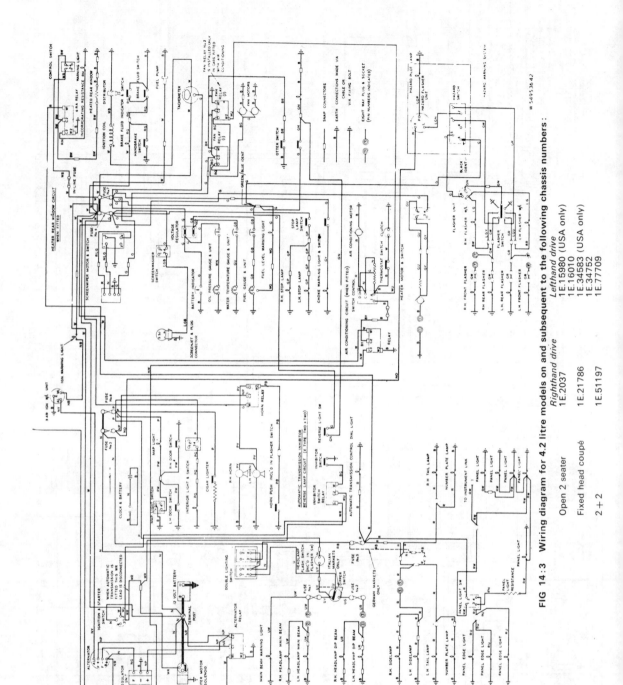

FIG 14:3 Wiring diagram for 4.2 litre models on and subsequent to the following chassis numbers :

	Righthand drive	Lefthand drive
	1E.2037	1E.15980 (USA only)
		1E.16010
Open 2 seater	1E.21786	1E.34583 (USA only)
		1E.34752
Fixed head coupé	1E.51197	1E.77709
2 + 2		

W 549536 42

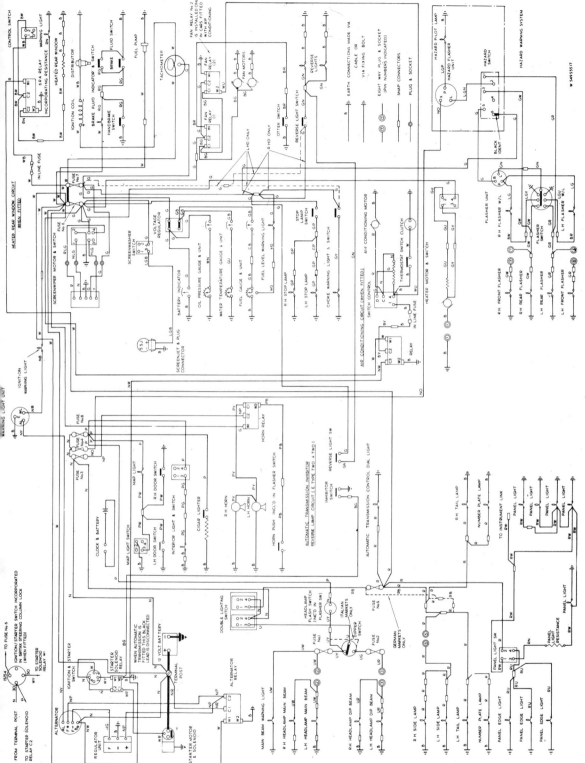

FIG 14:4   4.2 litre Series 2 Wiring diagram

HINTS ON MAINTENANCE AND OVERHAUL

There are few things more rewarding than the restoration of a vehicle's original peak of efficiency and smooth performance.

The following notes are intended to help the owner to reach that state of perfection. Providing that he possesses the basic manual skills he should have no difficulty in performing most of the operations detailed in this manual. It must be stressed, however, that where recommended in the manual, highly-skilled operations ought to be entrusted to experts, who have the necessary equipment, to carry out the work satisfactorily.

Quality of workmanship:

The hazardous driving conditions on the roads to-day demand that vehicles should be as nearly perfect, mechanically, as possible. It is therefore most important that amateur work be carried out with care, bearing in mind the often inadequate working conditions, and also the inferior tools which may have to be used. It is easy to counsel perfection in all things, and we recognize that it may be setting an impossibly high standard. We do, however, suggest that every care should be taken to ensure that a vehicle is as safe to take on the road as it is humanly possible to make it.

Safe working conditions:

Even though a vehicle may be stationary, it is still potentially dangerous if certain sensible precautions are not taken when working on it while it is supported on jacks or blocks. It is indeed preferable not to use jacks alone, but to supplement them with carefully placed blocks, so that there will be plenty of support if the car rolls off the jacks during a strenuous manoeuvre. Axle stands are an excellent way of providing a rigid base which is not readily disturbed. Piles of bricks are a dangerous substitute. Be careful not to get under heavy loads on lifting tackle, the load could fall. It is preferable not to work alone when lifting an engine, or when working underneath a vehicle which is supported well off the ground. To be trapped, particularly under the vehicle, may have unpleasant results if help is not quickly forthcoming. Make some provision, however humble, to deal with fires. Always disconnect a battery if there is a likelihood of electrical shorts. These may start a fire if there is leaking fuel about. This applies particularly to leads which can carry a heavy current, like those in the starter circuit. While on the subject of electricity, we must also stress the danger of using equipment which is run off the mains and which has no earth or has faulty wiring or connections. So many workshops have damp floors, and electrical shocks are of such a nature that it is sometimes impossible to let go of a live lead or piece of equipment due to the muscular spasms which take place.

Work demanding special care:

This involves the servicing of braking, steering and suspension systems. On the road, failure of the braking system may be disastrous. Make quite sure that there can be no possibility of failure through the bursting of rusty brake pipes or rotten hoses, nor to a sudden loss of pressure due to defective seals or valves.

Problems:

The chief problems which may face an operator are:
1 External dirt.
2 Difficulty in undoing tight fixings
3 Dismantling unfamiliar mechanisms.
4 Deciding in what respect parts are defective.
5 Confusion about the correct order for reassembly.
6 Adjusting running clearances.
7 Road testing.
8 Final tuning.

Practical suggestion to solve the problems:

1 Preliminary cleaning of large parts—engines, transmissions, steering, suspensions, etc.,—should be carried out before removal from the car. Where road dirt and mud alone are present, wash clean with a high-pressure water jet, brushing to remove stubborn adhesions, and allow to drain and dry. Where oil or grease is also present, wash down with a proprietary compound (Gunk, Teepol etc.,) applying with a stiff brush—an old paint brush is suitable—into all crevices. Cover the distributor and ignition coils with a polythene bag and then apply a strong water jet to clear the loosened deposits. Allow to drain and dry. The assemblies will then be sufficiently clean to remove and transfer to the bench for the next stage.

On the bench, further cleaning can be carried out, first wiping the parts as free as possible from grease with old newspaper. Avoid using rag or cotton waste which can leave clogging fibres behind. Any remaining grease can be removed with a brush dipped in paraffin. If necessary, traces of paraffin can be removed by carbon tetrachloride. Avoid using paraffin or petrol in large quantities for cleaning in enclosed areas, such as garages, on account of the high fire risk.

When all exteriors have been cleaned, and not before, dismantling can be commenced. This ensures that dirt will not enter into interiors and orifices revealed by dismantling. In the next phases, where components have to be cleaned, use carbon tetrachloride in preference to petrol and keep the containers covered except when in use. After the components have been cleaned, plug small holes with tapered hard wood plugs cut to size and blank off larger orifices with grease-proof paper and masking tape. Do not use soft wood plugs or matchsticks as they may break.

2 It is not advisable to hammer on the end of a screw thread, but if it must be done, first screw on a nut to protect the thread, and use a lead hammer. This applies particularly to the removal of tapered cotters. Nuts and bolts seem to 'grow' together, especially in exhaust systems. If penetrating oil does not work, try the judicious application of heat, but be careful ot starting a fire. Asbestos sheet or cloth is useful to isolate heat.

Tight bushes or pieces of tail-pipe rusted into a silencer can be removed by splitting them with an open-ended hacksaw. Tight screws can sometimes be started by a tap from a hammer on the end of a suitable screwdriver. Many tight fittings will yield to the judicious use of a hammer, but it must be a soft-faced hammer if damage is to be avoided, use a heavy block on the opposite side to absorb shock. Any parts of the steering system which have been damaged should be renewed, as attempts to repair them may lead to cracking and subsequent failure, and steering ball joints should be disconnected using a recommended tool to prevent damage.

3 If often happens that an owner is baffled when trying to dismantle an unfamiliar piece of equipment. So many modern devices are pressed together or assembled by spinning-over flanges, that they must be sawn apart. The intention is that the whole assembly must be renewed. However, parts which appear to be in one piece to the naked eye, may reveal close-fitting joint lines when inspected with a magnifying glass, and, this may provide the necessary clue to dismantling. Left-handed screw threads are used where rotational forces would tend to unscrew a right-handed screw thread.

Be very careful when dismantling mechanisms which may come apart suddenly. Work in an enclosed space where the parts will be contained, and drape a piece of cloth over the device if springs are likely to fly in all directions. Mark everything which might be reassembled in the wrong position, scratched symbols may be used on unstressed parts, or a sequence of tiny dots from a centre punch can be useful. Stressed parts should never be scratched or centre-popped as this may lead to cracking under working conditions. Store parts which look alike in the correct order for reassembly. Never rely upon memory to assist in the assembly of complicated mechanisms, especially when they will be dismantled for a long time, but make notes, and drawings to supplement the diagrams in the manual, and put labels on detached wires. Rust stains may indicate unlubricated wear. This can sometimes be seen round the outside edge of a bearing cup in a universal joint. Look for bright rubbing marks on parts which normally should not make heavy contact. These might prove that something is bent or running out of truth. For example, there might be bright marks on one side of a piston, at the top near the ring grooves, and others at the bottom of the skirt on the other side. This could well be the clue to a bent connecting rod. Suspected cracks can be proved by heating the component in a light oil to approximately 100°C, removing, drying off, and dusting with french chalk, if a crack is present the oil retained in the crack will stain the french chalk.

4 In determining wear, and the degree, against the permissible limits set in the manual, accurate measurement can only be achieved by the use of a micrometer. In many cases, the wear is given to the fourth place of decimals; that is in ten-thousandths of an inch. This can be read by the vernier scale on the barrel of a good micrometer. Bore diameters are more difficult to determine. If, however, the matching shaft is accurately measured, the degree of play in the bore can be felt as a guide to its suitability. In other cases, the shank of a twist drill of known diameter is a handy check.

Many methods have been devised for determining the clearance between bearing surfaces. To-day the best and simplest is by the use of Plastigage, obtainable from most garages. A thin plastic thread is laid between the two surfaces and the bearing is tightened, flattening the thread. On removal, the width of the thread is compared with a scale supplied with the thread and the clearance is read off directly. Sometimes joint faces leak persistently, even after gasket renewal. The fault will then be traceable to distortion, dirt or burrs. Studs which are screwed into soft metal frequently raise burrs at the point of entry. A quick cure for this is to chamfer the edge of the hole in the part which fits over the stud.

5 **Always check a replacement part with the original one before it is fitted.**

If parts are not marked, and the order for reassembly is not known, a little detective work will help. Look for marks which are due to wear to see if they can be mated. Joint faces may not be identical due to manufacturing errors, and parts which overlap may be stained, giving a clue to the correct position. Most fixings leave identifying marks especially if they were painted over on assembly. It is then easier to decide whether a nut, for instance, has a plain, a spring, or a shakeproof washer under it. All running surfaces become 'bedded' together after long spells of work and tiny imperfections on one part will be found to have left corresponding marks on the other. This is particularly true of shafts and bearings and even a score on a cylinder wall will show on the piston.

6 Checking end float or rocker clearances by feeler gauge may not always give accurate results because of wear. For instance, the rocker tip which bears on a valve stem may be deeply pitted, in which case the feeler will simply be bridging a depression. Thrust washers may also wear depressions in opposing faces to make accurate measurement difficult. End float is then easier to check by using a dial gauge. It is common practice to adjust end play in bearing assemblies, like front hubs with taper rollers, by doing up the axle nut until the hub becomes stiff to turn and then backing it off a little. Do not use this method with ballbearing hubs as the assembly is often preloaded by tightening the axle nut to its fullest extent. If the splitpin hole will not line up, file the base of the nut a little.

Steering assemblies often wear in the straight-ahead position. If any part is adjusted, make sure that it remains free when moved from lock to lock. Do not be surprised if an assembly like a steering gearbox, which is known to be carefully adjusted outside the car, becomes stiff when it is bolted in place. This will be due to distortion of the case by the pull of the mounting bolts, particularly if the mounting points are not all touching together. This problem may be met in other equipment and is cured by careful attention to the alignment of mounting points.

When a spanner is stamped with a size and A/F it means that the dimension is the width between the jaws and has no connection with ANF, which is the designation for the American National Fine thread. Coarse threads like Whitworth are rarely used on cars to-day except for studs which screw into soft aluminium or cast iron. For this reason it might be found that the top end of a cylinder head stud has a fine thread and the lower end a coarse thread to screw into the cylinder block. If the car has mainly UNF threads then it is likely that any coarse threads will be UNC, which are not the same as Whitworth. Small sizes have the same number of threads in Whitworth and UNC, but in the $\frac{1}{2}$ inch size for example, there are twelve threads to the inch in the former and thirteen in the latter.

7 After a major overhaul, particularly if a great deal of work has been done on the braking, steering and suspension systems, it is advisable to approach the problem of testing with care. If the braking system has been overhauled, apply heavy pressure to the brake pedal and get a second operator to check every possible source of leakage. The brakes may work extremely well, but a leak could cause complete failure after a few miles.

Do not fit the hub caps until every wheel nut has been checked for tightness, and make sure the tyre pressures are correct. Check the levels of coolant, lubricants and hydraulic fluids. Being satisfied that all is well, take the car on the road and test the brakes at once. Check the steering and the action of the handbrake. Do all this at moderate speeds on quiet roads, and make sure there is no other vehicle behind you when you try a rapid stop.

Finally, remember that many parts settle down after a time, so check for tightness of all fixings after the car has been on the road for a hundred miles or so.

8 It is useless to tune an engine which has not reached its normal running temperature. In the same way, the tune of an engine which is stiff after a rebore will be different when the engine is again running free. Remember too, that rocker clearances on pushrod operated valve gear will change when the cylinder head nuts are tightened after an initial period of running with a new head gasket.

Trouble may not always be due to what seems the obvious cause. Ignition, carburation and mechanical condition are interdependent and spitting back through the carburetter, which might be attributed to a weak mixture, can be caused by a sticking inlet valve.

For one final hint on tuning, never adjust more than one thing at a time or it will be impossible to tell which adjustment produced the desired result.

GLOSSARY OF TERMS

Allen key   Cranked wrench of hexagonal section for use with socket head screws.

Alternator   Electrical generator producing alternating current. Rectified to direct current for battery charging.

Ambient temperature   Surrounding atmospheric temperature.

Annulus   Used in engineering to indicate the outer ring gear of an epicyclic gear train.

Armature   The shaft carrying the windings, which rotates in the magnetic field of a generator or starter motor. That part of a solenoid or relay which is activated by the magnetic field.

Axial   In line with, or pertaining to, an axis.

Backlash   Play in meshing gears.

Balance lever   A bar where force applied at the centre is equally divided between connections at the ends.

Banjo axle   Axle casing with large diameter housing for the crownwheel and differential.

Bendix pinion   A self-engaging and self-disengaging drive on a starter motor shaft.

Bevel pinion   A conical shaped gearwheel, designed to mesh with a similar gear with an axis usually at 90 deg. to its own.

bhp   Brake horse power, measured on a dynamometer.

bmep   Brake mean effective pressure. Average pressure on a piston during the working stroke.

Brake cylinder   Cylinder with hydraulically operated piston(s) acting on brake shoes or pad(s).

Brake regulator   Control valve fitted in hydraulic braking system which limits brake pressure to rear brakes during heavy braking to prevent rear wheel locking.

Camber   Angle at which a wheel is tilted from the vertical.

Capacitor   Modern term for an electrical condenser. Part of distributor assembly, connected across contact breaker points, acts as an interference suppressor.

Castellated   Top face of a nut, slotted across the flats, to take a locking splitpin.

Castor   Angle at which the kingpin or swivel pin is tilted when viewed from the side.

cc   Cubic centimetres. Engine capacity is arrived at by multiplying the area of the bore in sq cm by the stroke in cm by the number of cylinders.

Clevis   U-shaped forked connector used with a clevis pin, usually at handbrake connections.

Collet   A type of collar, usually split and located in a groove in a shaft, and held in place by a retainer. The arrangement used to retain the spring(s) on a valve stem in most cases.

Commutator   Rotating segmented current distributor between armature windings and brushes in generator or motor.

Compression   The ratio, or quantitative relation, of the total volume (piston at bottom of stroke) to the unswept volume (piston at top of stroke) in an engine cylinder.

Condenser   See capacitor.

Core plug   Plug for blanking off a manufacturing hole in a casting.

Crownwheel   Large bevel gear in rear axle, driven by a bevel pinion attached to the propeller shaft. Sometimes called a 'ring wheel'.

'C'-spanner   Like a 'C' with a handle. For use on screwed collars without flats, but with slots or holes.

Damper   Modern term for shock-absorber, used in vehicle suspension systems to damp out spring oscillations.

Depression   The lowering of atmospheric pressure as in the inlet manifold and carburetter.

Dowel   Close tolerance pin, peg, tube, or bolt, which accurately locates mating parts.

Drag link   Rod connecting steering box drop arm (pitman arm) to nearest front wheel steering arm in certain types of steering systems.

Dry liner   Thinwall tube pressed into cylinder bore

Dry sump   Lubrication system where all oil is scavenged from the sump, and returned to a separate tank.

Dynamo   See Generator.

Electrode   Terminal, part of an electrical component, such as the points or 'Electrodes' of a sparking plug.

Electrolyte   In lead-acid car batteries a solution of sulphuric acid and distilled water.

End float   The axial movement between associated parts, end play.

EP   Extreme pressure. In lubricants, special grades for heavily loaded bearing surfaces, such as gear teeth in a gearbox, or crownwheel and pinion in a rear axle.

Fade	Of brakes. Reduced efficiency due to overheating.
Field coils	Windings on the polepieces of motors and generators.
Fillets	Narrow finishing strips usually applied to interior bodywork.
First motion shaft	Input shaft from clutch to gearbox.
Fullflow filter	Filters in which all the oil is pumped to the engine. If the element becomes clogged, a bypass valve operates to pass unfiltered oil to the engine.
FWD	Front wheel drive.
Gear pump	Two meshing gears in a close fitting casing. Oil is carried from the inlet round the outside of both gears in the spaces between the gear teeth and casing to the outlet, the meshing gear teeth prevent oil passing back to the inlet, and the oil is forced through the outlet port.
Generator	Modern term for 'Dynamo'. When rotated produces electrical current.
Grommet	A ring of protective or sealing material. Can be used to protect pipes or leads passing through bulkheads.
Grubscrew	Fully threaded headless screw with screwdriver slot. Used for locking, or alignment purposes.
Gudgeon pin	Shaft which connects a piston to its connecting rod. Sometimes called 'wrist pin', or 'piston pin'.
Halfshaft	One of a pair transmitting drive from the differential.
Helical	In spiral form. The teeth of helical gears are cut at a spiral angle to the side faces of the gearwheel.
Hot spot	Hot area that assists vapourisation of fuel on its way to cylinders. Often provided by close contact between inlet and exhaust manifolds.
HT	High Tension. Applied to electrical current produced by the ignition coil for the sparking plugs.
Hydrometer	A device for checking specific gravity of liquids. Used to check specific gravity of electrolyte.
Hypoid bevel gears	A form of bevel gear used in the rear axle drive gears. The bevel pinion meshes below the centre line of the crownwheel, giving a lower propeller shaft line.
Idler	A device for passing on movement. A free running gear between driving and driven gears. A lever transmitting track rod movement to a side rod in steering gear.
Impeller	A centrifugal pumping element. Used in water pumps to stimulate flow.
Journals	Those parts of a shaft that are in contact with the bearings.
Kingpin	The main vertical pin which carries the front wheel spindle, and permits steering movement. May be called 'steering pin' or 'swivel pin'.
Layshaft	The shaft which carries the laygear in the gearbox. The laygear is driven by the first motion shaft and drives the third motion shaft according to the gear selected. Sometimes called the 'countershaft' or 'second motion shaft.'
lb ft	A measure of twist or torque. A pull of 10 lb at a radius of 1 ft is a torque of 10 lb ft.
lb/sq in	Pounds per square inch.
Little-end	The small, or piston end of a connecting rod. Sometimes called the 'small-end'.
LT	Low Tension. The current output from the battery.
Mandrel	Accurately manufactured bar or rod used for test or centring purposes.
Manifold	A pipe, duct, or chamber, with several branches.
Needle rollers	Bearing rollers with a length many times their diameter.
Oil bath	Reservoir which lubricates parts by immersion. In air filters, a separate oil supply for wetting a wire mesh element to hold the dust.
Oil wetted	In air filters, a wire mesh element lightly oiled to trap and hold airborne dust.
Overlap	Period during which inlet and exhaust valves are open together.
Panhard rod	Bar connected between fixed point on chassis and another on axle to control sideways movement.
Pawl	Pivoted catch which engages in the teeth of a ratchet to permit movement in one direction only.
Peg spanner	Tool with pegs, or pins, to engage in holes or slots in the part to be turned.
Pendant pedals	Pedals with levers that are pivoted at the top end.
Phillips screwdriver	A cross-point screwdriver for use with the cross-slotted heads of Phillips screws.
Pinion	A small gear, usually in relation to another gear.
Piston-type damper	Shock absorber in which damping is controlled by a piston working in a closed oil-filled cylinder.
Preloading	Preset static pressure on ball or roller bearings not due to working loads.
Radial	Radiating from a centre, like the spokes of a wheel.

Radius rod	Pivoted arm confining movement of a part to an arc of fixed radius.
Ratchet	Toothed wheel or rack which can move in one direction only, movement in the other being prevented by a pawl.
Ring gear	A gear tooth ring attached to outer periphery of flywheel. Starter pinion engages with it during starting.
Runout	Amount by which rotating part is out of true.
Semi-floating axle	Outer end of rear axle halfshaft is carried on bearing inside axle casing. Wheel hub is secured to end of shaft.
Servo	A hydraulic or pneumatic system for assisting, or, augmenting a physical effort. See 'Vacuum Servo'.
Setscrew	One which is threaded for the full length of the shank.
Shackle	A coupling link, used in the form of two parallel pins connected by side plates to secure the end of the master suspension spring and absorb the effects of deflection.
Shell bearing	Thinwalled steel shell lined with anti-friction metal. Usually semi-circular and used in pairs for main and big-end bearings.
Shock absorber	See 'Damper'.
Silentbloc	Rubber bush bonded to inner and outer metal sleeves.
Socket-head screw	Screw with hexagonal socket for an Allen key.
Solenoid	A coil of wire creating a magnetic field when electric current passes through it. Used with a soft iron core to operate contacts or a mechanical device.
Spur gear	A gear with teeth cut axially across the periphery.
Stub axle	Short axle fixed at one end only.
Tachometer	An instrument for accurate measurement of rotating speed. Usually indicates in revolutions per minute.
TDC	Top Dead Centre. The highest point reached by a piston in a cylinder, with the crank and connecting rod in line.
Thermostat	Automatic device for regulating temperature. Used in vehicle coolant systems to open a valve which restricts circulation at low temperature.
Third motion shaft	Output shaft of gearbox.
Threequarter floating axle	Outer end of rear axle halfshaft flanged and bolted to wheel hub, which runs on bearing mounted on outside of axle casing. Vehicle weight is not carried by the axle shaft.
Thrust bearing or washer	Used to reduce friction in rotating parts subject to axial loads.
Torque	Turning or twisting effort. See 'lb ft'.
Track rod	The bar(s) across the vehicle which connect the steering arms and maintain the front wheels in their correct alignment.
UJ	Universal joint. A coupling between shafts which permits angular movement.
UNF	Unified National Fine screw thread.
Vacuum servo	Device used in brake system, using difference between atmospheric pressure and inlet manifold depression to operate a piston which acts to augment brake pressure as required. See 'Servo'.
Venturi	A restriction or 'choke' in a tube, as in a carburetter, used to increase velocity to obtain a reduction in pressure.
Vernier	A sliding scale for obtaining fractional readings of the graduations of an adjacent scale.
Welch plug	A domed thin metal disc which is partially flattened to lock in a recess. Used to plug core holes in castings.
Wet liner	Removable cylinder barrel, sealed against coolant leakage, where the coolant is in direct contact with the outer surface.
Wet sump	A reservoir attached to the crankcase to hold the lubricating oil.

NOTES

INDEX

Alfa Romeo Giulia 1962 on
Aston Martin 1921-58
Auto Union Audi 70, 80,
  Super 90 1966 on
Audi 100 1969 on
(Austin, Morris etc.)
  1100 Mk. 1 1962-67
(Austin, Morris etc.) 1100
  Mk. 2, 3, 1300 Mk. 1, 2, 3,
  America 1968 on
Austin A30, A35, A40
  Farina
Austin A55 Mk. 2, A60
  1958-69
Austin A99, A110 1959-68
Austin J4 1960 on
Austin Maxi 1969 on
Austin, Morris 1800
  1964 on
BMC 3 (Austin A50,
  A55 Mk. 1, Morris
  Oxford 2, 3 1954-59)
Austin Healey 100/6, 3000
  1956-68
(Austin Healey, MG)
  Sprite, Midget 1958 on
BMW 1600 1964 on
BMW 1800 1964-68
BMW 2000, 2002 1966 on
Chevrolet Corvair 1960-69
Chevrolet Corvette V8
  1957-65
Chevrolet Corvette V8
  1965-71
Chevrolet Vega 2300
  1970-71
Chrysler Valiant V8
  1965 on
Chrysler Valiant Straight
  Six 1966-70
Citroen DS 19, ID 19
  1955-66
Citroen ID 19, DS 19, 20,
  21 1966 on
Datsun 1200 1970 on
Datsun 1300, 1600
  1968 on
Datsun 240C 1971 on
Datsun 240Z Sport
  1970 on
De Dion Bouton
  1899-1907
Fiat 124 1966 on
Fiat 124 Sport 1966 on
Fiat 125 1967 on
Fiat 128 1969 on
Fiat 500 1957 on
Fiat 600, 600D 1955-69
Fiat 850 1964 on
Fiat 1100 1957-69
Fiat 1300, 1500 1961-67
Ford Anglia Prefect 100E
  1953-62
Ford Anglia 105E,
  Prefect 107E 1959-67
Ford Capri 1300, 1600
  1968 on
Ford Capri 2000 GT,
  3000 GT 1969 on

Ford Classic, Capri
  1961-64
Ford Consul, Zephyr,
  Zodiac, 1, 2 1950-62
Ford Corsair Straight
  Four 1963-65
Ford Corsair V4 1965-68
Ford Corsair V4 1969 on
Ford Cortina 1962-66
Ford Cortina 1967-68
Ford Cortina 1969-70
Ford Cortina Mk. 3
  1970 on
Ford Escort 1967 on
Ford Falcon 6 1964-70
Ford Falcon XK, XL 1960-63
Ford Falcon V8 (U.S.A.)
  1965-71
Ford Falcon V8 (Aust)
  1966 on
Ford Pinto 1970-71
Ford Maverick 1969-71
Ford Mustang V8 1965-71
Ford Thames 10, 12,
  15 cwt 1957-65
Ford Transit 1965 on
Ford Zephyr Zodiac
  Mk. 3 1962-66
Ford Zephyr V4, V6,
  Zodiac 1966 on
Ford Consul, Granada 1972
Hillman Avenger 1970 on
Hillman Hunter 1966 on
Hillman Imp 1963-68
Hillman Imp 1969 on
Hillman Minx 1 to 5
  1956-65
Hillman Minx 1965-67
Hillman Minx 1966-70
Hillman Super Minx
  1961-65
Holden V8 1968 on
Holden Straight Six
  1948-66
Holden Straight Six
  1966 on
Holden Torana 4 series HB
  1967-69
Jaguar XK120, 140, 150,
  Mk. 7, 8, 9 1948-61
Jaguar 2.4, 3.4, 3.8
  Mk. 1, 2 1955-69
Jaguar 'E' Type 1961-72
Jaguar 'S' Type 420
  1963-68
Jaguar XJ6 1968 on
Jowett Javelin Jupiter
  1947-53
Landrover 1, 2 1948-61
Landrover 2, 2a, 3 1959 on
Mercedes-Benz 190b,
  190c 200 1959-68
Mercedes-Benz 220
  1959-65
Mercedes-Benz 220/8
  1968 on
Mercedes-Benz 230
  1963-68

Mercedes-Benz 250
  1965-67
Mercedes-Benz 250
  1968 on
Mercedes-Benz 280
  1968 on
MG TA to TF 1936-55
MGA MGB 1955-68
MG MGB 1969 on
Mini 1959 on
Mini Cooper 1961 on
Morgan 1936-69
Morris Marina 1971 on
Morris Minor 2, 1000
  1952-71
Morris Oxford 5, 6 1959-71
NSU 1000 1963 on
NSU Prinz 1 to 4
  1957 on
Opel Ascona, Manta
  1970 on
Opel G.T. 1900 1968 on
Opel Kadett, Olympia
  993 cc, 1078 cc
  1962 on
Opel Kadett, Olympia
  1492, 1698, 1897 cc
  1967 on
Opel Rekord C 1966 on
Peugeot 204 1965 on
Peugeot 404, 1960 on
Peugeot 504 1968 on
Porsche 356a, 356b, 356c
  1957-65
Porsche 911 1964-69
Porsche 912 1965-69
Porsche 914s 1969 on
Reliant Regal 1962 on
Renault R4, R4L, 4
  1961 on
Renault 6 1968 on
Renault 8, 10, 1100
  1962 on
Renault 12 1969 on
Renault R16 1965 on
Renault Dauphine
  Floride 1957-67
Renault Caravelle 1962-68
Rover 60 to 110 1953-64
Rover 2000 1963 on
Rover 3 Litre 1958-67
Rover 3500, 3500S
  1968 on
Saab 95, 96, Sport
  1960-68
Saab 99 1969 on
Saab V4 1966 on
Simca 1000 1961 on
Simca 1100 1967 on
Simca 1300, 1301, 1500,
  1501 1963 on
Skoda One (440, 445, 450)
  1957-69
Sunbeam Rapier Alpine
  1955-65
Toyota Corolla 1100
  1967 on
Toyota Corona 1500
  Mk. 1 1965-70

Toyota Corona 1900 Mk. 2
  1969 on
Triumph TR2, TR3,
  TR3A 1952-62
Triumph TR4, TR4A
  1961-67
Triumph TR5, TR250,
  TR6 1967 on
Triumph 1300, 1500
  1965 on
Triumph 2000 Mk. 1, 2.5 PI
  Mk. 1 1963-69
Triumph 2000 Mk. 2, 2.5
  PI Mk. 2 1969 on
Triumph Herald 1959-68
Triumph Herald 1969-71
Triumph Spitfire Vitesse
  1962-68
Triumph Spitfire Mk. 3, 4
  1969 on
Triumph GT6, Vitesse 2
  Litre 1969 on
Triumph Toledo 1970 on
Vauxhall Velox, Cresta
  1957-72
Vauxhall Victor 1, 2, FB
  1957-64
Vauxhall Victor 101
  1964-67
Vauxhall Victor FD 1600,
  2000 1967-72
Vauxhall Victor FE Ventora
  1972 on
Vauxhall Viva HA 1963-66
Vauxhall Viva HB 1966-70
Vauxhall Viva, HC Firenza
  1971 on
Vauxhall Victor 3300,
  Ventura 1968 on
Volkswagen Beetle
  1954-67
Volkswagen Beetle
  1968 on
Volkswagen 1500 1961-66
Volkswagen 1600
  Fastback 1965 on
Volkswagen Transporter
  1954-67
Volkswagen Transporter
  1968 on
Volkswagen 411 1968 on
Volvo P120 1961-70
Volvo P140 1966 on
Volvo 160 series 1968 on
Volvo 1800 1961 on